# REAL TIME STRATEGY

## When Strategic Foresight Meets Artificial Intelligence

# REAL TIME STRATEGY

## When Strategic Foresight Meets Artificial Intelligence

By

Andreas Schühly

Frank Becker

Florian Klein

United Kingdom – North America – Japan
India – Malaysia – China

Emerald Publishing Limited
Howard House, Wagon Lane, Bingley BD16 1WA, UK

First edition 2020

Copyright © 2020 by Emerald Publishing Limited

**Reprints and permissions service**
Contact: permissions@emeraldinsight.com

**British Library Cataloguing in Publication Data**
A catalogue record for this book is available from the British Library

ISBN: 978-1-78756-812-9 (Print)
ISBN: 978-1-78756-811-2 (Online)
ISBN: 978-1-78756-813-6 (Epub)

ISOQAR certified
Management System,
awarded to Emerald
for adherence to
Environmental
standard
ISO 14001:2004.

Certificate Number 1985
ISO 14001

INVESTOR IN PEOPLE

To all our colleagues who contributed to this book. You give us the means to take the long view.

– Kudos to Maximiliane Brecht, Nadine Manger, and Niclas Vieten for their critical reviews and input along our journey.

And to our family and friends. You give us the reasons to take the long view.

Special thanks to Alina, Christine, and Paloma for their continuous support and patience.

– Andreas, Frank, and Florian

# CONTENTS

# LIST OF TABLES AND FIGURES

# AN INITIAL REFLECTION

This is an unorthodox book in a singular moment in history. Over the following pages, we will paint the picture of how strategic thinking and decision making is being disrupted before our very eyes.

For the record, let us be clear from the outset that the old world of strategic planning is neither dead nor dying. The established rules of the game still stand. The literature around the mechanics of competition and the sources of sustainable competitive advantages remains as valid as it has been for decades. What has changed is the world around us. Globalisation and the hyper-connectivity of people and markets have dramatically increased the volatility of our societies and economies. Among the victims of those developments are the validity and the lifespan of conventional strategic planning. What is the point of the most sophisticated 5- or 10-year strategic plans if they fail to take into account the next wave of populist policies, the next game-changing technology, or surprising changes in the consumer preferences of digital natives? This book is an attempt to establish the need for dynamic strategic management that is capable of reacting to sudden, unexpected moves in the context of our activities, yet still including the long-term focus of strategy.

However, there is an even more profound tectonic shift building up at this moment, and it concerns how people and in particular big, complex organisations, take strategically important decisions. Since humankind has evolved into societies and organisations, the really important and tricky decisions were taken by individuals such as kings, presidents or CEOs, or relatively reduced groups such as parliaments or executive committees. Decision makers base their choices on their own experience and on the advice of their 'inner circle'. The advisors, in turn, draw their wisdom from their experience and from established facts such as statistical offices or the state of academic literature.

By and large, that approach appears to have served us well for ages. However, there are several reasons why conventional decision making might not function as neatly in the future. Globalisation and hyper-connectivity are some of them. As the complexity of the decisions increases, decision makers hit the limit of what they are capable of factoring in. Given the multitude of issues and the limited attention span of high-ranking decision makers, there is a limit to how much decision makers can reasonably study, absorb, and reflect. Yet, this is not just an issue of the corporate world but also of our entire society. Humankind is failing to address many problems appropriately due to the sheer complexity of issues like climate change. There are just too many factors and viewpoints to take into account, and this leads to the second reason why conventional decision making is in crisis.

The basis for our decision making, the body of established facts, opinions, and ideas has grown beyond what decision makers and their advisors are capable of grasping. In our hyper-connected world, the speed of the discussions has accelerated in popular fora such as social media, and in professional arenas such as academia. Today, we are drowning in a tsunami of facts, figures, fake news, and individual opinions. Therefore, how could one expect professional decision makers to stay on top of this?

We propose a technology-based answer to this technology-induced problem. This book will speak about how we can improve the way we perceive what is going on around (through better, real-time sensing), and how we can enhance the way we process, interpret, and reflect on what we see (through broader, more holistic sense making). Using both levers, decision makers should be able to upgrade their capacity to perceive and understand complex problems and enhance their capability to act on them.

This constellation, the need to combine established strategic thinking with the brave new digital world of Big Data and Artificial Intelligence (AI), has brought the three authors together. Andreas Schühly is a digital native, scenario practitioner and scholar of the cultural aspects of scenario planning. Frank Becker is a complexity scientist and brings in technological expertise. Florian Klein is an expert strategist and scenario planner, and an observer of its evolution. Combining our perspectives, we would like to show you how the frontier between human-based strategic thinking and AI-based sensing has faded, and how decision makers and their advisors might use AI in the future to boost their capacity to take forward-looking decisions.

# 1

# THREE CHEERS TO UNCERTAINTY

Uncertainty is a fact of life. It surrounds us, forcing us to make difficult decisions. It is also the reason for evolution, as the survival of the fittest implies a capability to understand the rules of the game, anticipate future developments, and execute forward-looking strategies. It may be a nuisance, but it is also the only chance for the smart to prevail in competition.

Throughout history, humanity has always faced uncertainty, but at different levels and in the form of distinct issues. Early humans faced elementary uncertainty, typically related to basic needs such as security, food, or shelter. In our developed world with complex societies and intertwined economies, critical uncertainties have shifted.[1] Decision makers today are typically interested in rather abstract issues like future technology ecosystems, global trade regimes, or changing customer needs. As distinct as these problems may seem, they have one element in common: they reflect uncertainty from our particular perspective. When we seek to ensure survival for ourselves or our clan, or when we assess the potential for market growth for our company, we try to anticipate and solve a specific, defined problem for a particular stakeholder group. They are the type of problems that capable leaders with competent advisors should be able to figure out.

However, a new class of problems has popped up in recent history, and it seems that humankind is really struggling to cope with them. The common denominator among these wicked issues is that they concern not one particular stakeholder group but all of them at the same time, and hence, they involve unstable, complex, and holistic trade-offs. In other words, the traditional forward-looking problem-solving approach to ensure the survival of my clan does not work anymore, and that the logic to solve those problems is not as straight forward as 'faster, higher, and more efficient'. Questions around sustainability, depletion of commons, pollution, and climate change are such wicked issues. In addition, migration, global regulatory regimes, and some more profound social questions may also qualify. Our track record in decisively solving wicked problems is dismal, as the past centuries have demonstrated.[2]

The deeper reason why humankind is facing an increasing number of wicked issues may well be the tremendous success of our species. We have colonised almost all there is to colonise on the Earth, with only outer space as next frontiers. We have connected our societies and economies, and now we are hitting the limits to our growth.[3] Unless we quickly find ways to expand our playing field, we will increasingly have to dance to the tune of 'qualitative growth' instead of 'quantitative growth'.

We live in times where we see progress at an exponential pace. As consumers, we see every few weeks new phones with incredible features and extreme computer power. As tourists, we are staggered by buildings being constructed higher than ever before and we can easily travel across the globe. Just going forward without taking a step backwards is the slogan of our times. Had we asked an educated, ancient Greek or Roman at the times of Socrates or Augustus what the future might be like, would anyone have provided an answer describing the Medieval Times? Unlikely.

Furthermore, our time is not only characterised by advancements and success but also by failure and misinterpretation. We always strive for the best, but the best is not always suitable. Just think about aviation, an industry with long planning cycles – neither the fast Concorde[4] nor the large A380[5] did win. Times were changing too fast for this industry, and they did not fit into zeitgeist anymore. We do not always know what is going to happen and it is unlikely that at any point we will be able to do so – thanks to uncertainty. However, we need to find ways to cope with it – and make decisions despite uncertainty.

Philosophers across the world aimed at finding solutions to the fundamental questions we face. One of the core authors shaping modern, Western thinking was René Descartes. He must have been a rather suspicious fellow throughout his life. As a philosopher, he focussed much of his work on epistemology – or gnoseology, in the Greek term – in an attempt to answer some fundamental questions around knowledge. How can one know things? How can one acquire awareness and understanding? How can one be sure of certain facts, and which role does conviction and subjectivity play in the creation of certainty?

Quite unsurprisingly, in his early years, Descartes sought to address fundamental doubts about his own capability to create valid insights. In 1637, he published the fourth part of his *Discourse de la methóde* in which he established a principle upon which he would build his subsequent work: 'Je pense, doc je suis', usually translated as 'cogito, ergo sum', or 'I think, therefore I am'.

The point of Descartes was that 'we cannot doubt of our existence while we doubt [...]'.[6] This idea became a cornerstone of Western philosophy. In spite of doubt, this idea sought to shape a secure base of awareness. Descartes insisted that, while other awareness can be a figment of imagination, confusion, or mistaking, the very act of doubting one's own life was at least evidence of one's own mind. In this line of thinking, it is required to have a thinking entity to form thoughts, for example regarding itself.[7]

Some years later, in 1765, Antoine Léonard Thomas published an essay reflecting on the work of Descartes in which he aptly captured Descartes' intent: 'Dubito, ergo cogito, ergo sum'.[8]

The idea that 'I doubt, therefore I think, therefore I am' is one of the timeless insights of humankind. Doubt triggers us to reflect and think, and reflection and thinking are what defines us. Without doubt, there would be no research, no philosophy, and certainly no strategy.

## THE TRAP OF STATIC STRATEGY

Doubt enables us to have diverging opinions and make choices – and life is full of choices. Our existence is an endless string of decisions we take. Most of them are rather insignificant, but some are big, important, and even life-changing.

In certain circumstances, other people make calls on our behalf. We can experience this throughout our life. Right from the start, our parents make decisions in our best interest for us, even before our birth. In many cultures, they select our names and thereby shape the core of our own identity. Throughout our childhood, they continue to make decisions for us. Obviously, their rationale was to help and protect us, as we were too young to grasp the complexity behind many difficult decisions. We may have been too impulsive or inexperienced to think things through in a rational way, or we simply had other, more important, matters on our mind. The same sort of logic still applies today when we need medical treatment. Professionals will decide on the best course of action on our behalf. There are all sorts of benevolent dictators around us, and most of them take decisions to make our lives more comfortable, manageable, and structured.

Things get more complicated if decision makers decide on a course of action not only on our behalf but also on the behalf of other people. Teachers need to keep in mind the progress of the entire class, not only of the individual student, when they decide on how to structure their curriculum and how to grade performance. In a similar way, while the politicians we voted for are representing our interest vis-à-vis the rest of society, they should strive to find the best possible trade-off for all involved. In the worst of cases, they will have to make impossible trade-offs between human lives and the wider interest of society. As an example, one could take the case of whether to shoot down a hijacked passenger aeroplane on collision course with populated areas.

Another class of decision makers are managers, or 'agents', as economic theory would call them. They typically get their pay check for maximising the profitability of enterprises on behalf of their owners, the 'principals', leading to the classical agent-principal dilemma. Some managers will pride themselves for taking a short-term narrow view, but executives of the more prudent sort will balance that objective with other interests to keep the firm sustainable in the longer run. They need to incorporate the concerns of shareholders, employees, regulators, and the wider society – to name but a few – while striving to keep the company well positioned to compete in the market.[9] Throughout the past decades, we have seen many attempts to maximise profitability, which were purely driven by shareholder value interests, failing; the failed merger of Daimler-Benz and Chrysler, that was announced a 'wedding made in heaven' can be taken as cautionary tale.[10] Many managers, therefore, acknowledged the importance of combining shareholders' interests with stakeholders' concerns to achieve sustainable long-term profit.

This book is about improving decision-making processes in complex entities within a complex world, which – that much should be clear by now — is a considerable challenge in itself. This endeavour, however, is nothing new at all. The art and science of strategy has existed for thousands of years in the pursuit of the best possible course of action for armies, states, or enterprises. A comforting thought in our fast-paced world might be that its basic rules still apply. It boils down to knowing yourself and your competition, thinking ahead, and playing to your strengths with an intent to build a sustainable basis to win. If it were just that easy.

Finding and executing winning strategies is tremendously difficult. For one, we always develop strategies under restrictions, such as imperfect information, subjectivity, and time pressure. Next, it is safe to assume that our competitors are at least as smart, resourceful, committed, and agile as we are. Finally and most importantly, life is a bitch.

## TOWARDS DYNAMIC STRATEGIC THINKING

In today's world, decision makers have to navigate volatility. Societal values, the political context, and market sentiments are constantly at play with each other – at local, national, and global scale. These ambiguous drivers create unstable equilibria. This is the complex and shifting ground that strategists need to take into account when drawing up their best plans.

By way of example, the challenges that decision makers need to overcome when building their strategy are not just internal complexity and serious competition but to operate within an unruly world. Markets and societies are dynamic. Our world is aging, digitalising, unsure which news it should believe, at the brink of nervous breakdown and torn between short-term greed and a quest for long-term survival. This happens all at once, so of course our world is bound to be volatile, uncertain, complex, and ambiguous.

As a testament to how difficult this is, just consider all the firms, public entities, and societies that have taken manifestly questionable strategic decisions as of late. Mighty companies have fallen because they misjudged their power to keep their respective markets in check despite technological or societal evolution. The list of firms that once shaped and owned huge markets and that nevertheless were toppled from their thrones is long. Kodak, Blockbuster, and Nokia are just a few examples, among many others. Kodak, which owned the analogue photography market, tried to prevent progress threatening existing business, instead of using its unique position to shape the market.[11] Blockbuster, market leader in the video rental industry, missed out changes in the business model and sales channels and was eventually overthrown by disruptive players like Netflix (whom they could have easily acquired for $50 million; Zetlin, 2019). Mobile phone pioneer

Nokia, which was once an undisputed market leader, was unable to meet the customer expectations and hence was replaced by other players.[12] Former certainties such as the constant progress of globalisation, the supremacy of liberalism and democracy, or the ever-deeper integration of European states into one Union no longer stand unchallenged. Today, there are alternative views on what might be the logical course of world order.

Strategy is about making deliberate choices to ensure long-term success. Strategy originates etymologically from the ancient Greek noun *strategos* meaning *the art of army command*.[13] Like generals, corporate strategists need to make choices on what to do and what not to do. They need to define the battleground, their squad formation, and the weapons of choice before entering any battle. However, strategy is not only about immediate actions, but also the need to ensure way ahead that they have the required capabilities at their disposal. The seed planted today will not bear fruit immediately but will help in the future. Strategic decisions will not always benefit a decision maker directly but will definitely shape the course of action of the organisations and successors in the future. Instead of only basing their strategy on their gut feeling, many decision makers apply strategy frameworks. The problem is: strategy frameworks require us to understand and factor in the dynamism and complexity around us in order to lay sustainable and successful plans. However, in today's world of nested and compounded trends, strategic ambition and reality almost inevitably clash. Leaders have always faced uncertainty and dynamism while developing their plans, however in previous centuries, this aspect was less crucial. War was just a war which concerned only the involved war parties, as long as global supply chains did not exists. Nowadays, the consequences of wars go far beyond the involved parties and direct casualties. To name but a few dimensions, modern wars affect the global news landscape, as well as global supply chains and stock markets. The opinions of people on the other side of the globe was negligible, as long as it stayed there. Today, all of these factors potentially matter in almost any context, all of the time.

Such shifts in the context have a much deeper impact on strategy, as one might expect at first sight, for example the automotive captive bank sector. No need to worry for not having heard about captive banks yet. They are niche players between car producers and the banking sector. When you buy a car, you might come across one of them. Captive banks are typically associated with a car brand and are the preferred provider of financing solutions at the respective concessionary.

Captive banks will offer you a lease plan or a credit for your next car. They often have unbeatable conditions, and this is for several good reasons. For one, their financing terms are often cross-subsidised by carmakers, hoping to sell you a bigger car with more extras if your financial burden is less heavy. Up to this point, everything seems straightforward, but captive banks have an additional trump up on their sleeve when they make you an offer you cannot refuse: better information. Due to their connection with their mother company, they have access to much more data points than ordinary retail banks. This helps them to assess the current and future value of the car more accurately than ordinary retail banks. Hence, for ordinary banks, the residual value of the car is a higher financial risk than for captive banks, and hence the risk premium that captive banks need to charge can be lower. In this game, for once, all players apparently win the carmakers, the captive banks, and the car buyers.

As a result of this, the real competition for captive banks are other captive banks only. However, since carmakers usually have only one captive bank, even that competition does not really exist. In consequence, captive banks tend to be extraordinarily profitable, provided they do a decent job in estimating the future value of their mother company's cars. Hence, captive banks have contributed a very significant share to the profits of their mother groups over decades.

This happy story could continue until further notice if it was not for a chain of unforeseen events in the context of captive banking. For one, e-mobility is disrupting the automotive sector much faster and more thoroughly than previously expected. The only real uncertainty that exists at this point is when and how the sudden shift from a predominantly conventional car fleet to a fleet of e-vehicles will occur. Until recently, most carmakers thought themselves in control of that transition, as they could control the speed of adoption by price signals. Yet, several shifts in technology, public perception, and regulation have shown that this sense of certainty might have been an illusion. Battery technologies have matured more rapidly than anticipated. In consequence, the cost and weight of electrical power storage have come down more rapidly than previously assumed.

In addition, the Dieselgate scandal has turned the public opinion against conventional power trains, and more importantly, politicians and regulators in key markets seem to follow the lead of the public. One might argue that public opinion could turn again. This is undoubtedly true, but the damage is already done to captive banks: their predictions regarding the residual value of their cars have taken a hit. In this case, their association with carmakers might not have been a source of competitive advantage, but a risk. They have fallen into the trap of misjudging the future value of cars in line with their mother companies. Given that this sudden leap of uncertainty in the forecast models of captive banks hits all players simultaneously, one might be tempted to conclude that this is a minor blip. Eventually, the expert observer may argue, the industry will figure out the new competitive equilibrium, and until then, all market participants will have to navigate the same uncharted waters. However, that narrow technical perspective is treacherous. The landslide around captive banks is much bigger than just consisting of some risk indicators which need adjustment. The entire mobility sector is regrouping.

In the past, in most markets that were close to the heart of the automotive industry, the notion of being mobile typically included owning a car. However, will this dogma stand for 10 years? For starters, previously unattractive markets for carmakers are rapidly turning into the mobility hotspots of the future. Carmakers are looking at the large economies in Asia and emerging markets and start to wonder whether 'the joy of driving' and company car schemes will actually cut it there. In the markets of the future, the purchasing power of the new middle class, customer values, environmental pressure, and regulation will set the scene. Closer to home, in the mature economies of most carmakers, additional forces are at work. Our societies get older, urbanisation progresses, and younger generations are growing up as digital natives. The necessity to own a car disappears, while the meaning of owning a car is shifting. What once was a symbol for status it now turning into a mark of wastefulness.

If everybody in the sector knows about those elephants in the room, why is it so difficult for carmakers and their financing branches to prepare for them? The answers are complexity and inertia. Automotive groups are huge, multifaceted, globally acting entities that are deeply embedded in their societies. Starting a cultural, organisational, and technological transformation will take an extraordinary effort. In addition, starting the transformation without a clear-cut target picture – because we cannot be sure how our mobility world will look like in 15 years' time — has the potential to discourage even the most visionary CEO.

In addition, there is another root cause: cognitive bias within the organisation. On the surface, the conventional strategic planning approach of carmakers appears to be highly efficient. It turned them into some of the most valuable corporations ever. Corporations look at the world around them through the lens of technology and economics. Specialists identify growth potentials based on technical innovation and market demand for mobility. They devise their best strategic plans based on exhaustive analyses and draft those plans to cover periods of 3, 5, or 10 years. After that, the rest is easy: if you strive for maximum efficiency in executing these plans, you are on the safe side. After all, everybody with a voice in your organisation agreed on that plan. Some highly paid consultancy put a lot of time and effort into formalising it, so the logic of such a plan must be impeccable.

However, quite often, this is where the decision-making process derails: Decision makers tend to trust their strategic plans because their organisations have put in all available resources in developing them – after all, the strategy has to stand for many years, so we have to get it right! Inversely, the specialists who devised the plan will bend over backwards to instil confidence and certainty into their product – after all, top management bets the company on our plan, so we have to get it right!

The combination of these two notions spells trouble. All stakeholders in the process will do whatever they can to downplay the element of uncertainty in the final plan. A lot of deep thinking and research will be part of the solution. Nevertheless, in reality, strategic planners have little choice but taking shortcuts to arrive at neat, clear-cut, and unambiguous results. Therefore, they make explicit or implicit assumptions, formulate hypotheses, which turn into perceived facts somewhere along the way. We select our data and prioritise obvious strategic options over the ones that are far out. The result is often compelling in its simplicity and stringency, but it is essentially static and simplified strategic thinking. Static strategies tend to factor out complexity, create a misleading sense of confidence, and gravitate towards the safe middle ground in terms of strategic options, when they should at least consider bolder strategic moves as well.

Static strategic thinking is popular. Once we have figured out the way the market, society or technology sphere is most likely to behave, this way of thinking limits the choices one needs to make. Decision makers and their supporters can dedicate their full attention to detailing their plans quickly and with focus. The planning process proceeds splendidly, but at the cost of losing relevance. We chose to ignore important uncertainties, because the risk of doing so is apparently small. Both the decision makers and their advisors can live well with this bias. If everything goes according to plan, the advisor displays his deep insight into the industry and thus proves himself as a guru. If the decision makers, in turn, prove their leadership skills in maximising the efficiency of the process, everybody wins.

If life plays a trick on us and the unexpected happens, the liability of both the decision makers and their advisors is limited. In the worst case, the management team will be out of their current job. The next generation of static thinkers takes over. Consultants will move on their next project, managers change roles, and life will go on. The self-healing forces of competition in the market place politics will root out strategies that are mistaken, too slow, or too static. Eventually, some players will get it right, so we see evolution in its purest form.

Yet, our economy and our society pay the price of this ever-spinning wheel, because it takes time, resources, and effort to get to the right strategy. Static strategic thinking takes a toll on efficiency in the form of lower returns on investment, more red tape, and less agile organisations than we could have had. It is only now, in this era of digitally induced agility, that strategists wake up to this and ask the question whether there was a better way of planning. The analogy to all of this is: We all discovered years ago that there is an alternative to the printed, outdated road map. The digital, reactive map improved the efficiency and the experience of driving a car tremendously. Could a dynamic map of the volatile competitive landscape do the same to the navigation of a complex organisation? What would it take to build such a dynamic super strategy?

## DIMENSIONS OF DYNAMIC STRATEGY

Considering the shortcomings of conventional strategic planning, the public opinion about top managers and their strategic advisors is, unsurprisingly, not often kind. The general cliché is that decision makers are removed from reality, driven by the wrong priorities, and uninterested to engage with the real issues on the ground. No doubt, such criticism often has a point. However, before we condemn an entire profession, let us take a step back and consider. For complex, strategic decisions to turn out correct in a world of uncertainty, it would take an almost superhuman strategist. It would take nothing less than the combination of a saint, a Renaissance scholar, and Indiana Jones.

A saint, because ideal decision makers would need to take a holistic, unbiased, consistent, long view. They would have their ideas and priorities straight and would serve as a shining example by living those values in whatever they do. A Renaissance scholar, because ideal decision makers would have universal knowledge and be able to bridge the gaps between different fields of expertise as well as in between theory and practice. Last but not least, an element of Indiana Jones, as they would have to take on the world full front. They would engage with issues and people, would constantly explore, and would empathise with friend and foe alike.

In other words, to enhance the quality of decision making, a super strategist would need to strive for three ideals: *Clarity* – good strategic thinking starts with a clear and agreed set of assumptions, values, or principles. *Validity* – the thinking embraces and addresses the complexity within and around the organisation, and factors in dissident opinions and uncertainty. *Relevance* – good strategies need to be actionable and executable. They need to be exhaustive in identifying viable strategic options, create commitment to act in spite of uncertainty, and allow for strategic flexibility over time because of uncertainty.

## Clarity: Take the Long View

Strategy is about making choices[14] with the objective to create sustainable competitive advantages[15] and ensure long-term success. Before you think, 'piece of cake', be aware that there are libraries of footnotes, conditions, and disclaimers attached to these innocent looking statements. Doing strategy is an art and a science, and people will always disagree on what is a perfect strategy (while there is also the argument whether there is such a thing like a perfect strategy).

First, at the end of the day, strategy deals with people, their preferences, and the choices they make. Therefore, an element of reflectiveness and art is crucial to every good strategy. Good strategists need to be aware of their own 'frame', of how they see the world and how they judge the insights they gained about their environment. Equally important, they need to be mindful of other people's frames. Consequently, good strategists need to be self-aware and self-critical, as well as perceptive and empathetic of other people's values, opinions, and preconceptions.

This is a critically important notion. Strategy is about making sense of the things that we perceive from the world around us, and the only way to do this is using our judgement. The way you perceive and judge the world around you varies from person to person and from organisation to organisation. After all, we all have our own senses, our own set of values, and our own specific experiences, which we complement with an ever-growing set of other peoples' ideas that we picked up along the way. Some ideas we will try out, and the good ones we will save for future reference.

When we compete for the best strategy, ultimately, the quality of the things we perceive about the world around us *in combination* with the validity of our frame will determine whether certain decisions are particularly successful or not. In other words, the combination of superior perception (in the sense of detecting what is going on around you) and superior intelligence (in the sense of judging what those insights mean) will win the day. Hence, the concept of integrated strategic intelligence is one of the central ideas of this book.

We will focus on how to build a system that can help us to acquire and judge insights about this complex world in Chapter 2, which revolves around scenario thinking, and Chapter 3, which highlights the state-of-the-art in complexity science and artificial intelligence. However, for the moment, let us stick with what such a system would need to achieve – it should provide strategists with a dynamic 'map' that captures four dimensions:

- The current competitive landscape where we start our journey.

- Driving forces will determine the best course of action.

- The target picture, the objective we want to achieve.

- And as a consequence, a list of strategic options.

The first dimension is about the competitive landscape that we need to know and understand. Obviously, it is easy to narrow down a market to such an extent that you are always the number one. However, being number one does not matter when you have not understood your market. Maybe you are number one in your segment, but another segment is taking over yours, substituting your market and driving you out of the playing field. This has happened through the course of history, just think about the previously introduced downfall of Kodak brought by digital cameras or Blockbuster's decline incited by streaming platforms. It is pretty sure they were leaders in their competitive landscape. Nevertheless, the game changed, and they were not able to react.

Uncertainty and possible change are often not just falling from the sky. They are visible, yet not always apparent. A variety of driving forces might not have the power to shape the future individually. However, they can, when puzzled together, show the future way. Therefore, it is important to understand what is happening around us and open up the mind to look beyond our own noses. To do this, we must escape from our own narrow-minded thought models and show openness and curiosity. We need to take a look at other industries and geographies and understand what is shaping people's opinions. Once we know the driving forces surrounding us, we can start to make sense of them.

Knowing the playing field and its changing forces is not enough. We need to have objectives, a winning aspiration, that states what we want to achieve. Strategy shows us the way, but in order to choose the right route, we have to know the destination. Obviously, the aspiration is to be flexible and adaptable to changing environments while holding steady. Being the one to produce the leading DVD-player did matter in the past, but in the streaming world, it is losing its power. Just think about how often you have watched a DVD in the last 6 months and how frequently you have streamed or watched something online. Thus, we need to put our identity in our goals and pursue it with confidence to overcome the foe of uncertainty.

To achieve our goals and remain relevant, we need an array of strategic options that can help us to become, and remain, a winner. Some of the strategic options need to be robust, and they have to materialise regardless how the future is playing out. Other options need to be dynamic, enabling success depending on certain factors. While robust options bring consistency, dynamic options allow for agility.

Strategy is always at the intersection of combining short-term and long-term goals. Obviously, we want to maximise the outcome in the short run, but we also aim to ensure future success and profits. Combining those perspectives is a key challenge for corporate decision makers. Thus, one very basic element of how we frame our strategic thinking is the time horizon one applies to planning. The time horizon is the guiding star of strategy that enables us to track the chosen path accurately. By this, however, strategy is facing a problem humans have wrestled with throughout their entire history: do we consume now or rather later, economists call this the intertemporal optimisation problem Just take an ancient farmer just having brought home his harvest. He could either use it to instantly feed hungry mouths or he could store some of the harvest for the future. He could also take some investment decisions and use up some of the harvest to plant new crops or he could even sell his farming land. While instant consumption or asset sale will have the highest short-term impact, they present challenges for the future. The same applies for more future-oriented decisions. Saving seeds or planting more crops will increase the return in the future, yet create problems in the present. Decision makers of all kinds face such decisions. Today's world is driven by a sense of short-term thinking where decision makers often resort to merely reacting to sudden events instead of planning ahead. We no longer treat ourselves to the luxury of thinking about the future. We are often only interested in the here and now. The stock market assigns value to assets in a fraction of a second, not in generations. This is a challenge for all decision makers. They must tackle the problem at its roots and re-frame strategic management. The solution to this challenge lies at hand: accept the pain of a holistic and long-term perspective that factors in as much of the now as of the long-term future. This will bring pain and discussions. Yet in our view, if we don't try, we have already failed. Long-term planning is not a house of cards, it is a castle built for eternity.

While changing established mind-sets and well-worn processes seems very complex at first glance, the approach proposed in this book aims at simplicity, both in the process and in communication. You cannot always run away from the complexity surrounding us. To be able to cope with it, we need to carve up complexity and serve it in digestible pieces. However, this requires the commitment from all involved stakeholders to think about all factors without prejudice, see the world through the eyes of an unbiased child and listen to other opinions. Therefore, we need to zoom in to the details for every single moment and then zoom out again to see what is happening in the overall picture. The best analogy is probably a puzzle. We need to be able to understand each piece individually, but also be able to connect the pieces and understand the full picture. Furthermore, we need not only trust in the process itself, but also provide trust and support for the process. The chain is only as strong as its weakest link. If we doubt the achievement of long-term goals, we will not achieve them and remain trapped in the here and now, while the others go ahead and shape the future.

At the end of the day, decision makers need to receive, or at least perceive, benefits from their actions. This is why we also address the investment community: the aim must be to support long-term thinking and action. In this way, we counterbalance today's incentives to prioritise short-term over long-term objectives. Yet, what are the upsides of taking the long view? From our point of view, there are three key advantages. First, you increase the sustainability of your organisation, both towards the inside (long-term profitability) and towards the outside (value to society). Second, you increase the power of your strategy, because it will be easier to understand and follow. Third, you also increase the chances of your strategy actually succeeding because you have a clearer narrative.

## Validity: Embrace Uncertainty and Manage Complexity

Strategy seems stress-free: scan the market, draw your conclusions based on solid data and a profound market model, bring it into the organisation and evaluate your success; adapt if necessary. If you do not feel like doing it yourself, you can simply have a consultant to design the strategy for you. On paper, strategy is easy: you take the commonly accepted logic of the market and extrapolate it into the future. So much about the theory, but things get more complicated if one considers the increasing complexity and uncertainty around us. Throughout the strategic management process, planners aim to avoid them and instead draw a simple picture of the world. We often tend to assume that the world that surrounds us will extrapolate into the future. However, decision makers can partly control the complexity and uncertainty factoring into various settings in the internal organisational environment. Much more challenging and threatening is the complexity and uncertainty in the external environment. To overcome precisely this, decision makers must climb into the ring themselves, perceive the future in today and make decisions. No advisor or consultant can take this burden off the decision makers' shoulders.

Complexity and uncertainty often cause old recipes from success to fail, and thus, companies are being forced to adapt. However, companies do not always recognise the need for change, and even if they acknowledge that they have to adapt, they are often not able to take and enforce drastic decisions. External, environmental, and internal organisational sources of complexity and uncertainty present their very own challenges. The environmental uncertainty and complexity is endless. Researching it away is nearly impossible. Consequently, the challenge is to capture the breadth and the depth of what is going on around us and make sense of it, without overcomplicating things. At the same time, firms are challenged by organisational inertia and silo thinking. Therefore, they need to explore and to allow variety of opinions in a true dialogue.

To overcome those hurdles, we need to embrace uncertainty and manage the complexity. The task at hand seems impossible – do more research to lower the level of uncertainty, yet make systems and decisions less complex. The solution at hand is to build integrated intelligence systems, which are based on two key factors, technology and humans.

On the technology side, we experience a revolution enabling us to conduct things that have never been possible before. Automation is not stupid anymore. Artificial intelligence enables smart, self-learning algorithms, which conduct tasks in an efficient way. For the strategists, artificial intelligence provides raw analytical power and combines it with broad reach and strong pattern recognition. The strategist can easily observe and monitor a multitude of data points and get digested outputs, interpreted by the machine. Humans are limited in this capacity, and it is unlikely that we will observe a change in human nature. With machines, however, we observe a radical change, as they now have nearly endless analytical capabilities at high speed.

At this point, an ethical question also arises. Do we really want to be driven by some algorithm's decisions or don't we much prefer to equip ourselves with the best possible tools while still staying in the driver's seat? Assuming that technology is the sole differentiator, we would expect a monopoly of a few artificial intelligences. They would rule for us, and most strategies would be the same, assuming that every computer arrives at the same, perfect conclusion. However, there is no perfect, dominant strategy that will always work out – thanks to our friends, complexity and uncertainty. Thus, we believe that humans will remain relevant. Only humans can provide associative thinking and judgement based on their experience. Humans can take a look at the broad picture and combine machine output with their own judgement and gut feeling for the best possible result.

Embracing uncertainty while managing complexity requires a supportive, organisational environment, which needs to empower their decision makers and build a culture of critical thinking. This culture should instil an explorative, empathetic mind-set in each individual. We have to look not only at the cold, raw data, but also at the warm human, our feelings and intuitions. Therefore, decision makers need to be trained in focussing their efforts, yet incorporating their surroundings. To avoid the trap of group thinking and silo thinking, diversity is required. This should not be based on paper-driven quota satisfaction but on diversity in thinking. To make good decisions, we need to constantly focus and stay alert. Therefore, they require the best decision support tools at hand, which they combine with their own human judgement.

When embracing uncertainty and managing complexity in a successful way, you enhance the chances of your strategy being efficient, as you achieve a better understanding of the reality around you. This will help you speeding up the execution of your strategy, as you will have anticipated more hurdles than before.

## Relevance: Execute with Purpose

An African proverb says, 'For tomorrow belongs to the people who prepare for it today'. Yet, we observe too often good plans and strategies ending up in some drawer, instead of being implemented, or just failing because they do not meet reality. A core part of dynamic strategies' DNA is its action orientation to make it actionable. Any impactful strategy needs to be based on the three Ps, namely, purpose, principles, and pragmatism:

- *Purpose*: True passion requires purpose, understanding the reason for which we are doing something. We do not go into battle if we do not know what we are fighting for. Thus, any dynamic strategy starts with a significant strategic issue which needs to be solved by participants having understood the necessity to solve it and providing their buy-in.

- *Principles*: As in cooking, regardless of following a step-by-step recipe or already having internalised certain processes, we still need some key principles in our strategy for ensuring the validity and the achievement of our goals and avoiding chaos.

- *Pragmatism*: Sticking to a kitchen metaphor, to achieve great instead of merely good, chefs bring in their creativity and solve their tasks by combining an artful touch with pragmatism. Dynamic strategy requires going beyond cookie-cutter approaches and using intuitive sense making and pragmatic decisions.

It sounds intuitive to set-up and define a dynamic, action-oriented strategy that is responding to most urgent strategic issues. However, for many organisations, this presents a drastic shift, changing their legacy systems and mind-sets. Thus, the key challenge to execute a dynamic strategy is to replace established, static command and control systems and management styles. This change is often harder than developing the actual strategy, as it requires creating a culture of shared perception, purposeful exchange of ideas, and pragmatic yet principled management. Decision makers as well as entire organisations need to understand how we can use technology, such as artificial intelligence, to broaden our perception on what is happening around us. Decisions need to be informed; namely, in real time with a solid database. This requires trust in the technology and its outcome. Furthermore, we need to transform the fear of being replaced by technology into the curiosity of the new opportunities that results from technology-augmented decision processes. With new tools and a broader perception, a more liberal discussion culture emerges that goes beyond silos. The days of patriarchs sitting at the top of the hierarchy and seeing themselves as the only ones who have sipped from the fountain of knowledge are numbered. Relevant, actionable strategies do not segregate people with non-mainstream opinions; they understand dissident opinions as an asset. Instead of spending lots of time on collecting data, artificial-intelligence–enabled decision makers can focus on the interpretation of insights and discuss them in an open discourse based on trust and purposeful communication.

As strategy is neither pure science nor pure art but rather a combination of both worlds, each strategy process needs to find its own balance. The scientific aspects of strategy are focus, rigour, and coherence. As in every scientific work, principles are the core to understand the process and not leave out any aspects. However, pure scientific approaches are too narrow and thus require an artful touch to look beyond current horizons. The artistic aspects of strategy making are creativity, dialogue, and a certain amount of genius. This ensures that the process incorporates a novel and inspirational view providing a broader picture on the underlying strategic issues. Sometimes, strategy requires pragmatism to overcome the hurdles of scientific approaches and requires the gut feeling of decision makers. However, the task of defining and executing strategy is a privilege. The burden of this task ought to be shared among several circles: inner circle of decision makers, experts (external and internal to the organisation) as well as affected stakeholders.

To ensure flexibility yet in achieving the overall aspiration, the strategy needs to define a guiding star towards which we aim to move.

When implementing a relevant strategy with purpose, you are faster in the competition, which provides you with a competitive edge. While this process poses the risk of getting the strategy wrong, it also reduces the cost of course correcting.

In the next chapters, we will show how a scenario-thinking mind-set combined with artificial intelligence can help to facilitate the strategy process and ensure organisational success.

## NOTES

1. It should be noted that the struggle for basic needs is still real. According to the World Health Organization, in 2017 more than 820 million people are hungry (1 out of 9 people), with 151 million children younger than 5 being too short for their age resulting from malnutrition. Source: World Health Organization (2018). Global hunger continues to rise, new UN report says. Retrieved from: https://www.who.int/news-room/detail/11-09-2018-global-hunger-continues-to-rise---new-un-report-says

2. Wicked problems are unique, very difficult or even impossible to solve problems. There is neither a stopping rule nor right or wrong solutions to wicked problems. They often involve a variety of sources of complexity, such as technological or social complexity. Source: Camillus, J. C. (2008). Strategy as a Wicked Problem. Harvard Business Review. Retrieved from: https://hbr.org/2008/05/strategy-as-a-wicked-problem

3. See Meadows, D.H. ; Meadows, D.L. , Randers, J.; Behrens, W.W. III. (1972). The Limits to growth: A report for the Club of Rome's Project on the Predicament of Mankind. New York: Universe Books.

4. Despite being a modern plane, the Concorde was mainly grounded due to its low fuel efficiency, as it needs more than 100 tons of fuel for a flight from London to New York, while a Boeing 777 only needs around 44 tons. (For further information, please refer to:Bramson, D. (2015). Supersonic Airplanes and the Age of Irrational Technology. The Atlantic. Retrieved from https://www.theatlantic.com/technology/archive/2015/07/supersonic-airplanes-concorde/396698/ or Interesting Engineering (2017). Concorde: The Real Reason Why the Supersonic Passenger Jet Failed. Retrieved from: https://interestingengineering.com/concorde-the-real-reason-why-the-supersonic-passenger-jet-failed)

5. Airbus announced in 2019 to stop the production of its Airbus A380 in 2021, due to a change in customer needs, as airlines prefer smaller, efficient planes. (For further information, please refer to: Jolly, J. (2019). A380: Airbus to stop making superjumbo as orders dry up. The Guardian. Retrieved from: https://www.theguardian.com/business/2019/feb/14/a380-airbus-to-end-production-of-superjumbo or

Flottau, J. (2019): Die wohl größte Fehleinschätzung in der Geschichte der Luftfahrt. Süddeutsche Zeitung. Retrieved from https://www.sueddeutsche.de/wirtschaft/airbus-a380-aus-produktion-1.4329816)

6. See Decartes, R. (1853). *The Meditations and Selections from the Principles of Philosophy* (p. 115). Edinburgh: Sutherland and Knox.

7. See Störig, H. J. (2006). *Kleine Weltgeschichte der Philosophie* (p. 355ff). Frankfurt am Main: Fischer Taschenbuch.

8. See Thomas, A. L. (1765). *Éloge de René Descartes*. Whitefish, Mont: Kessinger Publishing.

9. For further information on the pricinpal-agent theorem please refer to Eisenhardt, K. (1989). "Agency theory: An assessment and review". Academy of Management Review. 14 (1): 57–74 or Rees, R., 1985. "The Theory of Principal and Agent—Part I". Bulletin of Economic Research, 37(1), 3–26 and Rees, R., 1985. "The Theory of Principal and Agent—Part II". Bulletin of Economic Research, 37(2), 75–97.

10. For further information on the failure of DaimlerChrysler please refer to Watkins, M.D. (2007). Why DaimlerChrysler Never Got into Gear. Harvard Business Review, retrieved from: https://hbr.org/2007/05/why-the-daimlerchrysler-merger or Wearden, G. (2007). From $35bn to $7.4bn in nine years. The Guradian. Retrieved from: https://www.theguardian.com/business/2007/may/14/motoring.lifeandhealth or Süddeutsche Zeitung (2010). Hochzeit des Grauens. Retrieved from: https://www.sueddeutsche.de/wirtschaft/daimler-und-chrysler-hochzeit-des-grauens-1.464777

11. See Mui, C. (2012). How Kodak failed. Retrieved from https://www.forbes.com/sites/chunkamui/2012/01/18/how-kodak-failed/3/#6c6f293e4a97

12. See Hern, A. (2016). Nokia returns to the phone market as Microsoft sells brand. Retrieved from https://www.theguardian.com/technology/2016/may/18/nokia-returns-phone-market-microsoft-sells-brand-hmd-foxconn.

13. See Hungenberg, H. (2014). Strategisches Management in Unternehmen (p. 5). Ziele-Prozesse-Verfahren. 8. Auflage. Wiesbaden. Springer-Verlage.

14. See Lafley, A. G., & Martin, R. L. (2013). *Playing to win: How strategy really works*. Harvard Business Press.

15. See Porter, M. E. (1980). *Competitive strategy: Techniques for analyzing industries and competitors*. Free Press.

# 2

# THE VALIDITY OF TRADITIONAL
# SCENARIO PLANNING

## WHAT ARE SCENARIOS?

Key decision makers, regardless if in private life, corporations or the public sphere, shoulder major responsibilities when making crucial decisions. Many are therefore aware of the need to be dynamic and prepared to break with the status quo if they want to be future winners. However, they face an environment that is so fast-changing that it is difficult for them to steer away ahead with confidence. Individually, decision makers are only able to observe and interpret a few of the signposts and indicators that can help anticipate change. Often, once they do recognise the forces at play, it is already too late for them to act and shape their playing field. They can only react on a playing field dictated by external conditions out of direct control. One could argue that this is quite a narrow field. However, it is not only C-level executives or high ranking politicians who have to make high impact decisions in conditions of high uncertainty caused by various factors such as new technologies and changing marketplaces. We all face those decisions in our everyday lives. Just think about your decision regarding a job and a career path. While some cultural environments are used to flexibility allowing for bold career changes, this is in many cultures a life-shaping decision, impacting a professional career of around 40 years. How can we be sure that a particular career is the best choice to reach personal and professional goals throughout our life? Our assumption is that hardly anyone can be sure that the choices they made are the best. Thus, the decisions of a CEO to acquire another firm or invest in a plant are similar to many decisions every one of us makes. The one kind is shaping the future of a firm; the other kind is shaping the future of a person. Yet, we have to make some judgement calls despite we don't know how our decisions play out. One way to ease the burden of our decisions is to use scenarios, or rather apply a scenario mind-set. Scenarios are an indispensable strategic tool for decision makers in the public, private, and non-profit spheres. They support C-level executives taking tough strategic decisions as well as anyone in a real-life situation, to cope with this dynamism and uncertainty. Strong decisions often have a long-term impact. Therefore, we like to avoid them and struggle from day to day, focussing on the immediate, short-term. Because of this, we are often living on the substance of the past, not laying out the harvest of the future. Scenarios help us avoid the mistake of focussing only on immediate problems and responses. With our focus on today's issues, we often underestimate the change on the horizon. It is not the question whether we want to buy a DVD with or without bonus material. The question is whether we will buy DVDs at all. For now, Netflix has answered the question with its streaming offering. It changed the industry landscape and paved the way for many competitors in the streaming business. This problem is famously framed by Bill Gates:

> We always overestimate the change that will occur in the next two years and underestimate the change that will occur in the next ten. Don't let yourself be lulled into inaction.[1]

Therefore, decision makers need to pose the right questions and look through the right time lenses into the future.

While the future is uncertain, scenarios help to gain an insight into a potential future. They enable decision makers to set sails and travel through a storm of uncertainty and turbulence. Through this journey, scenarios help open the eyes of any organisation or individual to the possible ways that the future could play out and to the forces that will shape it. In this way they help to change our mental maps. Our mind is organized like a map, guiding our decisions. However, we are often rather like the early explorers relying on maps based on assumptions of people who have never seen a geography than being modern tourists equipped with a GPS navigator. Just imagine an explorer in the 16th or 17th century on the shores of the Americas, only equipped with a map of a Dutch mapmaker who has never seen the Americas and is basing the entire map on hearsay. Inaccurate maps are not a problem in and of itself, but it is what we do with the map that becomes the problem. As explorer this could have severe consequences, e.g., running out of water as the map would expect a river where there is no river in reality. The same happens in decision making. We base our decision making on our mental maps, and never challenge our assumptions. Yet, if we get the facts that are the basis of the map wrong, we end up with a wrong map that leads us in the wrong direction or triggers the wrong decisions and actions. And as soon as we believe the map is correct, it is really hard to change our mindset. This is the starting point of scenario planning, that challenges your mental maps. In addition, the scenario development process can bring future order to present chaos and ultimately contribute to the decisions made with confidence about the future. They help break down complex phenomena into subsystems that are easier to analyse and are, consequently, the tools of choice for dynamic strategic planning. In this way, the immediate concerns and the game changers at the horizon are both taken care of.

Pierre Wack, a French executive at Royal Dutch Shell, was among the first to institutionalise scenario planning and thereby introduce it to the private sector. For him, scenarios make sense when 'the speed of the business environment is faster than your own ability to react'.[2] Scenario planning forces us to go beyond thinking in stock-market–driven quarters; instead, it encourages a focus on long-term thinking while simultaneously incorporating short-term thinking and actions. Thus, it is a way to combine the best of two worlds: the microscope to zoom in to the close things that happen in the short-term, so close that you might oversee them, and the telescope to take the long view at the distant future, difficult to see with the pure eye. Yet, this is not all. Scenarios also provide you with a Kaleidoscope that enables you to take on wholly different perspectives.

Scenarios are not a tool for everyone. Openness and imagination are core prerequisites to embrace uncertainty when 'thinking the unthinkable', to quote one of the originators of the scenario planning method. Herman Kahn, a leading futurist, was initially employed as a military strategist at the Research and Development (RAND) Corporation in the 1950s.[3] By embracing uncertainty, scenario planning allows us to challenge long-held positions and schools of thought in our surroundings, an organisation or ourselves. Yet, we do have to combine openness and imagination with hard facts. We need to know what is happening around us and what are the given mechanics. Those principles are caught in Pierre Wack's statement:

> *Scenarios deal with two worlds: the world of facts and the world*
> *of perceptions. They explore for facts, but they aim at perceptions*

*inside the heads of decision makers. Their purpose is to gather and transform information of strategic significance into fresh perceptions.*[4]

By re-perceiving the environment and thus questioning all the hypotheses about how the world functions, we can see and feel the world from varying perspectives, like using a kaleidoscope. This gives us a clear view to question existing hypotheses. Despite having the knowledge about certain developments and mechanics, openness is still required to break out of the common themes. Thus, thinking in scenarios is an art rather than a science. It follows scientific principles while requiring, at the same time, an open mind-set and out-of-the-box thinking.

Scenarios deal with uncertainty and turbulence. However, the different perceptions each individual holds about uncertainty and how to deal with it mirror into scenario planning literature. Thus, there is no precise definition of scenarios, neither in academic theory nor in practice. The word *scenario* is often related to terms like planning, forecasting, or analysis. Let us, therefore, consider some of the definitions (logically, rather than chronologically) of this method, used by managers to explore and reach crucial decisions. Herman Kahn, quoted above, is said to be the originator of scenario planning. He defined scenarios as 'a set of hypothetical events set in the future constructed to clarify a possible chain of causal events as well as their decision points'.[5] Harvard Professor Michael E. Porter[6] regarded as the founder of the modern strategy field and one of the most important management thinkers as well as founder of the strategy-consulting firm Monitor Group,[7] further defined scenarios as 'an internally consistent view of what the future might turn out to be – not a forecast, but one possible future outcome.'[8] Peter Schwartz, founder of the most influential scenario think-tank Global Business Network (GBN), saw their relevance as 'a tool for ordering one's perceptions about alternative future environments in which one's decisions might be played out.'[9] In his view, the process of 'scenario planning is the methodical thinking of the unthinkable. It searches for wisdom in unusual places. It assumes that there will never be enough information on which to base a decision, if that decision requires certainty about the future. Therefore, it is important to prepare a wide range of possible decisions based on an entire range of possible futures. Never being wrong about the future is better than occasionally being exactly right'.[10]

An examination of these definitions highlights some similarities. Scenario planning derives from the experience that it is impossible to know precisely

how the future will play out. Precise predictions are not feasible, as Albert
Einstein notes:

> *When the number of factors coming into play in a phenomenologi-*
> *cal complex is too large, scientific method in most cases fails. One*
> *need only think of the weather, in which case the prediction even*
> *for a few days ahead is impossible. Nevertheless, no one doubts that*
> *we are confronted with a causal connection whose causal compo-*
> *nents are in the main known to us. Occurrences in this domain are*
> *beyond the reach of exact prediction because of the variety of fac-*
> *tors in operation, not because of any lack of order in nature.*[11]

The words of Einstein resonate in the large number of forecasts and projec-
tions that failed. The world is too complex for a worst and a best case. Let us
take a journey into the past – for example at the rise of the CD. Large-scale
investments were made, based on the assumptions of how many CDs will be
sold in the future. Would those investments have been made with the knowledge of the iPod and Netflix? Probably not. However, were those developments imaginable at the time, when the Internet was starting its growth story,
and the MP3 technology was already in the development? Very likely, yet not
at first sight. Thus, decision makers need to think in robust ways: what needs
to be true for a decision to enable my firm or me to be a winner. And even more
important, as often overlooked: what needs to be true for a decision to lead to
total failure. Linear predictions are probably not the way to go. Yet, sound and
robust decisions or strategies should work in a number of possible, alternative
futures that we can explore with scenarios. In this way, scenarios help companies and individuals being flexible regarding setting strategies or making
decisions, while being innovative at the same time since scenarios contribute
to creative thinking about the future demands. They are models that build
distinct but plausible worlds, combining facts and fiction. Therefore, they are
articulated as stories or narratives of alternative end-states of the world in the
future and the respective development towards those states. Scenario design
observes trends, events, and forces, clustering them into related patterns to
tell plausible stories. The emphasis is on plausibility, not on the probability.
Scenarios have the aim of combining the novelty with the expectations derived
from historical determinism into a fruitful relationship. By plausible, we mean
that they could play out; we do not mean that they will play out with any
degree of certainty, as the concept of probability suggests. Scenarios are a contribution to deterministic chaos – the world around us is too complex to make

sound, reliable predictions. There have been approaches aiming to model the world based on probability, yet they lacked the computional power to process all data required. Today's world is subject to exponential change, consequently with increasing processor speed, and with the further development of artificial intelligence, the world of plausibility can be merged with the world of probability, as we will discuss in Chapter 3. However, let us disregard the ability of future technologies to make some kind of reliable predictions for now and base our initial thinking on the plausibility principle. While we assume that certain natural laws hold true, no one will ever have a glass ball to predict the future. Some might make predictions that will hold true to a large extent. However, there is no security that the next prediction will also materialise. We have seen many 'gurus' who were right in predicting a stock-market crash but then failed to repeat their success; even 'gurus' are just humans. Thus, plausibility is the dominant approach of scenario planning. With their focus on plausibility rather than probability, scenarios can help avoid the tendency to under- or overestimate risks in the long term. The Nobel Laureate, psychologist and behavioral economist Daniel Kahneman and his collaborator, psychologist and decision researcher, Amos Tversky brilliantly illustrate this in their prospect theory, which has become famous in business and economic research. This theory is derived from the understanding that individual risk-taking varies, depending on the expected probability of an event; however, expected utility is not important. If the expected outcome is positive, individuals prefer known, but small rewards to unknown but higher gains, and are thus risk-averse. If the expected outcome is negative, they are prepared to take risks, as individuals prefer outcome that are unknown yet imply high losses compared to an outcome with a small but unknown loss.[12] Hence, probability is not always the best measurement and we should more often focus on the bigger picture – something scenario planning is a good and suitable tool for.

In the following, we will present two core principles of scenario planning: outside-in thinking and embracing uncertainty. Key decision makers use a wide range of strategic tools to be dynamic and win in the market place; among these are traditional analysis tools such as the Boston Consulting Group (BCG) Matrix or Porter's five forces.[13] They try to combine external forces with a firm's competitive positioning, yet start from the firm's internal view. However, in contrast to these tools, we start the scenario process by analysing the external environment, rather than by starting with the organisation or the close environment. This approach is based on an outside-in way of thinking as a crucial scenario principle. For us, outside-in is the best view for making strategy, as the importance of external factors will continue to rise for any strategy. This is not to say that internal factors are not also integrated into the development process, but they do not provide the starting point for the scenarios. A further core principle of scenario design is to embrace uncertainty; compared with other strategy tools, uncertainty, volatility, and complexity are integral parts of the process. By focussing on the uncertain items, which might be highly volatile, scenario planning by nature takes on a high level of complexity which is then boiled down to make the complexity manageable. Uncertainty can happen in a variety of ways and areas. As strategy consultants, we like 2 × 2 matrixes and thus aim for two axes which in combination help us to understand an issue. Regarding uncertainty, we see two key drivers relevant for decision makers. First, do we know what is going to happen? When lacking this knowledge, we already face uncertainty. Yet, sometimes we can plan despite uncertainty. For frequent travellers, a daily example are the security instructions in planes before taking off. No one knows what is going to happen, however, the stewards provide instructions what to do in case of an emergency. However, often we lack the knowledge of what to do. When we combine the lack of knowledge about what is going to or what might happen, with the lack of knowledge on how to deal with it, we face true, total uncertainty. From our experience, we see scenarios as the only tool that helps to lighten true, total uncertainty. Uncertainty often creates a level of chaos that decision makers can hardly manage or not even bother thinking about controlling. Thus, scenarios help to order the perception of participants and manage uncertainty by using a structural approach. Scenarios should be designed as engrossing yet provocative and plausible stories that are capable of encouraging stakeholder involvement and of learning; they should challenge us to generate conceivable hypotheses about the future and also highlight the risks and opportunities associated with strategic issues.

However, when decision makers are not involved in the scenario development process, they might be reluctant and defensive because they lack experience of the scenario journey and have no knowledge on how to make sense of the prevailing uncertainty. Consequently, scenarios are a core tool for organisational learning. Lacking involvement creates a low level of ownership that might prevent the scenarios and necessary strategic consequences being brought into the organisation. Nevertheless, scenarios are tools for recognising and adapting to change over time; they are not the final word but need to be continuously monitored and adapted. Scenario planning is, therefore, a hands-on, practitioner-driven methodology.

The aim of scenario planning is not to identify and predict with certainty future occurrences but to emphasise the major factors that could shift the future in diverse directions, and hence incite thinking beyond the current assumptions. Scenarios aim, proactively and intelligently, to make these forces visible and manageable. This enables us to recognise forces for change when they materialise and assist us in making better decisions for the future already today. They provide an advantage to those organisations who have a scenario mind-set as they have already thought through a number of potential events and circumstances along with their implications, yet without aiming to plan for all potential events and outcomes. Therefore, scenarios bridge the gap between lack of planning – leading to surprises – and over planning – leading to inertia. This is a key advantage, especially in turbulent times, as organisations will need less response time and are consequently in a competitive 'pole position'. Scenarios thereby allow us to think about, and respond confidently to, the enormous number of potentially influential factors that affect any of our decisions by finding a way to cut through complexity. Ultimately, scenarios help us invent and consider various detailed, plausible futures and use them to create sound and future-proof strategies that will work in any of the potential futures.

Scenarios are hypotheses, not predictions. We deliberately talk about scenarios in the plural and not a scenario; this means they should provide diverging yet imaginable paths forward. A number of different scenarios are created in the search for robust and future-proof decisions and strategies, whereby each scenario diverges considerably from the others. Working on numerous scenarios enhances understanding and minimises the consequences of the unexpected. Multiple scenarios allow us to rehearse each scenario as a unique future. They teach us, particularly decision makers, the reality of a world that is too complicated and uncertain for us to predict its future. Therefore, rather than erroneously presuming how the future will play out, we can understand, based on multiple scenarios, how to make decisions when confronted with a high level of uncertainty.

Imagining the future is the easy part. Literature and Hollywood have often indulged in what have been regarded as wild fantasies about the future, which have then been politely characterised as science fiction or deemed, less politely, as unrealistic or crazy – until fantasy became reality.

For example, in 1865, the French author Jules Verne published his novel *From the Earth to the Moon* that talks about and actually predicts various aspects of the actual moon landing. In his novel, three men made the journey. He also predicted costs of around $5.5 million, the equivalent of about $13 billion in 1969, which is not far off the actual cost of around $16 billion. Other ideas that have made it from science fiction into real life are 3D printers or tablets used in *Star Trek* or the heads-up displays from the 1958 *Minority Report* that already showcased today's air touch technology.[14]

Those examples show that thinking about the future is based on two things: a good understanding on what is happening in the world around us, combined with pure creativity. It is much harder, however, to make this imagined future credible and to persuade stakeholders to act on this basis once they have been convinced. To achieve a credibility that leads to action requires a deep understanding of the world today and the disruptive forces that might change it in the future. Scenario planning is not a rocket science; however, it requires an open mind and the ability to embrace uncertainty.

## How Scenarios Differ from Predicting or Forecasting the Future

Looking into the future has always excited humans throughout mankind's history; the demand for futurism answers a deep urge to predict the destiny of people. The science fiction author Bruce Sterling defined futurism in a timeless way:

> *Futurism is the art of re-perception. It means that life will change, must change and has changed; it suggests how and why. It shows that old perceptions have lost their validity, while new ones are possible.*[15]

In human history, futurism was often connected with a religious or spiritual element. An example of ancient futurism is the High Priestess of the Temple of Apollo at Delphi, the Pythia in ancient Greece, commonly known as the Oracle of Delphi. She sat on a tripod with vapour rising from a crack in the earth beneath her. The vapour contained gas, sending her into ecstasies while she made her prophecies in opaque language that required an experienced priest to interpret.[16] Today, fewer people would bet on the prophecies of an oracle; nevertheless, there is a demand for theories and accounts of the future.

In their thinking process, scenarios follow the Hegelian premise in that they court contradiction and paradox. Decision analysis and forecast methods, on the other hand, follow the Leibnizian search for the one truth and representation of reality.[17]

Beyond the broad concept of scenarios introduced above, there exist a comprehensive set of different ideas and concepts relating to an understanding of what scenarios are. We, therefore, need to differentiate scenarios in the sense of how we understand and use them; we have to distinguish our understanding of scenarios from those ideas that talk about scenarios or use the term scenario without, ultimately, containing scenarios. Scenarios represent more than just different paths through a decision tree. We do not develop just one scenario, but rather a set of multiple scenarios they do not set out to accurately tell or forecast the future, nor do they provide precise probability distributions. As much as we would like to show how the future would play out, we do not own a crystal ball that predicts the future like it does in fairy tales. If we had one, we would be better engaged in playing the stock market than in consulting or writing books. Hence, despite thinking a lot about the future, we don't know more or less about it than anyone else. Scenarios do help gaining a better understanding of uncertainties that influence the future, but they downplay probability. Therefore, they simplify the vast amounts of data by telling an overseeable number of stories that incorporate the interaction of various factors under defined conditions. While past attempts to make the future more probable failed due to lacking technological capabilities, new frontiers of scenario planning are going to involve probabilities, thanks to technological progress. This is leveraging Moore's law, and the consequent computer power, with the abilities of AI, neuronal networks,[18] and machine learning. Also, we are just at the starting point of this development, which is disrupted and revolutionised bi-weekly. Developments like quantum computing[19] start to materialise beyond pure theory and provide a boost to the probability stream.

A key principle of scenario planning is that it is an art rather than science. Thus, let us work with an analogy from art. Scenarios do not paint an accurate picture of the future. However, they provide ways of applying the right brush on the right canvas with the right colours. When looking at the same prospect, one painter will get a Van Gogh picture of the future; one will get a Picasso; one a Rubens, and the fourth a Warhol on the same subject matter simply by differently arranging the same colour pixels. And as in painting, different viewers of a painting interpret them differently, scenarios will also be differently interpreted. Nevertheless, compared to art, conducting the scenarios does not require genius artist skills, once you understand the mechanics behind it. Yet, as in art, you need to know some basic principles which we aim to give you an understanding of throughout this book.

Scenarios do not exist simply, so we can choose the future we favour and bet the farm on it, in the hope only this future will come to pass; rather they are there to challenge existing mind-sets and ideas. As a collection of narratives, scenario thinking tries to focus on aspects with high impact and high uncertainty which risk being overlooked in traditional planning approaches. Therefore, we need to differentiate between four distinct kinds of futures:

- Possible futures – something that might happen with a certain likelihood based on knowledge and expectations about the future.

- Plausible futures – something that could happen based on our current knowledge, yet does not have to be likely to happen.

- Probable futures – something that is likely to happen based on curent trends and the extrapolation of it without incorporating uncertain events.

- Preferable futures – something we want to happen based on our own judgement, regardless of its plausbility or likelihood.

Various techniques have been used to look into the future and produce accurate forecasts serving as a basis for robust strategic planning; these include extrapolation or sensitivity analysis, complex simulations or contingency planning. They are based on *probable* futures, whereas scenarios focus on *plausible* futures. Contingency planning focusses purely on a limited number of uncertainties and looks for an answer if the limited number of uncertainties is not happening as aspired in the base-case. Scenarios in contrasts include a large variety of uncertainties and their interplay. Economic forecasts take a one-track approach based on a linear projection with a most likely end-state. In a sensitivity setting, most indicators are kept stable while only one or few variables are changed. While this makes sense in an environment with narrow changes, it will not be able to respond to change in a complex and fast-changing environment. Scenarios therefore change various variables at the same time and refrain from keeping something stable. Therefore, they have the goal to constitute a plausible future state with major changes in key drivers. Forecasters use complex quantitative models to predict the future, with uncertainty being implicit in the forecasting. In contrast, scenarios regard uncertainty as explicit and its development as unreliable. Scenario planners create a number of potential scenarios with distinct developments that are all plausible in various ways and that question existing assumptions. Forecasts are often the quantified understanding and judgement of a third party and take the place of independent thinking; quantified forecasts are then used as an argument or defence for any action. Accepting only this expert judgement fails to empower optimal decisions, as it often comes with a lack of understanding of the forces. Alternatively, as the physics genius Stephen Hawking once said: 'I have noticed that even those who assert that everything is predestined and that we can change nothing about it still look both ways before they cross the street.'[20] Forecasts bear the danger to be taken as truth, yet they only project today's assumptions as if tomorrow's world will be the same as today. André Bénard, a former group managing director at Shell, expressed the Shell thinking: 'Experience has taught us that the scenario technique is much more conducive to forcing people to think about the future than the forecasting techniques we formerly used.'[21]

Throughout history, various predictions and forecasts have shown a high level of failure with a substantial impact on all stakeholders, as Danish physicist and Nobel Laureate Niels Bohr famously observed: 'It is very difficult to predict — especially the future'.[22]

- In 1903, the President of the Michigan Savings Bank warned Henry Ford's lawyer Horace Rackham against investing in the Ford Motor Company with the words: 'The horse is here to stay, but the automobile is only a novelty – a fad.'[23]

- In 1946, Darryl Zanuck, president of 20th Century Fox, expressed his indifference to the competition from television: 'Television will not be able to hold on to any market it captures after the first six months. People will soon get tired of staring at a plywood box every night.'[23]

- Not only executives fail in their predictions but also powerful strategy consultants. In the early 1980s, the US telecommunications giant AT&T asked strategy consulting firm McKinsey & Company to give a forecast of the mobile phone market until 2000. The forecasted number of 900,000 mobile phones led AT&T to pull out of the market. The prediction was less than 1% of the actual 109 million phones. Having recognised the real development of the number of mobile phones, AT&T re-entered the market by acquiring McCaw Cellular for $12.6 billion. Obstacles at the time, such as the heavy weight of the devices, short battery time, patchy network coverage, and the high cost per minute were taken into account. However, in the prediction, they were static. Scenarios, on the other hand, take those obstacles as uncertainties and include them in order to simulate various what-if situations.[24]

Other examples are the rejection of the use of aeroplanes in offensive warfare in the early 20th century or the decline of US automotive companies due to the failure to imagine that customers might want to have a smaller car. We could zoom into any industry or sector at more or less any given time and find the omnipresent guru predicting something with certainty that eventually played out very differently, either because it went far beyond what the guru predicted or in the opposite direction. While many forecasts failed, there are also a lot of forecasts that materialize with a large share of accuracy. However, whether this is luck or skill remains undecided. Yet, we would just refer to the statement of Princeton-Professor Burton Malkiel: 'a blindfolded monkey throwing darts at a newspaper's financial pages could select a portfolio that would do just as well as one carefully selected by the experts'.[25] This statement led to a lot of investigations. The Chicago Times used for several years the monkey Adam to select five stocks from the Wall Street Journal that bet most of the years the Dow Jones. Adam Monk was not on his own, in Russia the chimpanzee Lusha belonged to the top-five percent of all Russian invesment fund managers by chosing 8 out of 30 stocks (as he selected building blocks that represented the stocks). In the US, the chimpanzee Raven was allowed to throw arrows on a list of 130 Internet companies. His portfolio grew by 79 percent in the first year and by 213 percent in the second, making Raven the 22nd of several hundred American investment managers in 2000. Yet, not only monkeys are good investors. In South Korea a parrot took part in a six-week stock market game together with ten professional stock brokers. In the end he had the third best performing portfolio by picking his shares with his beak.[26] In 2012, those outcomes motivated Aon Hewitt and London based Cass Business School to empirically compare random 'monkey' portfolios (10 million portfolios for each year between 1968 and 2011) with 13 stock market indicators, surprisingly (or not) most monkey portfolios bet the indices.[27]

In the retro-perspective, those examples sound far off and are hard to imagine today. Yet, the underlying assumptions were quite legitimate at the time of making those statements. However, they were limited by the lack of what-if thinking – a spice which scenario thinking brings into strategic planning.

Most non-scenario-related forecasting techniques are mainly based on regression analysis. We can differentiate between scenarios, forecasts, and predictions by using a number of different measures (Table 1).

**Table 1: Comparison Forecasts, Predictions, and Scenarios.**

|                | Forecasts | Predictions | Scenarios |
|----------------|-----------|-------------|-----------|
| Type of future | Most-likely futures | Continuation/Variation of the past based on some variables | Futures that could plausibly happen |
| Focus | Focussing on certainty | Focussing on certainty or uncertainty, pending on the developer's intention | Focussing on uncertainty |
| Illustration | Quantitative | Quantitative and pressured | Qualitative or quantitative |
| Core strength | Strong for a short-term time frame with a low degree of uncertainty | Strong for short-term time frame with strong political pressures | Strong for a medium-to-long-term time frame with a large degree of uncertainty |

*Source*: Adapted from Lindgren, M., & Bandhold, H. (2003). Scenario planning: The Link between Future and Strategy. New York: Palgrave Macmillan.

Complex simulation models often incorporate a large variety of potential outcomes as the result of a computer-generated algorithm. However, this is purely based on what has happened in the past, as it is difficult to include new regulations or innovation in those models, thus scenarios can help to overcome this number based, subjective analysis by incorporating subjective judgements.

It is a commonly held belief that hard information requires quantification in the form of tables, graphs, and figures, or at least in proper academic language. However, most questions on the future are too complex for scholarly language or quantitative hypothesis. Already, Socrates philosophized if 'a good decision is based on knowledge and not on numbers'[28] Scenarios are not a highly formalised methodology; rather they are a gentle way of structuring thoughts that uses the language of narration, often found stories, and other narratives. They allow the explanation of reasons that aid understanding and thus provide the required knowledge for sound decisions. How we develop scenarios is the focus of our attention in what follows.

## A Short History of Scenario Planning

Defining desirable future states is a part of human culture; people have, therefore, used scenarios or narratives for centuries as a tool for indirectly exploring the future and its impact on society, organisations, and institutions. From the edge of today, we can describe five stages in the evolution of scenarios as a tool to improve decision making: Four that paved the way and a fifth that is laying the future's foundation. The first wave is the 'ancient' process that not yet adequately formulated as scenario planning, yet still answering what-if questions. The second wave is Herman Kahn and the RAND Corporation that initiated modern scenario planning by using a formalised approach that went beyond the immediate battlefield. The third wave is the development of scenarios in the business world through their leading proponent and innovator Shell. The fourth wave was the worldwide diffusion of scenario planning by consulting firms like GBN. The fifth wave is currently taking place, as the scenario process is undergoing significant digital transformation to make it faster, more reliable and cheaper than ever before (Fig. 1).

In the first wave, scenarios were seen as potential futures encapsulated in the form of utopias or dystopias. Plato, for example, described the ideal *Republic*[29] in the ancient world, while Thomas More's *Utopia*[30] depicted the ideal society in the sixteenth century. George Orwell, on the other hand, painted a dark picture of surveillance in his dystopia *1984*.[31] As a strategic planning tool, scenarios find their roots in the military. Military strategists used them as war game simulations, to conduct what-if analyses before making any actual move. Despite its long military history, the first documentation of scenarios only appears in the writings of the Prussian generals Carl von Clausewitz[32] and Helmuth Moltke (the Elder)[33] who lived at the turn of the eighteenth and nineteenth centuries. They are also credited with being the first to formulate the principles of strategic planning.[34]

**Fig. 1:   Timeline of Scenario Planning.**

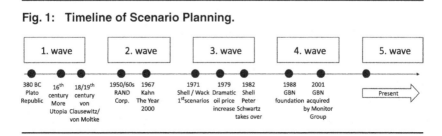

The second wave, the modern form of scenarios, started just after World War II. The US Air Force used scenarios for military purposes to help them imagine the competitive responses of their enemies. These scenarios were to enable them to fund the best weapons systems for the future. The task faced a high level of uncertainty, especially as weapon development processes had (and still have) long lead times and their outcome is often highly uncertain. Even today, in the time of computer simulations, military projects are complex, and failures are major news items (e.g. the Airbus A400M).[35] Furthermore, the onset of the Cold War changed global politics significantly, so the future political environment was unclear after World War II. Ultimately, the efficiency of weapons is highly dependent on the weapons themselves and the countermeasures developed by the enemy. The US military, therefore, needed an approach that encompassed all the different streams of thinking, brought them into alignment and enabled them to simulate the outcome and effectiveness of the to-be-developed weapon system. This requirement led to the development of the Delphi technique by the RAND Corporation during the 1950s and 1960s. The RAND Corporation was a research organisation established by the US Air Force and Douglas Aircraft technology in 1946 for researching new forms of weapons technology. By using a structured and interactive communication approach, different opinions could be synthesised. Experts answer questionnaires in various rounds, in which they are confronted with an anonymised summary of all the experts' forecasts and reasoning from the prior round. This process was meant to encourage them to revise their answers and converge towards one group answer.[36] One of the participants in the weapons' development programme at RAND Corporation was Herman Kahn. The use of Delphi techniques and system analysis at RAND inspired Kahn, who 'was the ranking authority on Civil Defense and strategic planning at the RAND Corporation', to invent a method that he called 'future-now' thinking. At this point, in-depth analysis met imagination in producing reports that purported to be written by people in the future.[37] By combining facts with logic, Kahn showed that US military strategy was based more on wishful thinking or even fantasy than reasonable justification and thoughtful process. It led to the foundation of his work on thinking the unthinkable, a scenario on the consequences of 'nuclear war by miscalculation'. Although this approach was already developed in the 1950s, Kahn did not receive wide public attention for his thoughts before he published his book *On Thermonuclear War*[38] in 1960. With this research, he wanted to prevent nuclear war by raising awareness. When he initiated his method of structuring thoughts in the 1950s for the Air Defense Missile Command (a large-scale early warning system), the term *scenario* had fallen out of use in the Hollywood film industry (having been replaced by the term *screenplay*), so Kahn reframed it for his own work. Previously, scenarios had been scripts for films or theatre plays. By using the term 'scenario', Kahn wanted to show the fictional character of scenarios, understood as stories needing exploration rather than accurate predictions.[39]

In the 1960s, Kahn established the Hudson Institute after leaving the RAND Corporation. The Institute had the purpose of developing stories about the future to support clients in thinking the unthinkable. In moving into the civilian world, Kahn was able to win over established companies like Shell, Corning, IBM, or General Motors to the scenario movement. In 1967, he published *The Year 2000*, 'which clearly demonstrates how one man's thinking was driving a trend in corporate planning'. Ted Newland saw this work as the starting point for initiating future thinking at his employer – marking the birth of the renowned scenario planning at Shell.[40]

When Kahn left the RAND Corporation, his colleagues Olaf Helmer and Theodore Gordon also departed and set up their own institute, the Institute of Future. They started, jointly with members of the Stanford Research Institute (SRI) and the California Institute of Technology, to offer long-range planning for civilian clients who saw various drivers such as political or economic forces as sources of change influencing their businesses. They conducted scenario planning to analyse and plan for enormous societal changes; for example, the US educational landscape, which SRI analysed to create five future scenarios for the year 2000, incorporating a number of different factors such as population growth or ecological destruction. An 'official' future was then chosen, while the others were largely disregarded. At the start of Nixon's presidency, the 'official' future arrived at the US Office of Education, where it was deemed impossible on account of its incompatibility with the values of the ruling administration. This did not stop the SRI and the cutting edge futurists like Willis Harmon, Peter Schwartz, Thomas Mandel, and Richard Carlson to move on to conduct scenarios with the Environmental Protection Agency. Kahn and the SRI were not alone in initiating scenario thinking. Jay Forrester, a Professor at the Massachusetts Institute of Technology, also used a similar way of thinking to describe supply and demand chains. In his approach, he applied scenarios to develop a model that would, at the same time, facilitate an understanding of the nature of growth and stimulate public debate.[41]

The third wave of scenario planning started at Royal Dutch Shell. Until 1955, Shell had focussed its planning process on physical planning. In the next decade, planning shifted its focus towards financial considerations on a project by project basis. In 1965, Shell then introduced the *Unified Planning Machinery* system to provide information for the entire oil value chain, from the extraction and transportation of oil until its arrival at petrol stations. The system included global activities and had a six-year planning horizon. While the first year's planning was very detailed, the following five years were planned in broader terms. As its involvement in the oil industry is a long-term business, Shell decided that the six-year planning process was too short a time frame. Therefore, in 1967, they set up a study called *Year 2000* to investigate the world of the future in that year. This study found that the then-current year-on-year growth in the oil industry was unlikely to continue until 2000. It was also anticipated that the oil price discontinuities and fluctuating interfuel rivalry would shift from a buyer's to a seller's market. They also expected oil players to become large, highly engaged and less agile organisations, compared with dinosaurs who could not deal with fast-changing settings. As a result, Shell asked a number of national Shell entities to participate in the *Horizon Planning* exercise to find a new way of planning and anticipating within a 15-year time frame. Inspired by Hermann Kahn's methods, Pierre Wack, who was the lead economist at Shell France, began to develop scenarios in France. Although an economist, Wack did not consider economic modelling as a high-value-adding approach due to it being a poor substitute for thought and its selective use of intuition. For him, France was the perfect testing ground, as natural gas was available, though undeveloped, at the time, and there was a high level of uncertainty in political discussions on the national energy regime. His initial attempts were unsuccessful, as they failed to give any insight beyond what was already known, due to only combining uncertainties that were already known. However, it helped gaining an understanding about applying the methodology. His team therefore sought to gain a deeper understanding of the various uncertainties surrounding the French energy market.

When the different strands of the *Horizon Planning* initiative validated the findings of the *Year 2000* process, Shell started, in 1971, to experiment with scenarios as an improved approach for corporate planning and thinking about future developments. However, the company was cautious in the first year and simultaneously ran the *Unified Planning Machinery* system that had been used until that time. Pierre Wack and Ted Newland, collaborators in what they called the Group Planning department, started to look out for far-reaching, profound drivers that had an impact on the oil price, in particular factors and events. Their intention was to give Shell sufficient lead-time to adapt to disruptive forces and changes in the oil industry.[42]

After World War II, the oil price had risen only very gradually. The advanced economies were highly dependent on a low oil price, as oil was the lubricant of their economies. At the time the Group Planning department was established, there was change in the air. The US were exhausting their known oil reserves while the members of the Organization of the Petroleum Exporting Countries (OPEC) started to flex their muscles in favour of the Arab world by threatening oil importers with price rises. Wack realised that scenarios were an excellent way to get inside the minds of Shell managers to trigger strategic actions, and they, therefore, incorporated all these factors in running the first versions of scenario planning at Shell. They investigated the possible drivers of oil prices within a long-term horizon for the year 2000. In their analysis, they found that oil exporters could occupy a position of significant market power by increasing the oil price on which the developed economies were highly dependent. They could see what would happen, but there was no clear indication about when it might occur. They knew that old oil contracts were to be renegotiated as part of the Tehran renegotiation in 1975 and assumed that prices would be drastically increased before the negotiations to up the pressure. From their investigation, they developed two different scenarios: the first described a world with stable oil prices subject to new technologies and new oil resources in non-OPEC countries; the second scenario, in contrast, described a world with an oil price crisis incited by OPEC members. On presenting their conclusions to the decision makers at Shell, the executives listened carefully to the scenario planners and realised the massive impact these developments could have on their business. They did not initiate any changes, as they were presented with strong uncertainties without any grounds for exercising their decisions. Consequently, Pierre Wack started to change their approach and move towards stories that made the future vivid and more imaginable, so that Shell decision makers could better understand the nature of these uncertainties. It was a timely move; in 1973 the Yom Kippur War (also called Ramadan War, October War or 1973 Arab–Israeli War) started, oil prices quadrupled, causing a cascade of events that began with an increase in inflation. This contributed to market over-reactions by various players, thereby boosting the inflation rate.[43]

By mid-1974, the demand for oil had contracted below production capacities causing an economic domino effect resulting in deflation. Because of their planning, Shell was prepared and able to adapt quickly to the changing environment, as they had made a much more robust use of scenario planning. They were aware that economies would reflate; only the timing was uncertain. When the slowdown in economic growth became visible, Shell managers adapted their business plans and were able to anticipate changes and exploit the oil price shocks, such as the tripling of the price in 1979. The scenarios and the rapid responses of the Shell managers helped transform Shell from being one of the weaker companies among the 'Seven Sisters', the name given to the seven most important oil companies, into one of the two most powerful. Furthermore, the strategic advantages coming from the scenarios transformed Shell into the most profitable oil company of the time.[44] Hence, the scenarios are seen as a cornerstone of Shell's leading position in the oil industry and made Shell into the core user and ongoing developer of scenario methodology in the business world. The oil industry is a good applicant of scenarios, where several actions have changed the entire industry. The industry has learnt how disrupting technologies can change the knowns of the past, for example fracking that led to a new boom of oil exploitation in the US. And who would have anticipated some decades ago, that US oil production can cover partial production cuts of Saudi Arabia?

At the same time, Shell was developing scenarios, General Electric (GE) joined the movement with scenarios on global and domestic (US) political and economic developments, although the team at GE around Ian Wilson gained little publicity, while Shell became the celebrated scenario organisation. Scenarios that follow the intuitive logic methodology are thus often referred to as the Shell approach.[45] This success inspired a large number of companies to incorporate long-term thinking and use scenario planning; for example, the number of US companies using scenarios after the oil crisis in the 1970s doubled. At this time, scenarios were notably used by large corporations in capital-intensive industries with long lead times, such as aerospace or petroleum.[46] For example, the Airbus A380 started with initial feasibility studies in the 1980s. After that, Airbus had discussions with its most prominent competitor Boeing to jointly build a superjumbo. When those talks failed, Airbus began developing their large-scale plane in 1995, setting up a Large Aircraft Division. It was not until 27 April 2005 that the maiden flight of the aircraft took place, and only in October 2007 was the first A380 delivered to an airline, Singapore Airlines, entering service on 25 October 2007 with flight number SQ380 from Singapore to Sydney.[47] In the early 1980s, half of all Fortune 1000 companies were using scenario planning. However, this success was temporary, as the economic recession of the 1980s brought staff reductions and cost-cutting that reduced the application of scenarios. Some argue that the recession was not the sole reason for this; over-simplified use of scenarios by planners who confused narrative scenarios with quantitative forecasting also contributed.[48]

In the mid-1980s, the fourth wave of scenario planning began. Peter Schwartz took over at Shell from Pierre Wack as the head of scenario planning (who had been employed there from 1961 to 1982). Wack spent his first decade at Shell France as Chief Economist and thereafter led the Group Planning team in London that conducted scenario planning.[49] Schwartz joined in 1972 the Stanford Research Institute. Here he worked on strategic planning and futurist topics, starting to work with scenario planning. At Stanford Research Institute he rose to director of the Strategic Environment Center, yet moved in 1982 to Shell to lead the scenario planning team.[50] Under Schwartz's lead, they continued the success story of scenario design at Shell. He and his team drew up three possibilities for Shell, including an oil price crash to 16 USD per barrel. Shell's top management took this very seriously and saved money to invest once prices had fallen. While other oil players stockpiled their reserves after the outbreak of the Iran–Iraq War in 1980, Shell sold its excess before prices dropped in 1986. As they had anticipated this price collapse, they were able to set up a 3.5 billion-investment programme; through buying oilfields, they gained a long-term cost advantage over their rivals. The success of his scenarios at Shell (he also anticipated the collapse of the Soviet Union) led Schwartz to provide more organisations with the long-term planning school of thought and with four colleagues he founded the consulting firm GBN in 1987.[51] Their aim was to help organisations picking up emerging opportunities from a shifting, uncertain world. Beyond consulting, they offered trainings and established a network of visionary thought leaders. Among his co-founders were:

- Jay Ogilvy, a former philosophy professor at Yale University and the head of values and lifestyles research programme at SRI.

- Napier Collyns, who worked for 30 years at Shell's planning group and was part of Pierre Wack's original scenario planning team.

- Stewart Brand, a creator and an editor of the counterculture magazine *Whole Earth Catalog* and the co-founder of the WELL, an online community for globally intelligent and well-informed participants as well as the Long Now Foundation.

• Lawrence Wilkinson, the president of the film, TV, and digital entertainment firm Colossal Pictures.[52]

The corporate world acknowledged their Shell legacy, which gave them chance to get clients in the first place. In the meantime, strategy guru Michael Porter suggested in his influential writings that external forces give a basis for planning in the corporate setting. It opened the eyes of decision makers towards more outside-in thinking, going beyond pure extrapolation-based planning. This led to a proliferation of consulting firms in the scenario ecosystems and the re-emergence of scenarios. GBN brought together a number of people with different mind-sets and backgrounds to think in depth outside current public discussions. It was seen as an eclectic, if not eccentric consulting company that started to codify the scenario process. Many regard Peter Schwartz's book *The Art of the Long View*[53] as the seminal publication on scenario planning as it introduced the concept and vocabulary of scenarios to leaders and organisations around the world. GBN's head office was in Emeryville, California, in a converted factory in the shadow of Bay Bridge. It had more than 100 clients; in the private sector, these included IBM and AT&T and, with clients like the Pentagon, the Central Intelligence Agency (CIA), the Government of Singapore, and the National Education Association, they also had a strong foothold in the public sector.[54] In 2000, GBN was acquired by the strategy-consulting firm Monitor Group, which in turn was acquired by the global professional service firm Deloitte in 2013.[55]

Beyond its consulting work, GBN gained extensive publicity mainly for its work in cinema. They collaborated with DreamWorks on the science fiction disaster film *Deep Impact*, which is about the behaviour of people when they know a comet is going to collide with the Earth. In essence, the film illustrates the essential structure in scenario building, namely a 'what if?' question. Due to their extensive contribution, Peter Schwartz and other GBN members are mentioned in the film's credits. For *Minority Report*, GBN assembled a team, including Peter Schwartz and 20 futurists, to develop a scenario of the world in 2058. According to Schwartz, the futurist team conceived all the details in the film, apart from the basic story. They also helped in the conception of other films, including *Sneakers* or *War Games*.[56]

Historically, mainly large companies have used scenarios, as they have the necessary resources and the motivation to try out new tools. After decades of experience, scenarios can now also be easily applied in the context of smaller business based on lean processes and the advanced information technology. However, they have also been applied for small firms prior to the digital revolution, for example by Peter Schwarz for the firm Smith & Hawken as outlined in the book *The Art of the Long View*, yet only more rarely.

Throughout history, scenario planning has experienced its highs and lows. The 9/11 terror attacks, regarded as one of the most catastrophic and disruptive events in this century, triggered a chain of events that continue to have repercussions in the present (the European Refugee crisis, instability in the Middle East, and the rise of ISIS). Consequently, the level of uncertainty increased, leading decision makers to the conclusions that they require certain tools to make sense out of the external turbulence. According to the biennial survey *Management Tools & Trends* of the consulting firm Bain, the use of scenarios rose to 70% among those executives surveyed, compared to 30% in 1999. Scenario planning was also widely used at the start of the Global Economic crisis in 2007. After that, its application diminished, according to the Bain reports, in line with other management tools. According to management author and Deloitte corporate strategy expert Michael Raynor: 'It's sort of like flood insurance. Everybody runs out and buys flood insurance the year after the flood.'[57] Yet, if you have read the book closely so far, you should have noticed that this behaviour leads us to treat the symptoms but not the root causes. Ideally, scenario planning should go down after certain events, as planners have thought about certain chains of events and can act directly. Instead, planers use it just after the uncertainty as a cure to steer through the uncertainty. Authors' own illustration based on Bain Management Tools and Trends Surveys is depicted in Fig. 2.

In 2008, consulting firm McKinsey showed in its study *How Companies Act on Global Trends* that executives in the corporate world evaluate scenario planning as an essential tool for winning in a world that, deluged with information from all quarters, is liable to sudden disruptions with catastrophic consequences. Nearly, 70% of the executives who participated in the survey agreed that global trends gained more or even much more critical for corporate strategy in the last five years. Nevertheless, the survey also showed a wide gap between acknowledging the disruption and taking action. While around 75% of the executives stated that a higher pace of technological innovation and the growing

**Fig. 2:   Usage of Management Tools.**

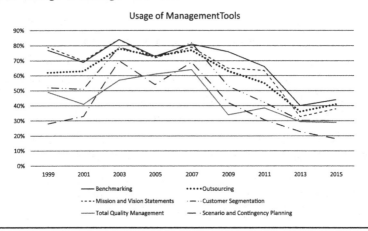

Usage of ManagementTools

*Source*: Own illustration based on Bain Management Tools and Trends Surveys.

availability of information would affect their company's profits, only 50% of the executives maintained that they had taken action on those two trends.[58]

In 2010, the McKinsey report *Global Forces: An Introduction* showed that executives were increasingly acting on key global forces. Around 75% of the respondents stated that they had taken action over the shift from developed to emerging markets. Nearly 66% said that they had incorporated the level of connectedness of the global economy, and around 50% said that they had addressed the clash between the increasing resource demand and supply restrictions.[59]

The fifth wave of scenario planning is just emerging and will greatly change the way we make decisions. The emergence of artificial intelligence and new digital technologies not only change the way scenarios are developed but also change the way they are perceived. The following sections in this book will show how the fifth wave of scenario planning has emerged and how it will change the way of strategy making.

## SCENARIO PLANNING APPLICATION

The ultimate aim of scenario planning is not to elaborate science fiction like stories of the future; rather it is to provide us with a deeper understanding of the world and our surroundings. Scenario planning is a well-established tool that has been applied to a wide range of situations where uncertainty and discord exist. It informs strategy and facilitates better decision making, both regarding immediate and future decisions. This is achieved by the ability of scenario planning to help us order and frame the complexity of the world towards a long-term orientation and thereby provides a confident platform for action. Therefore, scenarios are especially useful for strategic questions about long fuse, big bang problems such as market entries, portfolio adjustments, or large-scale investments; such decisions can entail a big bang in that they might have an impact on the success or survival of an organisation. Moreover, as already discussed, scenarios are not only a corporate strategy tool but can also facilitate major decisions in the personal sphere as well. In both the business world and in the private sphere, many of the answers will take some time to play out and materialise. We can use scenarios on a number of areas in the development of strategy and strategic questions. Scenarios can enlighten a specific issue and then facilitate our decision making and develop a strategic agenda. Yet, they do not only support individual decision making but also build a platform for strategic conversations that go beyond scenario building where decision makers can exchange their assumptions and combine different viewpoints. Based on the what-if principle, scenarios can be used as risk management tool, as scenarios help to assess risk and opportunities by investigating how different combinations of factors play out and shape the world. They thus help us to simulate potential outcomes of future developments and how initial ideas need modifying to bring success. As a combination of the perception of the world and the risk reduction approach, scenarios can also be used to test existing strategies and to analyse their robustness, meaning how sensitive they are to certain developments. By inserting a strategy or strategic idea into each scenario to stress-test it, we can see the open flanks and try to close them to ensure future proofness of the strategy.

Based on the different angles in which scenarios can be applied, scenario research has identified a number of roles for scenarios. Technology forecaster and futurist Stephen M. Millett says that scenarios support strategic thinking by depicting the future business environment and the consequent evaluation of strategic options.[60] The scenario practitioner Gill Ringland states that scenarios need to be integrated into an organisation's concerns to serve as a useful tool for discussing the future.[61] For the consultants Mats Lindgren and Hans Bandhold, scenarios facilitate strategic robustness and responsiveness.[62] The academics Thomas J. Chermack and Louis van der Merwe see scenarios see scenarios as leading to 'a strategic conversation that enables

organisational learning, by shifting current assumptions in the minds of decision makers'.[63] We can conclude that the role of scenarios is twofold, they
provide an important end product, however the process to achieve the scenarios is at least as important.

Examples of long fuse, big bang problems that require an in-depth understanding of the environment and how different factors could play out are
frequently found in mergers and acquisitions. There are ample cases where
the result was positive, for example the merger of Shell and Royal Dutch
Petroleum in 1907. A statistical analysis found, when looking at 1,305 deals
in 59 industries between 1990 and 1999, that mergers and acquisitions create wealth with an average return for the combined shareholders of 3.5%.[64]
On the other hand, there are negative examples like the Daimler-Chrysler
merger that can be described as a total failure and a costly disaster; Daimler
and Chrysler were never integrated into a unified whole. Consequently, the
potential synergies that drove the deal went unrealised. Yet, another study
showed that merger-related losses for shareholders have increased. The
acquiring firms' shareholders lost from 1998 through 2001 on average 12
cents per dollar spent on acquisitions around acquisition announcements,
resulting in a total loss of $240 billion. In the 1980s, they lost $7 billion that
is equal to 1.6 cents per dollar spent.[65] On the basis of such positive and
negative examples, should companies enter those deals or should they shy
away from them? As Mergers and Acquisitions (M&A) deals are a result of
the portfolio strategy, decision makers need to ask how they should structure
their company portfolio. In another critical field for organisations, the sourcing process, they need to find answers on make-or-buy decisions. Using only
traditional analysis, these questions are often hard to answer, it is just not
possible to clarify all uncertainties that influence the success of a big bang,
long-fuse decision like the M&A deal by pure traditional research.[66] Not
only decisions on a corporate level are relevant here; in the private sphere,
there are plenty of examples, like: what to study and where, marriage, starting a family, changing jobs – everything can be made more accessible with
scenarios.

The development process involves a number of exercises where teams
need to combine their creativity and investigate together the uncertainties
their organisation is currently facing or could face in the future. Though
developed as a decision-making tool, we can divide applications into those
that are more exploratory and those that are more decision oriented.

An exploratory application reduces the complexity in an existing system that is otherwise hard to ascertain, thereby allowing decisions to be made. Stakeholders can use the scenarios to articulate their mental models about the future within a systematic approach and reduce overconfidence by thinking about possible futures that have not yet been considered. A further exploratory application is organisational learning – what Shell's former head of corporate planning, Arie De Geus defined 'as the process whereby management teams change the shared mental models of their company, their markets, and their competitors'.[67] A proper organisational learning process should consist of three stages: first, mapping mental models; second, challenging existing mental models; and third, improving existing mental models. These phases are all covered by scenario planning which also serves as a tool for inquiry, reflection, and the construction of mental models.[68]

Nevertheless, changing the hearts and minds of managers is a more demanding process than scenario building itself. It is therefore vital to involve decision makers and leaders in the building process and overcome what has been termed 'availability bias', which argues that people undervalue things they have great difficulty in imagining or recalling.[69] Involving key leaders in the development process improves their learning experience, gives them ownership over the scenarios, and thus helps to overcome the availability bias. Managers need to be involved in developing the scenarios, otherwise they might reject them, leading to the very likely failure of the exercise. Scenario guru Peter Schwartz defined scenarios as building blocks in designing strategic conversations; they independently stimulate organisational learning on crucial questions. At this moment, the ability of executives to understand and anticipate change is shaped.[70]

When participants in the scenario journey gather and transform information on a topic into a new perception, they experience a moment of revelation that takes strategic minds beyond current thinking, thereby fundamentally shifting the position from which they see the future. Reaching this point is one of the critical challenges facing a scenario facilitator. Scenarios are successful when managers give a structure to uncertainty. This is based on a sound analysis of current developments and the ability to change their assumptions about the world, in case they are wrong or insufficiently supported by facts. Scenarios can also strengthen their assumptions due to affirmation of their believes.

Innovation, creativity, and new solutions that result from the scenario process are an exploratory use case. Looking into alternative but plausible futures helps identifying threats and opportunities, and in doing so, finding those opportunities necessary for potentially successful innovation. Closely connected to this is risk awareness, the capability to anticipate and connect external risks to business risks. Another exploratory use case is scenario-based innovation to generate new ideas to succeed in future worlds. Therefore, participants imagine they would be in the given scenario and identify what they would need to be a winner in such a scenario. A decision-oriented use case is the process of winning stakeholders over to a new or shared vision. The development process offers a safe environment for thinking extreme thoughts and exchanging ideas usually deemed unfruitful in any average strategy discussion as they go beyond the normal planning horizon. Scenarios help with collectively shaping the understanding of an issue. By combining existing ideas with new perspectives and insights, collaborative solutions can be found which no one had previously considered. Furthermore, scenario-based strategy formulation facilitates the development of robust and flexible strategies, leading eventually to decisions being made in uncertain conditions. Scenarios can assist in identifying growth opportunities and circumventing potential future traps. Organisations are confronted with vital decisions when they want to grow in an uncertain environment: will the business be commodified, will digitalisation disrupt it, or will new players emerge? Consequently, scenario planning is a way to align the viewpoints of a new management team. A new CEO can test the viewpoints of this management team and see if their future vision is aligned with his, of they should either make a change in strategy or the management team to be a winner.

Probably, the best example of bringing different opinions and people into alignment is offered by the Mount Fleur scenarios, developed in 1991 by a diverse group of 22 prominent South African leaders from different parts of society, including community and union activists, leaders from politics and the business world, as well as academia, all with different ideological mindsets. The process took place when Nelson Mandela was released from prison, political parties and organisations such as the African National Congress were legalised, and the first all-race elections were being planned. The entire country was discussing how the end of the Apartheid regime would play out. The group came up with four scenarios:

- Ostrich: a situation where no negotiated solution to the crisis was reached in South Africa and a government that was not representative remained in authority.

- Lame Duck: a negotiated solution was accomplished but a slow and indecisive transition to the new division of political power, and wealth distribution was also part of this scenario.

- Icarus: a rapid transition scenario where the state is pursuing unsustainable, populist economic strategies.

- Flight of the Flamingos: a scenario in which sustainable government strategies are achieved on an integrated route of development and democracy.

Later, the Mount Fleur scenarios were widely published and promoted throughout South Africa to establish a common language and mind-set that helped facilitate public debate about South Africa's future. The scenario process was highly successful and smoothed the path towards the democratic rainbow nation South Africa eventually became.[71]

Frequent professional scenario users are industrial associations or companies in the business world (from large multi-billion, multinational corporations to small and medium companies). However, scenarios are not only a tool in the corporate world but have also been used in a variety of other settings, for example at a national level for governments, government agencies or Non-Governmental Organisations (NGOs) They do not necessarily focus on a single entity, as various organisations can be included in the process to derive common understanding. Scenarios can even be used in personal decisions, like family or career planning. Participants in the development process and the audience for the end product are therefore different; it may be for a specific expert audience or for a broad, general audience.

The following checklist helps us clarify whether a situation is appropriate for scenarios. Scenarios should not be used when:

- an issue is not central to an organisation and its strategy, and the solution is clear and straightforward;

- the outcome of a strategic issue is highly predetermined by internal and external driving forces;

- decision makers do not want to initiate change as they prefer the status quo;

- a high level of urgency in the planning process does not allow participants to take a step back and reflect on potential developments;

- the desired outcomes are out of kilter with the resources made available.

Although scenarios may be applied in any decision-making process, we
can stress some critical characteristics of common situations for scenarios:

- the problem is a strategic issue with an unclear solution;

- the environment is highly volatile and uncertain, or it is facing a high
degree of change;

- decision makers support the scenario process;

- the organisation is open to change and discussion;

- necessary resources are available to enable a successful initiative;

- the lack of sufficient and reasonable options to pursue;

- the absence of common understanding, shared aspirations, or opinions.

Scenarios make great sense but are only useful when they help change
thinking (or at least trigger to challenge existing views and mind-sets) or
affirm existing views, yet having them checked with a valid analysis and
thereby influence actions for a more positive outcome.


## GUIDELINES FOR DESIGNING SCENARIOS

According to Pierre Wack, scenario planning is a method to incite inspirational
and entrepreneurial thinking and action 'in contexts of change, complexity,
and uncertainty'.[72] In our opinion, this can be achieved by relying on the
following seven principles:

- taking the long view;

- outside-in thinking;

- plausibility;

- engaging a holistic view;

- embracing uncertainty;

- zoom-out, zoom-in; and

- combining machine objectivity with human intuition.

It is also essential to think about the number of scenarios to be developed and to have a diverse, open and innovative team composition.

## The Long View

Daily work in many organisations is often driven by short-term actions and urgent requirements. Hounded by expectations to produce measurable outcomes in the short term, for example the expectations of the stock market for corporations or voters for governments, planning horizons are often near-sighted and constrain strategies within short-term planning. In contrast, scenario planning requires us to look beyond these short-term demands and far enough into the future to observe new options and chances, asking 'What if?' Participants therefore need to extend their thinking beyond the current setting to avoid focussing on a narrow option, or as Mike Tyson framwed it, 'everyone has a plan until they get punched in the mouth'.[73] Long-term perspectives may seem peripheral to an organisation's more instant issues, but taking the long view is crucial in sustaining a position or facilitating crucial change, as it empowers organisations in the following ways:

- By addressing deep-rooted problems with a more enthusiastic and antici-patory approach;

- By seeing challenges and opportunities with greater clarity when they occur; and

- By considering long-term outcomes and potential unplanned results of actions otherwise taken by an organisation.

These factors are arguments for applying scenarios in a more significant number of small- and medium-sized enterprises (e.g. the backbone of the German economy, its famous Mittelstand), which already have the perfect mind-set, as they think in generations rather than months or weeks. Since their owners are often large shareholders in the companies, they also bear a high risk. Scenarios are a perfect tool to support them in decision-making (in Chapter 3, we will elaborate this point under the time aspect).

## Outside-in Thinking

Unexpected events often lead to surprise among individuals and organisations as they spend most of their time considering the factors their own field, or organisation is aware and also knowledgeable of. They start their decision-making process by considering factors from the inside, the parts that they can regulate, and then go out to the wider world that they would like to form. For organisations caught in a cycle of responding to needs as they emerge, the area of control, the organisation's peripheral vision, is very narrow, making them highly exposed to blindsiding. Conversely, thinking from the outside starts by assessing external factors that may have a profound impact on the organisation over the course of time. For instance, an apparently insignificant technological innovation that could be advantageous for the provision of services or a geopolitical change that could lead to unforeseen social requirements. Outside-in thinking can help anticipate and getting ready for such 'surprising' possibilities. Outside-in thinking can be illustrated, as in Fig. 3, by our environmental onion framework:

- At the core are the attributes of the organisation or the specific issue at stake.

**Fig. 3:  Environmental Onion.**

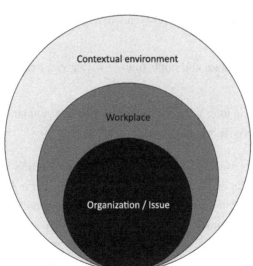

- The medium circle is the instant workplace with change forces like partners, clients/customers, and rivals as well as other stakeholders that can be partly influenced.

- The external circle is the contextual environment, including significant driving forces, such as values, global and local political developments, or sustainability. This is the key focus of the scenario planning, with Social, Technological, Economic, Environmental, and Political forces that are out of direct control.

The two outside circles are able to merge rapidly and blur. However, the distinction is productive because it stimulates us to consider not only direct externalities but also modifications in the contextual setting that are often disregarded in long-term planning. External changes in the broader global context and the working environment can be investigated with scenario thinking. The core, the organisational dimension, only comes into play for the implications once the scenarios have been developed. Most planning procedures begin with an organisation focus and then push out into the external environment; thus, the outside-in approach feels awkward at first glance. Once the notion has been understood, though, outside-in thinking can stimulate accessible and creative ideas about a variety of otherwise unseen future changes and strategies. Often, traditional planning fails to include all the dimensions, focussing just on one, such as the company, the working environment, or the contextual environment.

## Plausibility

The advantage of focussing on plausibility instead of probability is that we can identify a broad range of risks and opportunities that are at the long tail of distribution and not just in the probability confidence interval. Plausible further means that the stories are developed with a particular logical flow that provides them with a validity that they could indeed take place. Thus, the interplay and combinations of the various drivers need to be logic and in line with common sense. They start from the past and move into the present and the future while reflecting today's wisdom. Plausibility is, therefore, an important measure, and better than giving a particular forecast with a certain probability. Scenarios aim at highlighting opportunities that might make a significant effect on the organisation. Each story is augmented with careful research and rich in detail to make it vivid, while seeking future surprises and unexpected leaps of understanding. The decisions we make today can be tested in those worlds to see how they might be played out. However, the silver bullet is combining both methods; this will be elaborated on in the next chapter where we show that observing probabilities over time with the help of AI will help make sounder strategies.

## Holistic View

The introduction of various viewpoints — different voices that shed new light on a strategic issues and challenges — helps us gain a better under-standing of our own and others beliefs about the future. This is distinct from the management of several stakeholders, which many companies are very good at. If you are surrounded by enthusiastic consensus, it is easy to ignore voices of disagreement. The deliberate presentation of these voices exposes the respondents to fresh concepts, which can guide their views and help them see the broader image.

The scenario planning approach provides a compelling platform for align-ing different (and often divergent) perspectives. This widens the peripheral vision of an organisation; revealing new threats and opportunities that might otherwise have been missed. By being holistic, scenarios overcome confirma-tion bias, that is, the tendency to look for and interpret things in such a way that they confirm pre-existing beliefs or hypotheses.

## Embrace Uncertainty

Uncertainty can be terrifying for many people. The unknown represents an abundant source of disasters and even a complete loss of control over the future. Uncertainty leads to risk, which is a crucial source of business profit. Risk requires entrepreneurial decisions, as there is no free lunch. Risk-free returns need to be regarded with caution. Some industries, such as the tech-based start-up world or pharma, embrace this risk by engaging a number of options that can cope with different situations. However, the typical response of decision makers is either to deny change and uncertainty or to incorporate it to such a large extent that every possibility is planned for. Scenario design embraces uncertainty but also cuts through complexity to enable feasible planning. By embracing uncertainty, one first needs to acknowledge how little we consciously know, or to use the words of the ancient Greek philosopher Socrates: 'The only true wisdom is in knowing you know nothing'.[74] By embracing uncertainty and anticipating change, decision makers can gauge different options and structure their strategic decision making accordingly. When the future unfolds based on what they have anticipated, they can select which option to take and which ones to abandon.

## Zoom-out, Zoom-in

To provide meaningful and actionable results, scenarios follow the zoom-out, zoom-in approach and thus avoid 'just' telling stories about alternative futures. They zoom-out for strategic vision and to lure decision makers out of their comfort zone, and then zoom-in to trigger action. In zooming-out, long-term horizons of frequently 10–20 years are used, while the actionable zooming-in looks at 6–12 month time frames. Scenarios start by zooming out of today's situation and anticipate that the world of today is going to change radically. This step provides awareness and foresight. When zooming out, there is the recognition that a disruptive scenario will not be a precise prediction, as this is not possible. In looking at radical change, it is better to take a long horizon and push scenarios to their extremes to explore the limits of imagination and possibility. When the path to this zoom-out point has been travelled, strategic initiatives for short-term execution are developed in the zoom-in process, which focusses on action and progress. The zoom-out, zoom-in approach aims at challenging traditional 3–5-year planning processes that give false confidence. Firms in the Silicon Valley have begun to apply the zoom-out, zoom-in approach. Since it helps firms escaping the risk of falling into incremental, reactive strategies, zoom-out, zoom-in has found its way into scenario methodology.[75]

## Machine Objectivity Meets Human Intuition

Scenarios require expertise and knowledge. Yet, human expertise is often narrow, while machines and algorithms can incorporate various sources and viewpoints (when fed with concrete data) and analyse it objectively. However, in the past, scenario planning was mainly a human process as approaches including complex algorithms and machines failed to be of value or were too complicated to apply. Since the revolution that came with the emergence of artificial intelligence, machine objectivity can aid human decision making, despite initial attempts to replace it. Yet, scenario planning as a combination of perception and facts will always include human intuition to make final judgement calls. We will expand on the technological revolution in the following chapters.

## Number of Scenarios

The question of how many scenarios should be used is discussed in the large body of research. Various researchers and practitioners raise the questions: *How many scenarios should be developed for one issue/focal question?* Pierre Wack suggests never using more than four (otherwise it becomes unmanageable for most decision makers). More than three scenario narratives is not useful, as the

> First, is the surprise-free view (showing explicitly why and where it is fragile), and then two other worlds or different ways of seeing the world that focus on critical uncertainties.[76]

Kees Van der Heijden, who helped found the GBN after working as a scenario planner at Royal Dutch/Shell, proposes using between two and five scenarios as a useful quantity. He believes they enable reflection about future uncertainty, promote the development and discussion of concepts through multiple disciplines, show current results in a concrete real-world framework, and use a causal, intuitively convenient model of reasoning.[77]

Peter Schwartz suggests using four scenarios. The development of too many scenarios blurs their distinctions so that they are neither meaningful nor useful. From Schwartz's experience, teams often have problems in remembering more than four scenarios; this is in line with researches into the field of memory capacity.[78] It has been shown, for example, that young adults can recall only three or four longer verbal chunks, for example idioms or short sentences.[79]

Three scenarios might lead to the 'middle of the road' trap where 'large, medium, and small' versions of the future are developed. This might induce scenario workshop participants to use one, often the middle one (also called the 'middle of the road scenario') as the most likely scenario. These scenarios then fail to radically challenge decision makers and do not require a large palette of strategic options. They are also often regarded as predictions, while the other scenarios are left out, making the entire exercise more or less useless. Four scenarios are also very manageable, as they can be put into the classical scenario matrix that we also frequently apply. Hence, we are strong supporters of the number 4. To develop scenarios, participants on this journey are required to bring at least some creativity that allows this 'imaginative leap into the future', as Shell's scenario pioneer and co-founder of the GBN, Napier Collyns, described them.[80]

We believe that scenarios should be based on a systematic approach consisting of axis that form a framework with a number of four scenarios. One scenario is not a choice, it's a dogma. Two scenarios are rather black and white thinking; and of three scenarios is often leading to only one evolutionary path. Therefore, we use four scenarios, as they enable us to have diverging scenarios, based on two critical uncertainties. Using a third critical uncertainty would lead to eight scenarios, which are difficult to handle, thus less is more in this case.

## Scenario Team

Scenarios require a diverse set of opinions and multiple points of view. As scenarios should be developed in a team, a very wide team composition with diverse voices is vital for success in shedding new light on strategic challenges. Scenario development benefits enormously from visionary thinkers who help overcome passionate convictions that can easily make people deaf to contrary opinions. The scenario process team should include a diverse and holistic participant set from various interest groups. They should include participants from outside the organisation's domain and on the cutting edge of new dynamics. Participants in the scenario process need to adopt a speak-up approach and be willing to express their opinions and thoughts. They may be external experts, clients, partners, or event competitors. Apart from their different backgrounds, participants should also include a broad range of corporate functions such as marketing, R&D, finance, operations, or HR. This can also provide economies of scale, as different decision makers have to think about the way they see the future playing out and bring their own opinions into the process. Bringing them together can help anticipate possible developments in a chosen industry and further increase the source credibility of the scenarios. The advantage of external participants who do not commonly interact with the organisation is that they can contribute original but also unorthodox points of view to the process.

By excluding unorthodox thinkers who challenge conventional wisdom, scenarios might fail because game-changing ideas are left out. In introducing those who are radical in their thinking and leaders in their field, decision makers can be taken out of their comfort zone and provided with better and more robust scenarios. The scenario process, therefore, builds an ideal platform for bringing together many different voices, which can help expand an organisation's peripheral vision, as newly emerging challenges or favourable circumstances are detected.

Participants typically:

- stand out from the majority in intellectual resourcefulness;

- are masters of their chosen field;

- are enthusiasts and unendingly curious;

- are generators of ideas;

- are accessible and open;

- are astute and perspicacious;

- contribute unique insights;

- push the boundaries; and

- think in the future already.

If you or your organisation do not want to include external participants in the actual development process, you should aim at bringing them into the driver development stage, via interviews or group discussions, for example. This helps avoid the risk of groupthink in an organisation and can introduce new controversial perspectives.

There are those who are unable to conduct scenario planning, as they aim for a mathematically derived correct answer and need to attach a calculation to any problem. A good facilitator, therefore, needs to stress that there are no right or wrong, good or bad scenarios; merely a set of clear and plausible futures that could happen. A good scenario facilitator is close to both the organisation's leadership team as well as the ground team working on the overall process. He needs to push participants beyond current short-term thinking in extreme, yet plausible directions. Moreover, he has to support the identification of blind spots and introduce external challenges that can change perspectives. He should be engaged in the entire process, identify the focal issue, adapt the specific requirements of the process, and facilitate continuing strategic conversation. Our experience has shown that a combination of two facilitators is best. The lead facilitator is an experienced scenario practitioner who owns the entire process. He is supported by a senior industry expert. Although the scenario expert leads the process, he can also bring in new ideas that are extraordinary or not even accepted in the industry; he, therefore, does not require a broad industry background. However, it should be stressed that his role is the methodology expert. His deputy brings in industry knowledge that goes beyond the organisation's thinking but allows the facilitator team to be at eye level with the participants.

Once the scenarios have been developed, the team needs to be downsized and changed in order to come up with strategic responses to their implications. Only top executives with decision-making power and responsibilities should be included, for they have to develop their strategy and face the consequences.

The development of scenarios is highly dependent on the culture and industry background, among other factors, of participants in developing successful scenarios. The facilitation style might, therefore, need to be adapted to those needs. We provide our perspective on development and point out some of the cultural issues that have occurred in our everyday work practice.

## NOTES

1. See Bill, G., Myhrvold, N. & Rinearson, P. (1996). *The Road Ahead* (p. 316). New York, NY: Penguin Books.

2. See Sharpe, B., & van der Heijden, K. (Eds.). (2007). *Scenarios for success: Turning insights in to action (Oxford Futures Forum)* (p. 28). Chichester: Wiley.

3. See Varum, C. A. & Melo, C. (2010). Directions in Scenario Planning Literature: A Review of the Past Decades. *Futures*, 42(4), 356.

4. See Wack, P. (1985a). Scenarios: Shooting the rapids. *Harvard Business Review*, 63(6), 140.

5. See Kahn, H., & Wiener, A. J. (1967). *The year 2000: A framework for speculation on the next thirty-three years* (p. 6). New York, NY: Macmillan.

6. See Michael E. Porter is Bishop William Lawrence University Professor and part of the faculty of the Harvard Business School. For further information please refer to: https://www.hbs.edu/faculty/Pages/profile.aspx?facId=6532.

7. Monitor Group was founded in 1983 by Michael Porter, Mark Fuller, Joseph Fuller, Michael Bell, Mark Thomas and Thomas Craig with strong relations to the Harvard Business School. The firm's objective was to establish the theoretical aspects of Michael Porter's work in the corporate world. Monitor Group was acquired in 2013 by Deloitte and is called today Monitor Deloitte. See: Denning, S. (2012). What Killed Michael Porter's Monitor Group? The One Force That Really Matters. Forbes. Retrieved from: https://www.forbes.com/sites/steveden-ning/2012/11/20/what-killed-michael-porters-monitor-group-the-one-force-that-really-matters/#506c74a747b5.

8. See Porter, M. E. (1985). *Competitive advantage* (p. 63). New York, NY: Free Press.

9. See Schwartz, P. (1991). *The art of the long view: Planning for the future in an uncertain world* (p. 45). New York, NY: Doubleday.

10. See Garreau, J. (1994). *Conspiracy of Heretics*. Retrieved from: https://www.wired.com/1994/11/gbn/.

11. See Einstein, A. (1954 [1982]). *Ideas and opinions* (p. 47). New York, NY: Three Rivers Press.

12. See Kahneman, D., & Tversky, A. (1979). Prospect theory: An analysis of decision under risk. *Econometrica, 47*(2), 263–291.

13. For further details refer to Hunger, J.D. & Wheelen, T. L. (2011). Essentials for Strategic Management. New Jersey: Pearson Education, pp. 47ff; pp. 88ff.

14. See BBC. (2016). Science fact: Sci-fi inventions that became reality. Retrieved from http://www.bbc.com/news/health-38026393

15. See Sterling, B. (2002). *Tomorrow now: Envisioning the next fifty years* (p. XII). New York, NY: Random House.

16. See Jones, G. H. (2013). *Pythia. Ancient History Encyclopedia*. Retrieved from: https://www.ancient.eu/Pythia/.

17. See Schoemaker, P. J. (1993). Multiple scenario development: Its conceptual and behavioral foundation. *Strategic management journal, 14*(3), 194.

18. Moore's law refers to a 1965 prediction of Intel co-founder Gordon Moore that the amount of transistors on a computer microchip will double each year, which he adjusted in 1975 to doubling every two years. Hence computing power is increasing, while prices for computers decrease. Source: Simonite, T. (2016). Moore's Law is Dead. Now What? Technology Review. Retrieved from: https://www.technologyreview.com/s/601441/moores-law-is-dead-now-what/

19. Instead of using only 0s or 1s like classical computers, quantum computers calculate on the basis of the probability of the status of the object before measurement, which ensures that they can store more information exponentially compared

to traditional computers. Source: Sciencealert (n.d.). How Do Quantum Computers Work. Retrieved from: https://www.sciencealert.com/quantum-computers

20. See Reddish, T. (2016). *Science and Christianity: Foundations and frameworks for moving forward in faith* (p. 92). Wipf and Stock Publishers.

21. See Wack, P. (1985b, September–October). Scenarios: Uncharted waters ahead: How Royal Dutch/Shell developed a planning technique that teaches managers to think about an uncertain future. *Harvard Business Review*, 74.

22. See Mencher, A. G. (1971). IV. On the Social Deployment of Science. *Bulletin of the Atomic Scientists*, 27(10), 37.

23. See Szczerba, R. J. (2015). 15 Worst tech predictions of all time. Retrieved from https://www.forbes.com/sites/robertszczerba/2015/01/05/15-worst-tech-predictions-of-all-time/#6417b1ba1299

24. The Economist. (1999). A survey of telecommunications: Cutting the cord. Retrieved from https://www.economist.com/node/246152

25. See Malkiel, B.G. (2007). *A random walk down Wall Street* (9th ed., p. 24). New York: North & Company.

26. See Krämer, W. (2012). Die Affen sind die besten Anleger. Frankfurter Allgemeine Zeitung. Retrieved from: https://www.faz.net/aktuell/finanzen/meine-finanzen/2.2465/denkfehler-die-uns-geld-kosten-9-die-affen-sind-die-besten-anleger-11711132.html

27. See Clare, A., Motson, N., & Thomas, S. (2013). *An evaluation of alternative equity indices Part 2: Fundamental Weighting Schemes.* Cass Business School.

28. See Plato (380 bc). Laches, or Courage [Translated by Jowett, B.]. Retrieved from: http://classics.mit.edu/Plato/laches.html

29. See Plato (2016). The Republic. Translated by Jowett, B. Digireads.

30. See More, T. (2003). Utopia. Translated by Turner, B. 2nd Edition. London: Penguin.

31. See Orwell, G. (1961). 1984. New York: Signet Classics.

32. See von Clausewitz, C. (1989). Translated by Howard, M. & Paret, P. Princeton: Princeton University Press.

33. See Hughes, D. J. (1983). Moltke on the Art of War - selected writings. New York: Random House.

34. See von Reibnitz, U., & Hammond, P. (1988). *Scenario techniques*. McGraw-Hill Hamburg.

35. See Süddeutsche Zeitung. (2010a). Airbus: Pannenflieger A400M: Pleiten, Pech und Peinlichkeiten. Retrieved from http://www.sueddeutsche.de/wirtschaft/airbus-pannenflieger-iami-pleiten-pech-und-peinlichkeiten-1.65920

36. See Rescher, N. (1998). *Predicting the future: An introduction to the theory of forecasting.* SUNY Press.

37. See Bradfield, R., Wright, G., Burt, G., Cairns, G., & Van Der Heijden, K. (2005). The origins and evolution of scenario techniques in long range business planning. *Futures, 37*(8), 795–812.

38. See Kahn, H. (1961). *On Thermonuclear War* (2nd ed.). Princeton: Princeton University Press.

39. See Bradfield, R., Wright, G., Burt, G., Cairns, G., & Van Der Heijden, K. (2005). The origins and evolution of scenario techniques in long range business planning. Futures, 37(8), 795–812; Chermack, T. J. (2003). *A theory of scenario planning*. University of Minnesota; Millett, S. M. (2003). The future of scenarios: challenges and opportunities. *Strategy & Leadership, 31*(2), 16–24.

40. See Ringland, G. (1998). *Scenario planning: Managing for the future* (pp. 11–28). Chichester: John Wiley and Sons.

41. See Bradfield, R., Wright, G., Burt, G., Cairns, G., & Van Der Heijden, K. (2005). The origins and evolution of scenario techniques in long range business planning. *Futures, 37*(8), 795–812; Chermack, T. J. (2003). *A theory of scenario planning* (pp. 8–9). University of Minnesota.

42. See Wack, P. (1985b, September–October). Scenarios: Uncharted waters ahead: How Royal Dutch/Shell developed a planning technique that teaches managers to think about an uncertain future. *Harvard Business Review*, 73–89.

43. See Jefferson, M. (2012). Shell scenarios: What really happened in the 1970s and what may be learned for current world prospects. *Technological Forecasting and Social Change, 79*(1), 186–197.

44. See Jefferson, M. (2012). Shell scenarios: What really happened in the 1970s and what may be learned for current world prospects. *Technological Forecasting and Social Change, 79*(1), 186–197; Kahane, A. (2012). *Working Together to Change the Future: Transformative Scenario Planning*. Oakland: Berrett-Koehler.

45. See Bradfield, R., Wright, G., Burt, G., Cairns, G., & Van Der Heijden, K. (2005). The origins and evolution of scenario techniques in long range business planning. *Futures, 37*(8), 795–812; Chermack, T. J. (2003). *A theory of scenario planning* (pp. 8–9). University of Minnesota.

46. See Linneman, R. E., & Klein, H. E. (1983). The use of multiple scenarios by US industrial companies: a comparison study, 1977–1981. *Long Range Planning, 16*(6), 94–101.

47. See Norris, G. (2005). Creating a titan. Retrieved from https://www.flightglobal.com/news/articles/creating-a-titan-199071/; Singapore Airlines. (2013). Singapore airlines – Our history. Retrieved from https://web.archive.org/web/20130209040833/http://www.singaporeair.com/en_UK/about-us/sia-history/ ; Süddeutsche Zeitung. (2010b). Die Geschichte von Airbus: Erfolgsgeschichte mit Problemen. Retrieved from http://www.sueddeutsche.de/wirtschaft/die-geschichte-von-airbus-erfolgsgeschichte-mit-problemen-1.516776

48. See Linneman, R. E., & Klein, H. E. (1983). The use of multiple scenarios by US industrial companies: A comparison study, 1977–1981. *Long Range Planning, 16*(6), 94–101.

49. See Chermack, T. J. (2017). *Foundations of scenario planning: The story of Pierre Wack* (pp. 109–129). Taylor & Francis.

50. See Knight, M. (1999). 2020 Visionary. Rensselaer Alumni Magazine. Rensselaer Polytechnic Institute. Retrieved from https://www.rpi.edu/dept/NewsComm/Magazine/dec99/visionary1.html; Wilkinson, A., & Kupers, R. (2013, May). Living in the Futures. *Harvard Business Review*. Retrieved from https://hbr.org/2013/05/living-in-the-futures.

51. See Garber, J. R. (1998). What if … ? Retrieved from https://www.forbes.com/forbes/1998/1102/6210076a.html#270aa2902995

52. Global Business Network. (2010). Where we started. Retrieved from: https://web.archive.org/web/20100105183523/http://gbn.com/about/started.php

53. See Schwartz, P. (1996). The Art of the Long View. New York: Doubleday.

54. See Crainer, S., & Dearlove, D. (2004). *Business, the universe and everything: Conversations with the World's greatest management thinkers* (pp. 37–42). John Wiley & Sons.

55. Global Business Network. (2010). Where we started. Retrieved from https://web.archive.org/web/20100105183523/http://gbn.com/about/started.php

56. See Wired (2012): Inside Minority Report's 'Idea Summit,' Visionaries Saw the Future. Retrieved from: https://www.wired.com/2012/06/minority-report-idea-summit/; Lohr, S. (1998). Long Boom or Bust; A Leading Futurist Risks His Reputation With Ideas on Growth And High Technology. *The New York Times*. Retrieved from: https://www.nytimes.com/1998/06/01/business/long-boom-bust-leading-futurist-risks-his-reputation-with-ideas-growth-high.html?scp=10&sq=%22Global+Business+Network%22&st=nyt.

57. See Tuna, C. (2009). Pendulum is swinging back on "Scenario Planning": JDS Uniphase prepares responses for a range of business situations, helping company react quickly to change. Retrieved from http://online.wsj.com/article/SB124683295589397615.html

58. See McKinsey. (2008). *How companies act on global trends: A McKinsey Global Survey*. The McKinsey Quarterly.

59. See McKinsey. (2010). *Global forces: An introduction*.

60. See Millett, S. M. (1988). How scenarios trigger strategic thinking. *Long Range Planning, 21*(5), 61–68.

61. See Ringland, G. (1998). *Scenario planning: Managing for the future*. Chichester: John Wiley and Sons.

62. See Lindgren, M., & Bandfold, H. (2003). *Scenario planning: The Link between future and industry*. London: Palgrave Macmillan.

63. See Chermack, T. J., & van der Merwe, L. (2003). The role of constructivist learning in scenario planning. *Futures, 35*(5), 445–460.

64. See Mulherin, J. H., & Boone, A. L. (2000). Comparing acquisitions and divestitures. *Journal of Corporate Finance, 6*(2), 117–139.

65. See Moeller, S. B., Schlingemann, F. P., & Stulz, R. M. (2005). Wealth destruction on a massive scale? A study of acquiring-firm returns in the recent merger wave. *The Journal of Finance, 60*(2), 757–782.

66. See Schühly, A., Vieten, N., Weiß, J., & Niggeloh, S. (2019). *Braving the wind of change – resilient portfolio strategy*. Munich: Monitor Deloitte.

67. See de Geus, A. P. (1988). Planning as learning. *Harvard Business Review, 66*(2).

68. See Chermack, T. J. (2003). *A theory of scenario planning* (p. 27). University of Minnesota.

69. See Esgate, A.; Groome, D. (2005). An Introduction to Applied Cognitive Psychology. Psychology Press. p. 201.

70. See Schwartz, P. (1991). *The art of the long view: Planning for the future in an uncertain world*. New York, NY: Doubleday.

71. See Kahane, A. (2012). *Working Together to Change the Future: Transformative Scenario Planning*. Oakland: Berrett-Koehle; Global Business Network. (2003). The Mont Fleur scenarios: What will South Africa be like in the year 2002? *Deeper News, 7*(1).

72. See Wack, P. (1985a). Scenarios: Shooting the rapids. *Harvard Business Review, 63*(6), 139–150.

73 See Berandino, M. (2012). *Mike Tyson explains one of his most famous quotes*. Deerfield Beach, FL: Sun Sentinel.

74. See Plato (n.d.). Apology. Translated by Jowett, B. Retrieved from: http://classics. mit.edu/Plato/apology.html

75. See Hagel, J. (2017). Crafting corporate narratives: Zoom out, zoom in. Retrieved from http://edgeperspectives.typepad.com/edge_perspectives/2017/08/ crafting-corporate-narratives-zoom-out-zoom-in.html

76. See Wack, P. (1985a). Scenarios: Shooting the rapids. *Harvard Business Review, 63*(6), 146.

77. See Chermack, T. J., Lynham, S. A., & Ruona, W. E. (2001). A review of scenario planning literature. *Futures Research Quarterly, 17*(2), 24.

78. Schwartz, P. (1991). *The art of the long view: Planning for the future in an uncertain world*. New York, NY: Doubleday.

79. See Gilchrist, A. L., Cowan, N., & Naveh-Benjamin, M. (2008). Working memory capacity for spoken sentences decreases with adult ageing: Recall of fewer but not smaller chunks in older adults. *Memory, 16*(7), 773–787.

80. See Schwartz, P. (1991). *The art of the long view: Planning for the future in an uncertain world* (p. XIII). New York, NY: Doubleday.

# 3

# THE TRADITIONAL SCENARIO
# PLANNING PROCESS

Having discussed what scenarios are and what they are not, primarily by differentiating them from forecasts, we now want to focus on the scenario development process and the tools and methods used along the way. Several different ways of conducting scenario planning have been developed, leading to methodological chaos. Following a short glance at earlier scenario methodologies, we shall examine in greater depth the GBN approach that has evolved from the methods used at Shell and has been called the 'gold standard of corporate scenario generation'.[1] Over decades of applied scenario thinking, a wide set of approaches and methods has been developed. This considerable body of work, however, created methodological chaos. Thus, we need to bear in mind that a more extensive range of methods and variations exists than is presented here. Many of these are only academic constructs that have not been widely used in practice and are unsuited for everyday business where time and resources are scarce. In contrast, the GBN approach we follow has been used for decades in a large variety of settings, hence it has been tested and proven to work by many practitioners.

There are also various other methods. One of these is the probabilistic modified trend scenario, such as trend-impact analysis developed in the early 1970s by the Future Groups. Another method is the cross-impact analysis developed by Herman Kahn's former RAND Corporation colleagues Theodore Gordon and Olaf Helmer in 1966. Furthermore, there is the French *La Prospective* approach, heavily reliant on computer-based mathematical models and algorithms. In practice, it has been acknowledged that applying complicated models and elaborate computer simulations is not the optimal way to develop scenarios. However, we see with current scenario development that they are an excellent way to monitor scenarios, and thus enhance their application.

The GBN approach is an *inductive*, *intuitive*, and *logical* approach. It goes back to Pierre Wack, who started to apply and refine Herman Kahn's concepts at Shell in the 1960s. He developed frameworks by firstly drawing the bigger picture of potential futures before zooming into the details. He believed that starting with the details would miss some critical dimension of the scenario development process. This process was then developed and refined over the years at Royal Dutch Shell.[2]

The GBN approach is a systematic process, which cuts through complexity and brings order to chaos. Scenarios require a full embrace of complexity and ambiguity; this permits a more balanced view of both risks and opportunities in the business environment. According to Peter Schwartz:

> *Anyone can create scenarios. But it will be much easier if you are willing to encourage your own imagination, novelty, and even sense of the absurd – as well as your sense of realism.*[3]

However, it is important to recognise that a scenario exercise is only successful if the involved leadership and decision makers are open to asking 'What-If?' questions and to voicing inconvenient truths. Without this ability and the recognition of the need for scenario planning, it will be a tough ride. Thus, if the involved leadership is willing to be open and participate in the scenario process, they will experience a new way to perceive the world that helps them to make better decisions (Fig. 4).

## FOCAL QUESTION

For every scenario planning exercise, there is an underlying strategic challenge. The first task is, therefore, to nail it down, to synthesise the actual strategic

**Fig. 4:  The Scenario Process.**

| 1. Focal question | 2. Driving forces | 3. Critical uncertainties | 4. Scenario framework | 5. Scenario narratives | 6. Implications & options | 7. Monitoring |
|---|---|---|---|---|---|---|
| Determine the scope and strategic direction | Identify drivers that have the potential to shape the future | Prioritize and cluster drivers into critical uncertainties | Combine critical uncertainties into a scenario frame | Define framework conditions for each scenario | Determine resulting implications and strategic reponses | Monitor and adjust strategy |

challenge you or your organisation faces from the external environment in the form of a question. Therefore questions are a powerful tool. 'The key to powerful thinking is powerful questioning. When we ask the right questions, we [set up our success as] thinkers. Thinking, at any point in time, can go off in thousands of different directions, some of which, by the way, are dead-ends. Questions define the agenda for our thinking. They determine what information we seek'.[4] Otherwise, we as scenario planners could tell an infinite number of stories about your future, whereas scenario planning actually aims at telling stories that enable better future decisions for a specific task at hand. The first step is therefore to identify and distil the issue the scenario exercise should address and agree on it with all the relevant and involved stakeholders. Even though scenario planning is based on outside-in thinking, we should not focus purely on external challenges, for example the growth environment, as this is likely to leave out important, company-specific information that will affect how the future plays out and how the company behaves.

This is not an issue that scenario planning is facing solely. For each strategy project, a market or issue needs to be clarified. In the marketing domain, already at the beginning of the 1960s, Theodore Levitt pointed out the problem of a too narrow, product-oriented market demarcation in his article 'Marketing Myopia', nowadays referred to as classic, using the example of the US American railway companies:

> *The railroads did not stop growing because the need for passenger and freight transportation declined. That grew. The railroads are in trouble today not because that need was filled by others (cars, trucks, airplanes, and even telephones) but because it was not filled by the railroads themselves. They let others take customers away from them because they assumed themselves to be in the railroad business rather than in the transportation business. The reason they defined their industry incorrectly was that they were railroad oriented instead of transportation oriented; they were product oriented instead of customer oriented.*[5]

Scenarios are best used when the underlying strategic challenge does not have a simple solution. It should rather face a high level of uncertainty so that an adequate solution is not straightforward because it depends on various uncertain events in the future. Scenarios are a tool to shed light on the strategic challenge and view it from different angles and take on different perspectives. Therefore, we can claim that the focal question sets the scope of the scenario planning exercise. Answering the focal question should help us find plausible solutions to any underlying strategic challenge.

Since the development of the focal question is the cornerstone of the entire scenario process, it should be undertaken deliberately while incorporating the following factors:

- First, we need to define the *time horizon* of the scenarios. Therefore, the first question is whether the scenarios should rather look at 5 years from now or 15. The time frame needs to be short enough to allow the development of the probable scenario, yet it must be far enough in the future to provide the opportunity to imagine that potential major changes influencing the future to take place. Scenarios can be applied for any period. However, the benefits increase when they are developed for the long term. This is because future uncertainty grows further we look into the future. With every step away from the present, uncertainty grows. From our experience, we strongly advise against using too short a time frame, as this will just lead to scenarios that are a mere projection of today's environment into the near future rather than an actual challenging exploration of the future. The final year of the scenario is called the horizon year.

- Second, the *regional focus* of the scenarios needs to be set. Sometimes, we develop global scenarios or even market agnostic scenarios that could be – to some extent and after some adaptation – inserted into any region. Very often, we focus in our scenarios on a specific market or region that incorporates global yet puts the spotlight rather on local uncertainties.

- Third, the *lens or perspective* of the scenarios need to be chosen to define how wide the strategic issue is and from where it is to be observed; scenarios can look at a strategic question from a number of different angles. They can be conducted through a customer's lens on the strategic challenge, from an employee's point of view or constructed with a general industry focus. There are various ways of looking at an issue.

After the initial focal question is defined, the scenario journey can begin, although the focal question is not something that is seen as cast in stone once it is established. A good focal question anchors conversations that wander off and lose relevance while still providing a platform for future discovery and exploration. People often start the scenario planning process with a narrowed focal question and then discover that forces far beyond the initial assumption affect the actual situation or issue. Focal questions need to be discussed and agreed on. This is an iterative process that might even last until the start of the actual scenario development process. However, the definition of the focal question is a key; a productive scenario design project has to be, in all circumstances, relevant to the organisation's research *objective*.

In our everyday work, we drew up our own checklist for a good focal question with the following definitions:

- precisely worded;

- no longer than one sentence;

- relevant to all involved stakeholders;

- specifies the scope and timing;

- should trigger immediate visions of uncertainty;

- allows for 'it depends on' [*the right answer?*] and avoids yes/no answers;

- is clearly linked to the underlying problem or dilemma;

- helps to achieve the strategic goal.

*Practical Example: European Bank – Shift from Industry to Customer-centric Focus:* In one of our projects, our colleagues asked us to support their corporate strategy project for a European bank with our scenario capabilities. The client had a long and proud history, but was acquired by a competitor and thus lived a life in the regional niche. To help our client, we discussed ideas with our colleagues and then presented our approach to the board and other key decision makers. They were instantly quite clear about their requirements: they wanted scenarios on the domestic banking market in 2030, a classic industry scenario. We started our approach with a focal question such as: 'What will the domestic banking landscape look like in 2030?' Very quickly, we had to go back to our client; they were not in good shape and made most of their revenue with private customers. Therefore, we had to tell them:

'Look, industry scenarios are nice to have. However, they will not help you in your current situation. You need to understand how your customers are evolving in order to provide them with the best possible service. Understanding them is a question of survival'.

After some discussions and iterations, we ended up with a focal question on the future of banking customers that would have helped our client develop solutions to put them in pole position in the local banking market. Unfortunately, the strategy project changed in scope from a forward-looking project to a restructuring project, so the scope of the exercise shifted from a forward-looking exercise into an inward looking exercise, and scenario planning was abandoned. The take away from this story is that forward looking strategy in general and scenario planning in particular require a strong commitment from leadership and decision makers.

*Practical Example: Fast-moving Consumer Goods (FMCG) Company:* When developing scenarios for a leading European FMCG company in the beverage industry, we started the initial discussions with the hypothesis that our client was interested in the future of the type of beverage they produce. However, our client soon told us:

> *Well, that is something that is very important for us – but the actual challenge for us is: how are customers interacting with fast-moving consumer goods companies, especially how do they identify with brands?*

This was another example of a client who understood his business and the underlying drivers very well.

*Practical Example: Healthcare Company:* When developing scenarios for a leading healthcare company, we started discussing with the client the development of scenarios covering the entire treatment area of their portfolio. We quickly realised that it might be feasible to combine all therapeutic areas into one set of scenarios, although the disadvantage would be that we would lose specific elements. We therefore deliberately decided with our client to divide the therapeutic area into a number of fields that covered their entire product and service portfolio. Hence, we focussed primarily on one therapeutic area and then developed subsequent sets of scenarios covering the other areas. This was in line with our guiding strategic principle of strategy, which is about making choices: the choice where to put our focus on and which areas to deprioritise.

## DRIVING FORCES

After defining the focal question, we start the process of identifying driving forces; these are the fundamental sources of future change, as they will drive the outcome of future scenarios. Driving forces shape the course of events and history and dramatically increase our ability to imagine future scenarios.

Without driving forces, there would be no way we could think in scenarios. They are the tool for honing initial thoughts and making decisions.

Research into driving forces begins with an outside-in thinking approach *by looking into macro environment drivers*. We apply the STEEP framework in order for this research to be holistic, looking for drivers from the Social, Technology, Environment, Economic, and Political spheres. Those drivers are particularly in the contextual environment, as reflected in our environmental onion framework. This wider context of social, political, economic, environmental, and technological domains offers both huge opportunities and significant threats to many organisations:

- Social drivers cover demographic, but also cultural issues such as values, lifestyle, and behaviour. For a telecommunications company that we supported, for example demographics and the related communication modes and preferences are the main driver impacting their business model.

- Technological drivers talk about direct, indirect, and enabling technologies. When discussing scenarios in any transactional field currently, blockchain is a key driver as it could remove intermediaries and thereby cut out the middlemen.

- Environmental drivers cover the behaviour of Mother Nature as well as sustainability issues. Climate change has been very widely acknowledged as a fact. Hence, reducing its levers is important in many societies; $CO_2$ reduction is, therefore, an important driver for heavy polluters like energy producers or manufacturers.

- Economic issues include both macroeconomic drivers that shape the economy as a whole, and microeconomic and industry-specific drivers as well as drivers within the organisation. For public drivers that, in particular, look at the whole economy, various economic key performance indicators (KPIs) like inflation rate or growth are of high relevance. Economic drivers also featured prominently in the historic Shell scenarios.

- Political drivers include electoral issues (e.g. how voters behave), legislative questions (how policies will be changed by parliaments), and regulatory factors (regulation and litigation issues affecting how courts behave). In discussions with organisations in heavily regulated industries, regulatory changes are often a question of life or death and therefore play a major part in the scenarios.

Applying this framework helps avoid omitting a significant source of future change. Assigning these drivers into the different STEEP categories is often not clear-cut; however, it is not necessary for further progress to resolve these ambiguities and correctly categorise the drivers. In terms of consulting-slang, they are not MECE (Mutually Exclusive, Collectively Exhaustive) – nor are they intended to be. The framework is for guidance so that drivers outside the organisation's normal realm of thinking are not omitted. Real issues are, to some extent, made up of all the STEEP forces. Yet, the STEEP framework is not the sine qua non of driver research. Social sciences have developed a variety of approaches to assess environmental forces, whereby STEEP is just one of them. As we believe that the discussion about which framework to use, is rather a linguistic than a content problem, other frameworks are possible. The only guiding principle is to be holistic. Thus, sometimes, we categorise those drivers subsequently in a way that is more in tune with the organisation's mind-set and therefore makes it easier for scenario participants to process them.

Often, we experience that the STEEP categorisation is not intuitive for our clients. When we developed scenarios for a business unit of a global Med-Tech firm, we allocated the driving forces into industry categories such as:

- Patient;

- Provider;

- Technology landscape; and

- Miscellaneous.

We applied the same approach when developing scenarios for a leading media company, where we used the following categories:

- Viewer/Customer;

- Advertising;

- Content; and

- Miscellaneous.

Our research into identifying drivers is based on four pillars: the first two pillars are classical desk-based research and the collection of primary data based on interviews; the other two pillars are our megatrend research and artificial intelligence-based driver identification.

Due to the major time and budget constraints on most scenario projects, it is important to select the most appropriate interview partners for providing relevant knowledge. Thus, one should interview on the one side relevant stakeholders and subject matter experts inside the organisation to get their buy-in. Often, it is extremely valuable to involve also the wider network of the client, such as their customers, suppliers or associations they belong to. However, to ensure an outside perspective and the most relevant insights for a specific topic, third party subject matter experts are indispensable. In our interviews, we ask participants in a very open way for their opinions about future drivers so that we can get their vision of the future and potential issues. We need to understand their hopes and fears, which in turn helps us to understand the rationale behind their actions. Consequently, there are no general rules to follow; however, you should:

- Introduce the project background to give context; and

- Explain the scenario process and how the data will be used.

In this context, it is very important to establish a high level of trust and to guarantee anonymity. This helps in accessing opinions that are not aligned with the organisation's point of view, when interviewing people inside the organisation. Interviewers need to be genuine listeners who pay a high level of attention and react spontaneously to the interview answers. When starting the actual interview, it is important to stimulate a far-ranging conversation.

Moreover, we continuously carry out trend scouting based on our megatrend research;[6] this is often used as the starting point for any research. These drivers affect a number of different industries and can be applied industry-agnostic due to their high relevance in the world we live in. However, these three categories do not differ from any scenario-driven research conducted in the past. By using the latest technology, we can raise the scenario process to a new level. Therefore, we make use of AI. This helps us extend, in a time-efficient manner, the research sources. Therefore, we differentiate our scenarios for real-time strategy from the old-school scenarios back in the days based on the knowledge of few experts.

We see a driver as a dynamic concept. Every driver has two extreme endpoints that both illustrate a plausible future end-state of the driver and how a driver might shift relative to where we are today. The actual development of the driver occurs on an axis between those endpoints, which represent a continuum of possibilities between the extremes. Scenario thinking is a process of thinking in extreme points. Some drivers have natural extreme endpoints, others lack them in clear-cut terms. This enables us to push participants of the scenario development process to the limits of their imagination so that they can see the full range of possibilities. If there is no extreme point, one can make comparisons with today, for example driver X is developing slower or faster than today.

Initially, we compile a long and exhaustive list of driving forces. We want to include anything that could affect our scenarios, regardless of the number of drivers on the list. For practical reasons, we try to reduce the longlist to a shortlist of 60 to 100 drivers. This is a highly iterative process where we discuss the role and relevance of each driver with industry experts to get a shortlist of potentially disruptive drivers. We eliminate some drivers and often merge many others to get a list that is both manageable and comprehensive in terms of the information included. Drivers need to be carefully researched and require innovative, out-of-the-box thinking – if they are badly researched, they create a *garbage in, garbage out* issue.

When we developed scenarios as part of a large corporate strategy project for a Wall Street company, our scenario team worked as holistically as possible in developing a long list of driving forces. Not all were straightforward, and thought was needed to connect them with the underlying focal question. Nevertheless, as scenarios need to think outside the box and be extreme, they had their place. However, when discussing these drivers with our firm's financial service experts, they expressed surprise about their relevance. They were imprisoned within the confines of their industry. We advised against rejecting them, but in the end, they owned the project. In the course of the scenario project, questions arose about some of the missing drivers we previously excluded, as they did not seem relevant for the industry experts at first glance – showing how important it is to think out of the box and go beyond current industry assumptions and conventions.

## CRITICAL UNCERTAINTIES

After having identified the most important driving forces shaping a subject or topic, we conduct a driver evaluation with internal experts from our client and peer-group, *and* stakeholders from our client and external subject experts. They need to assess all drivers both for their impact on the focal question and for the degree of uncertainty surrounding the forces themselves. Change often comes as a surprise when it occurs, yet it can often be foreseen with early indications. It is therefore vital to embrace this uncertainty. In any context, whether it is in the business, political or private sphere, surprise, and uncertainty are normal.

Therefore, decision makers and organisations need to find coping mechanisms to handle uncertainty and ambiguity. Actually, uncertainy also has some appeal to our human nature, as stated by the Prussian general and military theorist, Carl von Clausewitz 'Although our intellect always longs for clarity and certainty, our nature often finds uncertainty fascinating'.[7]

Commonly, researchers and practitioners have observed two characteristic responses to uncertainty. One reaction is the denial of uncertainty where the decision maker oversimplifies the fact and expresses false confidence. Being unable to interpret the imperatives for change is the most obvious source of refusal. However, there are more subtle expressions of negation. One example is when an organisation becomes attached to a particular business model that has driven their growth in the past but is not applicable to a changing business landscape. The organisation becomes stuck in a rut, as it is only looking for opportunities that fit their mind-set; they may even set their criteria to rule out any opportunity that does not fit their mind-set. They are running a significant risk of suffering in the future because they only apply the metrics from a stable, known world to a disruptive, less stable world. This is a powerful form of cognitive bias: failing to recognise that the environment is uncertain and disruptive and that man-made change is required. It is found in organisations of all kinds and can halt all creativity and expose organisations to surprise. A good example is Kodak. They invented the first digital camera in 1975, yet they saw it as a major threat to their business. Kodak engineer Steve Sasson, who invented this camera, summarised the management response to his innovations as follows: 'But it was filmless photography, so management's reaction was, "that's cute – but don't tell anyone about it"'. They saw digital photography as a major threat and retreated into denial. Kodak did not just have the blueprints for the digital camera in their drawer, they also conducted a major study in the 1980s on the future of digital photography that provided a very detailed picture of how disruptive digital photography would be for their business. Yet, the study provided them with at least 10 years' time to prepare. An opportunity Kodak missed with the consequence that they eventually had to file for Chapter 11 in 2012. Historically, Kodak's founder George Eastman was very good at understanding disruptive changes in the market. He initially gave up a profitable dry-plate business to switch to the film business. His second move was to invest in colour film at a time when it was demonstrably inferior to the black and white films where Kodak was dominant at the time. He laid the foundation for Kodak's success for decades.[8, 9, 10]

The second typical response is paralysis. Decision makers try to plan for everything and then wait and see which option comes true. Yet, in a highly complex system such as today's globalised world, it is often simply not feasible to plan for anything; there are too many variables. They may recognise the necessity of coming up with another course of action but display paralysis when those choices are presented. Explicitly or implicitly, they admit the level of uncertainty but are incapable of taking decisions on how to move on. The 'paralysis' issue is often triggered by an inability to select between available options. When technology changes quickly or new marketplaces are emerging, it is challenging to make the correct decision with confidence or to allocate the right resources at the right time. Decision makers will frequently wait for additional pieces of data or information that will bring into sharper relief or confirm what the right option is. However, such information rarely comes at the right time, so that opportunities may be missed as the environment has moved on. Less frequently, paralysis can also derive from an organisation misperceiving its competitive environment and its customers. They plan for much more intense competition and threats than they actually face. When actually facing a highly uncertain situation, as the market has changed or new technology has disrupted the industry, decision makers might overemphasise the threats and fail to see beyond the immediate challenge. In this way, some organisations tend to underestimate their own capability to influence and shape the market. Furthermore, different research outcomes show how today's work environment is causing paralysis:

- IQs of workers attempting to juggle messages fell by 10 points, as shown by psychiatrist Dr Glenn Wilson who monitored the IQ of workers throughout the day. This is comparable to the lack of a whole night's sleep and more than twice the four-point fall seen after smoking marijuana.[11]

- A Microsoft study that tracked email habits found that it took an average 24 minutes until a knowledge worker returned to a suspended task once they had been interrupted by an email or instant message notification. Various other studies showed that knowledge workers estimate that around 60%–80% of their emails are not necessary.[12]

- In 2009, research conducted by Basex estimated that information overload on the workforce costs the US economy $900 billion a year.[13]

During World War II, the British Prime Minister Winston Churchill issued a communiqué that probably went against the grain. Churchill, who once said that he was 'satisfied with the very best', was facing a dilemma. His urgent intention was to cross the English Channel to take the war to the European mainland; this put him in the difficult position of having to settle for something less than the very best for the greater good of the war. When Churchill got wind of the fact that the designers of the landing crafts for transporting the military and their equipment across the Channel were expending enormous efforts on discussing major design changes, he communicated this warning: 'The maxim "Nothing avails but perfection" may be spelt shorter: "Paralysis"'.[14]

Faced with the hazards of denial and paralysis, it is not surprising that many organisations face a dilemma when they have to imagine their future in order to sustain their position or grow. New initiatives frequently fail to gain traction and many attempts at growth fail completely. Scenario planning is a good method for bringing surprise to the surface. However, decision makers cannot plan for all eventualities and have to identify the ones to focus on. Scenario planning then helps cutting through this complexity and make the necessary choices.

Although we cannot look into the future and are thus subject to uncertainty, we can structure uncertainty into three distinct categories:

- Uncertainties that have sufficient historical precedent facilitating an estimation of the probability of occurrence yet retain an element of judgement and thereby inherit some level of uncertainty. An example of this is the reaction of the stock market to central banks' interest rate decisions. Financial institutions have developed a variety of tools to hedge this uncertainty.

- Structural uncertainties that appear when new changes occur without a statistical basis to fall back on for drawing possible conclusions. Each event is independent, and there is a lack of overall coherence so there is no evidence to judge possible likelihoods. Events could develop in various directions. This level of uncertainty is the playground for scenario design.

- Uncertainties that we cannot imagine at a certain point in time are called black swans.[15] They are surprising events but have a large magnitude and effect on the world we lived in before. Examples from the past are the Chernobyl nuclear disaster or digital dementia. Possible future black swans could be an attack from an alien civilisation or a genetically modified organism pathogen that kills most of humanity.

For our scenario approach, the second category of structural uncertainty is in the spotlight. The first category can be adapted into probabilistic models and thus do not require scenarios. Black swans, on the other hand, are difficult to capture since these events happen without advance notice, therefore it is difficult to plan for them.

We define uncertainty, the level of unknowingness and volatility that we measure, by using the standard deviation of our expert survey's rating of the possible endpoint of each driver. Let us take an example that was highly relevant when we started writing the book (and currently still is) to make it more vivid. After the Brexit vote on 23 June 2016, various experts had different opinions on the implications for the EU. One group of experts claimed that the EU would break apart because of Brexit; other experts argued that Brexit would lead to further integration of the EU. In our driver evaluation, the outcome (where experts from a wide background are selected) would provide a high standard deviation. This is a good example of a very uncertain argument, as there are convincing arguments for both outcomes.

Some trends and driving forces may have a high impact but have a high level of certainty. We define these as predetermined elements or trends as they are already on the way and outside our control. For those drivers, we can anticipate to a certain degree their occurrence and how they will play out. They are more or less a given for each scenario; however, they are likely to interfere with the scenario-specific events and gain momentum. It is important to separate them from critical uncertainties and understand the rationale of each driver. Therefore, when we develop the scenario narratives, they play a role in each narrative. However, they might have different origins such as:

- slow-changing phenomenon (development of infrastructure or demographic changes);

- constrained situations (the social security crisis many developed markets face or the need and drive of some countries to maintain a positive trade balance due to a lack of resources);

- trends already in the pipeline (the demographic shifts of populations through aging – excluding migration); and

- apparently inevitable collisions (branch banking vs. internet banking).

For the scenario development, we need to identify the most critical drivers. For this purpose, we use the impact/uncertainty grid, a classic

**Fig.5:  Impact-Uncertainty Grid.**

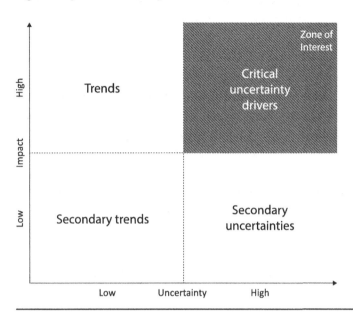

consulting 2 × 2 matrix, and pre-fill it with our initial expert rating. Kees van der Heijden initiated this approach at Shell in the 1970s to give structure to a large number of driving forces embedded in the scenario development process (Fig. 5).[16]

Those with high impact and high level of uncertainty – we call them the critical uncertainty drivers – are the zone of interest we focus on. They have the potential to tip the future in one direction or another. For strategy development purposes, they can be differently interpreted and therefore require the development of various scenarios to account for the uncertainty. By embracing this uncertainty, one accepts that it is impossible to research away from the uncertainty but one can reduce it and enable structured decision making. Drivers in the upper-left corner are trends, predetermined elements. They have high impact on our focal question and they enable stable planning as most subject matter experts agree that they will evolve in a certain direction. Hence, they are building blocks for all four to-be-developed scenarios. Drivers in the lower-left corner are secondary trends. We have confidence on how they will evolve, yet their impact is limited. Hence, we use them for future monitoring to see how they evolve, but otherwise only touch them in a light way in further developments. Lastly, in the lower-right corner are secondary uncertainties. While we do not know how they will play out, they have a limited impact and are consequently, as the secondary trends, rather only on the watch list for future developments than in the actual scenario development.

When we discuss driving forces in our workshops, we often move them around in our matrix. Some drivers look highly uncertain at first glance, but on closer inspection, we sometimes recognise them to be predetermined. On first thought, all drivers seem unique, but observation reveals some commonalities or common themes. Therefore, to cut through complexity, we synthesise and combine the drivers in the top-right corner that share a common theme into critical uncertainties. This means they share some commonality; they discuss similar concepts or push the world in the same direction. This process is based on associative thinking, a mental process:

> In which thoughts are defocused, intuitive, and receptive to a broad range of associations to a given stimulus, and analytical (convergent) thinking, the capacity to analyse, synthesise, and focus.[17]

In many of our scenario projects across industries, we can observe drivers that are related to data. Here, we can cluster such drivers as data availability, data regulation, data ownership, and also the role of technology players (not just the Googles, Facebooks, and Amazons of this world, but also Chinese players like Baidu or Tencent). The actual description of this cluster obviously depends on the focal question. These critical uncertainties are the building blocks for developing a set of scenarios. They are the key to answering the focal question. By ranking and clustering the drivers, we try to solve the dilemma of trying to understand all drivers and their relationship while having as few drivers as necessary to answer the focal question. We do not focus on isolated trends, since almost all trends interact with other trends that can move them in different directions. We, therefore, combine them to get a multidimensional model.

Participants are sometimes worried that reducing complexity will lead to a loss of value, yet in the later process, any driver left out at this stage can be re-integrated into the scenario narratives.

*Practical example – Media company:* When running a scenario project for a large media company facing a high level of disruption from new players and new business models in the market, we had a scenario workshop with top executives and strategists. In this project, we discussed how their entire industry would look like by 2030 and how they needed to adapt to be a winner in the future. During this workshop, participants felt a level of confusion about critical uncertainties. There was a lack of common understanding about how we define uncertainty. Therefore, we had to pay extra attention to clarifying critical uncertainties until we were able to get everyone to agree on our definition. Once having dealt with all the misunderstandings, we were able to achieve great scenarios. This project example showed us how important clarity in grammar and syntax are in getting everyone on board.

*Practical Example: Agrochemicals in Asia:* When our colleagues in a developed Asian nation were developing a go-to-market strategy refresh for a leading chemical company, they asked us to provide them with a glimpse into a plausible future. This was a very challenging project, as it was our first project in this cultural environment. For every step in the process, they wanted to know about its internal logic and rationale. Not every explanation suited the local mind-set, and so we had to look deeper at intercultural research. Logic is strongly linked to language and other cultural factors; this has a signigficant impact on the way people think and act. Consequently, we had to make small amendments to our process to suit their cultural mind-set. This project showed us the strong influence national culture can have on the entire scenario planning process.

What we can draw from our experience is that every scenario practitioner can steer the group far more effectively when he has gained experience across industries and cultures. The clustering of drivers into critical uncertainties is an art rather than a science. Especially with groups driven by numbers and quantified perfectionism, for example the stereotypical German engineer, this task is a challenge.

## SCENARIO FRAMEWORK

After the drivers in the zone of interest are clustered into critical uncertainties, the process of scenario framework development begins. First, we assess which of the critical uncertainties are most relevant. This is conducted by a simple rating exercise with the scenario workshop participants. Afterwards, the correlation between the critical uncertainties is tested, as we only want to combine elements that have a weak connection or lack a relationship; they should be causally independent of each other. This correlation can be either one-sided or mutual. A good example of correlated clusters is the combination of an oil price cluster with one that talks about economic development in the Middle East. As changes in oil price greatly affect economic development in the region, it is difficult to develop four distinct but plausible scenarios. Therefore, this combination should be rejected. Once there is a list of combinations of critical uncertainties that are not correlated, participants in the scenario development workshop rank to the different combinations in order to select the combination that is most appealing to the strategic issue at hand. The top-three combinations are then tested. Each critical uncertainty with its distinct endpoints provides one axis for the scenario framework. Therefore, the initial result is three scenario frameworks, consisting of two axes that each stand for a critical uncertainty. For each framework, initial logics are tested. The logic of a given scenario is characterised by its location in the matrix. Initially, we are therefore conducting high-level scenarios.

Often, we end up with more than one scenario framework. However, they can often be clustered clearly and logically.

*Practical Example – Manufacturing in Germany:* When developing scenarios on the future of manufacturing in Germany, we ended up with two sets of scenarios that made perfect sense and answered the focal question. However, we had to prioritise and focus only on one set. During the development of the scenarios, we soon recognised that we could put one scenario framework over the other and have a two-layered framework.

*Practical Example – R&D Strategy for a Global Med-Tech Player:* Another example where we gained two good sets of scenarios was in an R&D strategy approach for a global Med-Tech player. We designed two scenario sets that both made perfect sense. However, during the discussion, we came to the conclusion that one scenario framework was more the mid-term scenario and the other one would define the long-term playing field. Although the latter was much more radical and challenging to the client's business model, they decided to choose the mid-term one, which responded to the time frame in the focal question.

## SCENARIO NARRATIVES

Once we have developed three different scenario frameworks and discussed the initial logic of each of them, it is time to choose the favourite scenario

framework. Either this can be a process leading to just one scenario framework, because, for example, the other combinations have a weak logic; or
the need arises for a vote to select the most promising scenario framework
from the two or three frameworks with scenarios that make sense.

At this point, it might be useful to discuss deep causes. Deep causes are
the initiating source of either a condition or a causal chain that leads to
an outcome or effect of interest. In scenario planning, they are some of the
fundamental forces that will drive the dynamics in each scenario. Thus,
deep causes are reasons why the world might head up or down your verti-
cal axis.

Each of the four scenarios in the chosen framework then needs to be
fleshed out to transform the scenarios into vivid stories that enable the future
to be easily imagined. This helps reflect the viewpoints the scenario planners took on board. Narratives are an extremely powerful way of ordering
insights and complex issues and to make them imaginable. For Arie de Geus,
the former head of corporate planning at Shell under whom the scenario
planning was residing, stated that 'Scenarios are stories. They are works of
art, rather than scientific analyses. The reliability of [their content] is less
important than the types of conversations and decisions the spark'.[18]

Often, this part is undervalued. However, scenarios are only as good as
the way they are communicated to convey important messages. Humans tend
to rely mostly on tangible, causally coherent stories. Ideas that are otherwise
hard to believe can be brought to life by telling a solid story where inten-
tional and causal events are woven into real and fictional evidence as narratives. They should be written in a rich language full of imagery to improve
memorability and provide novel ideas. As scenarios have different audiences,
the stories need to be told appropriately. An industry scenario for experts
without industry language might lead to a loss of confidence, whereas a scenario with geek-speak could overtax a lay audience.

First of all, one needs to consider the trends, the predetermined elements,
the drivers with high impact and low uncertainty that will be part of each
scenario. Then for each scenario, the drivers within the critical uncertainties
are considered and how their given endpoints play out in each scenario. In
doing so, consideration needs to be given to how the drivers interact in a
dynamic way. Finally, all the other critical uncertainty drivers not captured
in the critical uncertainties need to be analysed. In a scenario workshop,
we often start by developing one scenario narrative with the plenary before

splitting up the group into working teams to develop the remaining scenario narratives.

For each scenario, there are six key dimensions that should be considered. Each scenario needs to be:

- *Challenging* of current conventional wisdom and not merely providing variations on the same theme to provide a new perspective. Blockchain technology is often a topic that gives a new perspective as it implies a decentralisation of business models. When developing an R&D strategy in Med-Tech, the client initially failed to recognise any use of blockchain until the recognition of the big bang effect it had on the business model sank in. Another example was in the oil industry. The client thought solely about technology and the oil price cycle. As they had a high-margin business, they were not really driven by efficiencies. Nonetheless, when developing scenarios we helped pose the central question of scenario planning: 'What-If?' and so challenged them with the proposition that we might have reached the point, with oil prices falling significantly, that the entire nature of the oil and gas business has changed, and even the largest and wealthiest players need to be more efficient.

- *Divergent* so that scenarios 'stretch' thinking in different directions. If the scenario process is properly followed, divergent scenarios will emerge as a matter of course as they are combinations of divergent extreme points.

- *Balanced* to strike a good psychological balance between positive and negative stories. This is required for the whole scenario set as a whole as well as in each particular scenario. There should be some scenarios that are more positive and some more negative. The aforementioned scenarios in Med-Tech where we produced two scenario frameworks showed that the long-term extreme scenario framework was of great concern to participants because it shook their business to its very foundations.

- *Plausible* so that each scenario could actually happen in some form, or in some segment of the market, and is believable in that it follows a causal logic.

- *Relevant* to the key strategic issues at hand, captured by the focal question so that strategy development and business adaptations are feasible.

However, scenarios aiming at the status quo or business-as-usual are not advantageous as they rarely cause participants to re-perceive their assumptions about the future. To achieve this, one needs to cross-check with the focal question on an ongoing basis.

- *Internally consistent* so that each event in the scenario is connected with causal lines of argument. Once the track of internal consistency is lost, the scenario exercise is likely to fail.

Each fleshed out scenario narrative is a prose description of the future conditions prevailing under different scenario assumptions. They play around carefully constructed plots that highlight the significant elements and their development over time. Each scenario needs to tell not only the end status but also narrate in detail the way in which this scenario will evolve over time. This enables sound monitoring of the trends that shape the future as well as better decision making, because executives get a clear picture of the factors that need to be true for a scenario to become real. In the scenario narratives, people, places, and things are organised into future outcomes that challenge the prevailing view. Scenario narratives bring alternative futures alive in ways that make them feel important to stakeholders. Sound narratives can significantly increase the content credibility of the scenarios. The way they are presented further increases their credibility; lively narratives attractively presented can make the difference.

The combination of deep causes is a good platform for creating the most compelling start to any one scenario. You should try not to use the same deep cause in two different scenarios. A key factor or trend should be considered at least in one scenario. However, many trends and uncertainties are likely to appear in many or even all scenarios.

Each of the key factors and trends should be given some attention in at least one scenario while some elements, are likely to appear in many or even all scenarios. For instance, demographic developments may be implicit in all situations but they may have different consequences based on how other STEEP variables affect them, for example education, migration, or consumption. It is sometimes clear how an uncertainty should be taken into account in a certain situation, yet there are also more complex situations.

Scenario narratives rely on classic storytelling techniques to succeed. Our brains are wired for stories; through stories, we make sense of the world.

Stories simplify complex data and can effectively convey the meaning of information. When they are properly told, stories create fresh perspectives and enable us to see new possibilities. Stories have a high cognitive and emotional impact, increasing memorability and meaning. In contrast, data by itself are necessary but are not sufficient to enable action. When developing scenarios, simply expecting change is not sufficient, scenario developers need to anticipate responses. Many planners of big and successful organisations often think that they can drive their future mainly by themselves. Every ecosystem has the ability to respond and self-correct: continual, fast economic growth might bring resistance, whereas the threat of war results in demands for peace. Or, to remain in the oil universe, that is, when oil prices are high, new fields are explored and new technologies are implemented to produce more oil that might eventually lower the price. This lead to an environment where innovation is low and those past changer drivers have a hard time, as has been seen with the fracking boom and global oil prices recently.

In the following paragraphs, we shall briefly present some of the tools and traditional plots for fleshing out scenarios.

Let us start with the tools. Systems thinking is useful for improving narrative plots; narrative construction is efficient in expanding fundamental concepts to narratives with origins, middles, and ends; protagonists are a tool for populating situations with important or illustrative people who personalise plots.[19]

- Systems Thinking: To explore the logic of a scenario, it can be useful
  to study the way that parts of a system interact. This means observing
  not only the outcome of the weather forecast but also its underlying
  causes, such as the Gulf Stream. Generally, in our society, we focus on
  single events and not the underlying causes of an event. Therefore, we
  just focus on the stock price crash that 'suddenly' appears, but not on its
  underlying reasons. The iceberg model helps to make this more explicit;
  an iceberg has just one-ninth of its volume above water and the rest
  remains beneath the surface of the sea. At the tip and above, the surface
  are events and things that we can easily see around us, such as elections
  or the rise and fall of corporations. However, many reasons are sub-
  merged beneath the surface and they need deeper investigation to reveal
  the patterns that these events suggest. They might be social issues or the

consolidation of players in an industry. Below these patterns lie vital organisational adjustments that can define significant scenario logic, such as basic shifts in beliefs or the reorganisation of sector. A helpful practice to assist the scenario team, when problems arise with relationships between distinct forces, is to have them map occurrences, patterns, and structure separately, and then work together to generate system diagrams of how distinct forces interact. This can be achieved by using sticky notes to identify and subsequently cluster (and re-cluster) occurrences, recognise and connect trends, and then identify the fundamental organisational problems.

- Building Narratives: Once the fundamental logic of the different worlds has been described, the parts should be fused together to create a narrative. This includes a start, a middle, and an end-state, and should respond to how the universe changes from the current reality to the future situation in the scenario. It should also respond to the demands for creating the end-state in a plausible and feasible way. A popular error is the temptation to settle for a single-state depiction of the potential end-state. This static image loses the chance to see how 'moving components' could interact, and then engage again, occasionally creating counterintuitive implications well down the path. Narratives are also crucial for capturing issues of timing and path dependency. Frequently, we may all agree on an end-state of technology, yet there might be different opinions about the winners and losers and their future paths, for example the struggle between Blu-Ray and HD-DVD to succeed the DVD. These paths are often characterised by shorter-term concerns of regulation, technology, economic competition, or industry consolidation. We often ask our scenario teams to write newspaper headlines that capture events or trends. The headlines are a fast and efficient way to define successive stages of a narrative. Good headlines may signal a dramatic start, then maybe a chaotic middle period, and a satisfactory conclusion. We often give instructions to focus on the format of tabloid journalism (in the US known as yellow journalism) that *The Sun* in the UK or *Bild* in Germany would use, instead of highly academic titles.

- Characters and Personas: Many scenarios use 'characters' as driving forces, organisations or institutions, even nations, while individuals are rarely used. However, the logic of the situation can sometimes be clarified and sharpened by a recognised or fictional personality, for example a charismatic leader gaining a following in radical change. A (true or imagined) person can personify the interaction of the key driving forces. Yet, when building the scenarios, not the entire plot should be built around an individual's personality or power. They could fail either with real-time events that might happen between scenario development and publishing or they can reduce their credibility due to an image transfer. Creating people living in scenarios is also a way to express the magnitude and direction of differences. In our practice, we rather prefer invented, generic personas instead of characters to capture most of the benefits while avoiding most of the pitfalls of characters.

Every scenario plot or logic for the narratives should be different while being relevant to the focal question. Developing narratives can be demanding, yet there are standard plot lines that help make the process easier. Once a plot has been chosen, imagination can be given free rein within the given framework. These archetype stories are developed from watching the angles and turns of our financial and political systems, from the increase and fall of technology, and from the swing of the pendulum in social topics. Valid and useful scenario narratives need to invite people to rethink their assumptions about the future. However, narratives that are too scary or unthinkable tend to be readily discounted and thus weaken the general importance of the scenario method. Although some archetypes already exist, scenario narratives cannot be developed according to a recipe. Moreover, the archetypes are only possibilities; there are plenty of other ways of tweaking scenario narratives.[20]

- A winners-and-losers plot is founded on a zero-sum game: one wins, while the other(s) lose. Conflict is often inevitable in this archetype. However, it is possible that the conflict, after a quick and intense flare up of hostility, relaxes or evolves into an equilibrium of strength. Sometimes, the future conflict is escalating to war, fought with either troops or economical means. A good example is the struggle in the smartphone world between Apple and Samsung. They are engaged in a fierce contest over the development of state-of-the-art smartphones. Yet, they also rely on each other, as Samsung is a supplier for Apple. This represents a scenario within the plot of the winner and loser framework but also with the added ingredient of balance. Sometimes, it is better to be a loser than a winner – as long as you are still alive or still in the game in the business world. Think of the *Iliad*, where victors like the warrior Achilles or the king of Mycenae Agamemnon died while a loser like Aeneas (said to be the founding father of the Roman Empire) laid the foundation for a new empire.

- A further archetype is the good-news–bad-news scenario. It is vital for well-balanced scenarios to include desirable and undesirable elements in the narrative. Especially when working with clients, it is often difficult to incorporate bad news about the organisation in the scenarios. However, it is indispensable to do so. Furthermore, good news might also have some downsides, whereas news that appears to be bad at first sight might offer opportunities or provide a key source of change to remain relevant in the future. A good example is an ancient Taoist parable:

  *A Chinese farmer receives a new horse, which quickly runs away. His neighbour says, 'That's bad news'. The farmer then replies, 'Good news, bad news, who can say?'*

  *One day, the horse returns and brings another horse with it. His neighbour says, 'That's good news!' The farmer then replies, 'Good news, bad news, who can say?'*

  *So he gives the new horse to his son. He rides it, then is thrown and badly injures his leg.*

  *'I am really sorry for your bad news', his concerned neighbour tells him. 'Good news, bad news, who can say?' the farmer replies.*

  *Quickly afterwards, the emperor's army comes and takes every able-bodied young man to fight in an upcoming war in a far part of the empire. Eventually, the farmer's son is spared from the warfare.*[21]

- A crisis-response-scenario is another common plot archetype. At first, one or more difficulties arise in the scenario, and then adjustment happens (or continues to happen). If the adjustment is effective, new winners and losers emerge and, ultimately, the rules of the game can be changed entirely. A sound example is the German *Energiewende*. Although the social-democratic and Green coalition government of Gerhard Schröder had decided to phase out nuclear power generation in 2000, the conservative-liberal government of Angela Merkel changed this law in 2010 to extend the operation period of nuclear power stations. In 2011, triggered by the Fukushima Daiichi nuclear disaster, they reversed their energy policy and pushed forward the process of phasing out nuclear power.

- Evolutionary change is another archetype that is based on the understanding that the rise and fall appear in all systems over time. Man-made systems tend to move forwards, especially during periods of growth, without too much thought being spent on the inescapable decline. However, even if the change is foreseeable, its type and size are rarely understood and therefore seldom managed properly. Another version of this archetype is co-evolution. The transformation in one system interacts with another system and thus changes this system as well. A good example is a technology that often provokes co-evolutionary change. New innovations are introduced and prosper (or perish). They might be the nucleus of other innovations while simultaneously interacting with social, political, economic, and environmental spheres. A good example is blockchain technology. While receiving a lot of public attention with its application in cryptocurrencies like bitcoin, blockchain technology has the potential to disrupt various processes by making them easier, safer, and faster at lower costs, making some industries and jobs redundant.

There are a number of other plot archetypes, which we present here in brief.[22]

- Revolutionary plots contain a sudden change. This can be either man-made, for example a breakthrough innovation like the discovery of penicillin, or natural disasters such as a tsunami.

- A tectonic-change-plot has structural alterations that bring with them tremendous disruptions, comparable to a volcano, with further major discontinuities that are, nonetheless, clearly foreseeable, for example the breakup of the European Union.

- As aspects of history happen in cycles, these provide an excellent archetype, as the timing of change is critical yet unpredictable, for example boom and bust in real-estate markets or the pork cycle.[23]

- The infinite-possibility archetype follows the seductive idea that continuous growth is achievable. An example is today's Internet economy with the likes of Google, Facebook, Amazon, and Apple.

- In a quest-scenario-narrative, an organisation or person has to fulfil a quest set against established rules and procedures. The main character sees himself often in a fight against a system that he perceives to be a corrupt, evil monster threatening his realm. Often this appears in scenarios where a start-up competes against an established market leader. It is a fight between first and second mover advantages, for example MySpace versus Facebook or IBM versus Apple.

- A scenario plot that focusses on demographics/generations reflects the rise of new cultures or groups with changing values and expectations, e.g. how will Gen Z change the workforce and workplace.

- A combination of the evolutionary and infinite-possibility archetype is called perpetual transition. This plot sees change as ongoing and foresees that change will be anything but uniform. A good example is the development of computing technology, that is not only about improving performance but also having new technologies like quantum computing, that bring systematic change.

After having developed scenario narratives that fulfil the scenario criteria, we need to find a catchy and memorable name for each scenario. This name should immediately convey the crucial changes in the world and how they affect the organisation. Furthermore, it should be crisp and capture the essence and underlying logic of the topic. This helps executives remember the scenario and facilitates recall, thereby inserting scenarios smoothly into a crucial part of the strategic thinking of an organisation. Often, we use scenario names that refer to something in the real world such as adaptations of book names, movies, TV shows, or even regions.

As the last step of the scenario narrative framework, we ask executives, 'So which is your official future that you would bet on?' Afterwards, one can put the qualitative models the scenarios constitute of into quantified models. Even though this is not the main goal of a scenario exercise, a quantitative model can often help check the internal consistency of the scenarios with high-level quantifications.

## IMPLICATIONS AND OPTIONS

By articulating demanding yet plausible paths forward, scenarios promote decision makers to 'think the unthinkable', foresee surprises, and consider new options; scenarios help overcome denial. After developing and considering alternative futures in the course of the scenario process, decision makers are enabled to conduct planning without the typical responses of denial and paralysis. In this way, they achieve sound decisions about future strategy, as they have experienced how the forces at work could play out and have acquired a systematic appreciation of their surroundings. At the same time, scenarios help cope with paralysis by explicitly structuring or framing the key choices of the organisation. The paralysis disappears when decision makers not only see new and desirable options but also gain a deep understanding of strategic options. After the process of building scenarios, participants have to start to think about what strategic options they want to pursue in the various scenarios and therefore need to return to the initial focal question. In doing so, the core team should examine the 'So-what?' for the organisation: the implications and options. The implications are the conditions under which the organisation needs to operate, while options are the range of actions that an organisation will take under the scenario conditions.

Implications are challenges that emerge, bottlenecks, and shortages the organisation faces as well as emergent needs or capabilities that the scenarios bring with them. There are some topics that are wide-ranging and form part of most discussions. Those are:

• How is my world looking like in this world?

• How are the marketplace and stakeholders evolving?

• How is regulation changing?

• How is my organisation affected?

However, the implication categories need to be tailored to actual needs. Thereafter, they need to be translated into executable options. As an intermediate step, we consider success factors for each scenario. Either for a specific segment or for all implication categories. Success factors are assets, alliances, capabilities, or other essential factors that help to win in a given scenario. The success factors then facilitate to translate implications into options. Options are responses, workarounds and fixes, new supplies, suppliers, other partnerships or changing products, service offerings, channel innovations or specific investments, or development activities that help to win under given circumstances. The categories used need to be tailored to actual demand. The strategy relies on the combination of existing and original, newly discovered options.

After having developed implications and options for each scenario, future-proof and robust strategic options need to be established. A robust strategy will outperform alternatives across a wide choice of alternative futures. To identify them, one needs to ask:

- What does success look like in this scenario?

- Which markets will you play in and which customers will you serve?

- How will you serve those customers?

- What capabilities will you need to have in place?

- How would you know if this scenario is going to come true?

The process of developing implications and options enables an organisation to test each decision in the scenarios. This process is a funnel exercise. While some of the decisions we make today will make sense across all of the scenarios, others will only make sense in a limited number of scenarios. Therefore, we first identify potential options for each scenario that are then synthesised to find options that make sense and are helpful in all scenarios and avoid options that that mostly bring disadvantages. This enables us to make robust plans and increase confidence. However, options that only make sense in one or few of the scenarios are challenging. They need to be observed, to have the right answer readily available once they emerge. Therefore, a flexible and dynamic strategy might require us to keep options open and possibly hedge against this option. Putting all our eggs in one scenario is more like gambling where decision makers bet the company; this is especially risky when the organisation has little control over the likelihood of a scenario being realised as it is mainly driven by external forces. Pursuing multiple scenarios at the same time until the future becomes clear is a scattergun approach that is also risky as its lack of focus.

Once we have developed strategic options, we stress-test them by using the wind-tunnelling approach. We start by testing the strategy of the organisation in the Strategy Choice Cascade (there is an excellent description in Roger Martin's and A. G. Lafley's book *Playing To Win*).[24]

In this part, an existing strategy can also be stress-tested and then be adjusted, based on the scenarios. The Choice Cascade is only an example of one framework we frequently use while also other strategy frameworks or corporate portfolios work. From our experience, the Choice Cascade is ideal for our stress-testing, which we call wind tunnelling, as it defines strategy as the result of choices, a set of interrelated and powerful choices that positions the organisation to win.

The wind-tunnelling analogy is taken from engineering; the strategy is subjected to extreme conditions similar to a car in the wind tunnel. It is an effort to see which strategic options can flourish and which flounder. Although the process is very simple, it requires in-depth thinking. Either in break-out groups or in plenary sessions, experienced leaders from the organisation put themselves into the world of each scenario. Good narratives and a vivid visualisation help achieve this. Once decision makers have become familiar with the scenario, we take each part of the strategy and challenge it: does it fit with the existing world and does it help the organisation to be a winner? Is this strategy helpful? If this world became reality tomorrow, how would the strategy work? This leads us to bold decisions; there is no 'maybe' or 'in between'. We need to make choices. Having conducted this analysis for all four scenarios, we then collect the results. Points in the strategy that are robust overall will be a part of the future strategy. Aspects that are clearly a no-go need to be ejected from the strategy. Following this, we need to discuss which parts of the strategy we want to keep because they match our official future; which parts of the strategy do we need to change to create a robust strategy. We also determine which of the strategic options are relying on certain developments. Those are the jokers or dynamic components. Once we can see certain changes that bring about one or the other scenario, we can adapt the strategy with the dynamic options. They need to be in-depth discussed and analysed as they might change the entire business model and support the decision as to where a company places its bets. After this discussion, we combine the wind-tunnelled strategy with the strategic options. We ask ourselves: which of those options are already in place and how do we need to adjust the strategy to incorporate the required options? This eventually provides us with a future-proof and robust strategy but also with a roadmap for strategic initiatives.

*Practical Example: African B2B Telco Operator:* When developing scenarios for an African B2B telco operator, we collected all their strategy documents as well as the tacit implicit knowledge of their strategy and fed them into our Choice Cascade framework. After having fleshed out the scenarios, together we challenged the strategy and all of its components in each respective scenario. We ended up with some robust elements, things the company should continue to do whatever happened.

We also had some elements that were good in some scenarios, although possibly providing an obstacle to being a winner in the future. In this process, we need the entrepreneurial skill of the top executives to make a judgement call. Finally, we arrived at a number of elements the company should definitely change, given the high likelihood of them jeopardising the company's success in the long term. This stress-testing helped the company to think about its strategy from different angles under a 'What-If?' assumption.

## MONITORING SCENARIOS WITH CUTTING-EDGE TECHNOLOGY

Often, we are surprised by the news that appear to be sudden. Something has happened that we could not conceive of before. Yet very frequently, these events have their roots in the past, roots that we can trace when looking closely enough at the ground. Monitoring is, therefore, an important part of scenario planning.

After we have developed the scenarios and outlined possible strategic options, it would be wrong to archive them in some drawer; rather, they should be actively monitored to know which scenario is the closest to the actual course of history. A sound strategy process is no substitute for insights. To gain those insights, it is vital to identify indicators that express key developments and dynamics. This mechanism will help an organisation track shifts in the competitive environment and the surrounding world and adjust its strategy accordingly. As the world is in motion, so should be the strategy. Once the implications that hold true for most of the plausible scenarios have been derived, understood well and are combined with the predetermined elements that are serious enough to consider, an organisation can act with confidence in the future and make well-informed decisions. Nonetheless, there will certainly be numerous implications an organisation chooses not to act upon, as they are depending on the future evolving in a certain direction. There will also be significant drivers that, although currently uncertain, have the possibility to becoming certain – or predetermined. To deal with this situation, a monitoring system helps identify and track indicators showing if a specific scenario is starting to materialise, leading to some implications to grow in significance and some uncertainties to become predetermined elements.[25]

Many strategy processes include monitoring of indicators; however, these are very narrow, focus mostly on the specific strategy, and therefore ignored as weak signals that partly lie beyond the strategy's horizon. Indicators can take the form of current events or plausible future signposts that present potentially significant change. The best scenario approaches and monitoring systems employ both. This can either be obvious, such as debated change in regulatory frameworks, or may be a subtle indication of a major change in society, like an increase in voluntary work. Some are easy to observe, for example economic data for economic trends, such as gross domestic product for economic development or Gini[26] coefficient for inequality. They are quantified and therefore easy to measure. However, some drivers are more difficult to measure as they are more of a qualitative nature, for example social behaviour changes, and thus it requires some time and effort to identify key indicators that enable the monitoring of these trends. Once we have identified them, we can track them to pinpoint when a particular scenario seems to be unfolding in the real world. In case the indicators are chosen prudently and imaginatively, they can assist as dominant signals that are necessary to adopt a strategy to the shifting environment. However, one needs to differentiate those signals from all the noise surrounding them. The advantage of scenario planning is that it follows a logical coherence; therefore, it allows us to draw logical implications from key indicators. Unfortunately, the monitoring stage is dropped on occasion when the time is scarce for developing a strategy. Nevertheless, setting up a monitoring tool can be a powerful approach to make an organisation aware of changes in the external environment while also maintaining the strategic conversation. Scenarios help monitor signals and indicators in a structured way. They further help to identify weak signals that appear to be less plausible at first glance, yet may turn into game changers. Once these topics have appeared, they often create the need to develop new scenarios.

A number of examples from the past exist that show that signposts and indicators have been present in the market; one is the aforementioned Kodak example. They already had indicating the advancement of digital photography. These studies were grounded on a variety of aspects, such as the cost of digital photography equipment, image quality, and the interoperability of various components (e.g. cameras, displays, and printers). Yet, Kodak failed to monitor those trends or take decisions based on those indicators, and that led to a total collapse of the firm. A once mighty blue-chip company was transformed into a penny stock that had to file for bankruptcy.

Another good example of an event that changed the world is the last global economic financial crisis. Different research shows that the entire global financial crisis was foreseeable and preventable, including that by Harvard Professor Jeffry A. Frieden. He says that around 2003–2004, many global economists and analysists were worried by growing global macroeconomic imbalances. Especially the US behaviour of borrowing between a half trillion and a trillion dollars each year from the rest of the world was of concern. This large monetary inflow was fuelling a financial and real-estate boom on credit. Financial institutions were using financial derivatives as a tool to benefit from this boom. In 2003, Warren Buffett was already calling derivatives, 'financial weapons of mass destruction'. Eventually, they caused the subprime crisis in the US, being a key trigger. Already by 2005, most economists agreed that imbalances would lead to severe issues, even though the specific outcome, as well as the timing of the problems, were debated. Economists of various ideological persuasions warned all through 2005 and 2006 of the dangers accruing in the real-estate and financial markets. Prevention was possible at this time. The US government could have reduced the deficits that spurred foreign borrowing as well as taking measures to slow down the overheated economoy. To reduce the credit book, the central bank (Federal Reserve) could have raised the interest rate as well. Also, the regulators of financial institutions could have been more strict. Yet, no one acted to prevent a crisis that had tremendous consequences for the world.[27, 28] Scenarios, particularly our approach based on AI, could have helped, as the signposts were quite clear. This way, stakeholders could have seen the potential outcomes instead of only seeing the status quo with a best and worst case that could go either up or down like a regression analysis.

Another example from the corporate world is Nokia, which was the undisputed cell phone leader (during times where phones were mainly a device to make calls and the battery duration was just incredible). In 2007, on November 12, *Forbes* magazine ran a cover page featuring Nokia's (then) CEO Olli-Pekka Kallasvuo holding a Nokia series 6xxx flip phone. They titled this picture: *Nokia, one billion customers – can anyone catch the cell phone king?* Just a couple of months earlier in 2007, on June 29, Apple released the first iPhone, which Steve Jobs had just announced in January 2007. Ten years later, Apple's iPhone is a key source of profit for Apple and became the most popular and recognisable smartphone in the world. Nokia at the same time sold its phone business to Microsoft for $7.2 billion in September 2013. In October 2013, Apple posted quarterly revenues of $37.5 billion and quarterly net profits of $7.5 billion. Most of these profits were generated by the 33.8 million iPhones they sold. For Microsoft, the acquisition did not pay off. In 2016, they sold the brand, which was worth around $300 billion at its peak, in two parts for a total of just $350 million. While the brand name was transferred to a new business established in Finland by former Nokia staff called HMD, iPhone manufacturer Foxconn purchased Nokia's production and commercialisation units, which also decided to construct the new Nokia HMD device. Apple with its iPhone was able to replace Nokia as the cell phone king because they understood and perceived several developments correctly, while Nokia overslept or could not integrate into their offering, such as an intuitive handling based on multi-touch capabilities for which customers were willing to pay high prices. The phone changed from being one out of many devices to a must-have device based on exponential technology and infrastructure advancements.[29, 30]

Monitoring of scenarios can be conducted today by the application of AI. In the past, a dedicated team was required to scan news to analyse events that might shift the future. Technological progress enables us to conduct this process in a resource-efficient manner. We shall explain our approach towards this in the upcoming chapters.

## NOTES

1. See Millett, S. M. (2003). The future of scenarios: challenges and opportunities. *Strategy & Leadership, 31*(2), 16–24.

2. See Varum, C. A. & Melo, C. (2010). Directions in Scenario Planning Literature: A Review of the Past Decades. *Futures, 42*(4), 356.

3. See Scearce, D., & Fulton, K. (2004). *What if? The art of scenario thinking for non-profits* (p. 22). Emeryville, CA: Global Business Network.

4. See Paul, R.; Elder, L. (1996). Foundation For Critical Thinking. Retrieved from https://www.criticalthinking.org/resources/articles/critical-mind.shtml

5. See Levitt, T. (1960). Marketing Myopia. *Harvard Business Review, 38,* 45–56.

6. See Klein, F., Bansal, M., Wohlers, J. (2017). *Beyond the noise: The megatrends of tomorrow's world.* Munich: Deloitte Consulting.

7. See Von Clausewitz, C. (1976). *On War.* Translated and Edited by Howard, M. & Paret, P. Princeton, NJ: Princeton University Press.

8. See Business Standard. (2012). Kodak files for bankruptcy, plans biz overhaul. Retrieved from http://www.business-standard.com/article/international/kodak-files-for-bankruptcy-plans-biz-overhaul-112011900119_1.html

9. See Deutsch, C. H. (2008). At Kodak, some old things are new again. Retrieved from https://www.nytimes.com/2008/05/02/technology/02kodak.html

10. See Mui, C. (2012). How Kodak failed. Retrieved from https://www.forbes.com/sites/chunkamui/2012/01/18/how-kodak-failed/3/#6c6f293e4a97

11. See Wainwright, M. (2005). Emails 'pose threat to IQ'. Retrieved from https://www.theguardian.com/technology/2005/apr/22/money.workandcareers

12. See Hemp, P. (2009). Death by information overload. Retrieved from https://hbr.org/2009/09/death-by-information-overload

13. See Spira, J. B. (2008). Information overload: Now $900 billion – What is your organization's exposure? Retrieved from http://www.basexblog.com/2008/12/19/information-overload-now-900-billion-what-is-your-organizations-exposure/

14. See Roberts, L. (2010). Analysis paralysis: A case of terminological inexactitude. *Defense AT&L*, January-February, p. 18–22.

15. For further information refer to Taleb, N.N. (2010). The Black Swan: the impact of the highly improbable (2nd ed.). London: Penguin.

16. See Wulf, T., Meissner, P., & Stubner, S. (2010). A scenario-based approach to strategic planning–integrating planning and process perspective of strategy. Leipzig: Leipzig Graduate School of Management.

17. See DeHaan, R. L. (2011). Teaching creative science thinking. *Science, 334*(6062), 1499.

18. See de Geus, A. (1997). *The living company: Growth, learning and longevity in business.* London: Nicholas Brealey Publishing.

19. See Ogilvy, J., & Schwartz, P. (2004). *Plotting your scenarios.* Emeryville, CA: Global Business Network.

20. See Schwartz, P. (1991). *The art of the long view: Planning for the future in an uncertain world.* New York, NY: Doubleday; See Ogilvy, J., & Schwartz, P. (2004). *Plotting your scenarios.* Emeryville, CA.

21. See Theiss, E. (2009). Parable of a Chinese farmer: How an ancient story resonates in today's hard times. Retrieved from https://www.cleveland.com/living/2009/02/parable_of_a_chinese_farmer_ho.html.

22. See Schwartz, P. (1991). *The art of the long view: Planning for the future in an uncertain world.* New York, NY: Doubleday; Ogilvy, J., & Schwartz, P. (2004). *Plotting your scenarios.* Emeryville, CA: Global Business Network.

23. The term pork cycle is an economic term, describing cyclical demand-supply fluctuations, with a time lag between supply and demand adaptations. Thus, the market is mainly characterized by under- and oversupply, while an equilibrium is rare. The term originates from research in livestock markets. Source: Deutsches Institut für Wirtschaftsforschung (2015). Meilensteine aus 90 Jahren DIW Berlin. Retrieved from: https://www.diw.de/documents/publikationen/73/diw_01.c.359465. de/gelehrtenrepublik_und_denkfabrik_2015.pdf

24. See Lafley, A. G., & Martin, R. L. (2013). *Playing to win: How strategy really works*. Boston, MA: Harvard Business Press.

25. See Scearce, D., & Fulton, K. (2004). *What if? The art of scenario thinking for nonprofits*. Emeryville, CA: Global Business Network.

26. The Gini coefficient was created in 1912 by the Italian statistican Corrado Gini, as a statistical distribution measure. It is frequently applied to calculate inequality or distribution of wealth. The coefficient ranges from 0 to 1, with 0 representing perfect equality and 1 representing perfect inequality. Due to negative income or wealth, also values over 1 are theoretically possible. Source: Investopedia (2019): Gini Index. Retrieved from: https://www.investopedia.com/terms/g/gini-index.asp

27. See Shen, L. (2016). Warren Buffett just unloaded $195 million worth of these 'weapons of mass destruction'. Retrieved from http://fortune.com/2016/08/08/mass-destruction-buffett-derivatives/

28. See Frieden, J. A. (2011). The financial crisis was foreseeable and preventable. *The New York Times*. Retrieved from https://www.nytimes.com/roomfordebate/2011/01/30/was-the-financial-crisis-avoidable/the-financial-crisis-was-foreseeable-and-preventable

29. See Farber, D. (2014). When iPhone met world, 7 years ago today. Retrieved from https://www.cnet.com/news/when-iphone-met-world-7-years-ago-today/

30. See Hern, A. (2016). Nokia returns to the phone market as Microsoft sells brand. Retrieved from https://www.theguardian.com/technology/2016/may/18/nokia-returns-phone-market-microsoft-sells-brand-hmd-foxconn

# 4

# HOW THE SCENARIO PROCESS
# IS CHANGING

So far, we have mostly discussed the scenario process as it has evolved along the first four waves and have only provided a few glimpses into scenarios 5.0 – the fifth wave of scenario planning. A number of new developments are changing the scenario process to make it more efficient, while also enhancing its quality; these include the crowdsourcing of ideas, the democratisation of the scenario process, speeding up the entire process, as well new ways of telling and presenting the scenario narratives.

## CROWDSOURCING IDEAS AND
## AI-GENERATED INSIGHTS

Crowdsourcing is a method of sourcing where a large, comparatively open and often quickly evolving group participate to source ideas to achieve a common result. The term crowdsourcing was coined at the end of 2005 by Jeff Howe and Mark Robinson, editors at *Wired* magazine, in internal discussions. They wanted to describe the process of business using the Internet to 'outsource work to the crowd'. Jeff Howe published his article 'The rise of crowdsourcing' in June 2006 in *Wired* magazine. While the term 'crowdsourcing' was coined in 2005, the concept existed before this, and there are numerous examples in history where crowdsourcing was applied before the Internet was even conceived:

- In 1714, the British government set up the *Longitude Prize*. They offered the public a financial prize to whoever came up with the best answer on determining a ship's longitudinal position.[1]

- In 1848, Matthew Fontaine Maury distributed 5,000 copies of his work *Wind and Current Charts*. Sailors received it free of charge on the condition that they returned a standardised log of their voyage to the US Naval Observatory.[2]

- In 1884, many volunteers catalogued words to produce the first version of the *Oxford English Dictionary*.[3]

The rise of the Internet subsequently led to various crowdsourcing businesses that are still active:

- iStockPhoto was founded in 2000 as free stock imagery website that enables the public to contribute to and receive a commission for their contributions.[4]

- The most prominent example is probably the launch of the 'free-access, free-content Internet encyclopaedia' Wikipedia in 2001.[5]

Nowadays, there is a number of use cases of crowd-based methods applied in different industries and settings. Two parts of the scenario process are highly attractive for crowdsourcing approaches: driver identification and driver evaluation.

Classical crowdsourcing can conduct driver identification. Volunteers can support the identification of trends and drivers that shape the future. They can either be directly engaged in tasks to identify driving forces or the crowd can be used as experts. While interviews are limited by the availability of researchers to conduct them, technology facilitates large-scale, tech-based information gathering instead of asking questions in person. This can happen either in text, audio, or on video-based platforms. Automated, artificial-intelligence–based language transcription applications enable the processing of large amounts of data that can then be tapped into. This data can then be easily analysed with natural language processing software that helps examine and visualise the crowdsourced information. By automatically drawing connections between big ideas, they provide the scenario planner with more time to think in depth. One can then ingest the ideas and opinions expressed in those interviews to find patterns and commonalities. Therefore, technology is opening up an opportunity of broad mass involvement that has never been possible in the past.

In addition to the use of one's own generated data, it is possible to tap into the many sources the crowd is already providing online to go across billions of data points and documents. For this, we can use databases that comprise company-specific and deal-specific M&A information, news, professional articles and blog databases, and patent databases. Therefore, we can incorporate the latest ideas of the Chinese PhD student as well as the thought-leadership of the Ivy League Professor. The keyword here is Big Data, which is one of the most discussed themes in the Data Science realm. Most Big Data attempts are presently concentrated on describing ground-level information in the data sets without ever knowing the greater interactions that can be observed by investigating the data as logical, interrelated clusters. We apply ground-breaking Data Science approaches. They enable us to make sense of large data sets by using natural language processing and Big Data visualisation methods. Based on these approaches, we can explore and understand complicated connections and relationships in a data set.

For driver evaluation, crowd voting can help gain a wider picture of the impact and uncertainty of the drivers. A large group's opinions and judgements on a certain topic are collected. Scenario planners can use online ratings where knowledgeable people from the crowd can participate. There is a wide variety of crowd voting especially in product design, such as Coca Cola's bottle design or Domino's Pizza crowd voting. Also, the movie industry is using crowdsourcing to test new movies, either based on trailers or on the basis of pilot episodes, as is Amazon for its own productions. While we were only able to ask a few experts in the past, we are now able to collect a huge amount of data from a large variety of experts to unveil the real uncertainty.

## DEMOCRATISING SCENARIO PROCESSES

Scenario planning in the past was a tool for elites. Executives met with key opinion leaders for some face-to-face workshops in unusual meeting places, such as a romantic chateau in France or a hotel at the foot of Fuji Mountain in Japan. In the present (and the future to come), technology enables the democratising of the process. The crowdsourcing approach described above is a crucial tool for democratising the scenario process and involving a more substantial number of participants; it also gives more organisations access to scenario think-ing. While the standard approach is accessible to any organisation, traditional research for inputs required much time and dedicated resources. Because of the democratisation of the process, the knowledge gathering and analyses do not nec-essarily differ between large-scale projects and efforts made on a smaller budget.

## SPEEDING UP THE SCENARIO PROCESS

Compared to other methods from the standard toolkit of a strategist, scenarios have turned into a fast tool. Traditional scenario planning projects often last at least five months or even up to a year just for the development of the scenarios, without diving too much into the strategy. Much time was required to conduct interviews with all the relevant subject matter experts, fly them to the workshops and conduct effective communication approaches. By applying the latest technol-ogy, that is based on crowdsourcing and democratisation, we can increase the speed for each project and run efficient scenario projects in four to six weeks with-out losing quality. Due to higher shares of remote work, there is less demand for travelling, hence scenario planning is also reducing its environmental footprint.

## NEW WAYS OF TELLING STORIES

Scenarios are stories. Stories need to be told illustratively and persuasively and therefore require distinct storytelling capabilities. Every era or genera-tion in human history has contributed something to our combined narrative so far; we now have more methods than ever before of communicating our thoughts and feelings. Humans have the need to tell stories, something that is unique to our species. However, the ways they did so have changed tremen-dously from the early cave drawings to the YouTube video blogs, Instagram stories or TikTok videos of today. Thus, we need to broad Kurt Tucholsky's statement 'If you want to have an impact on other people, you need to first speak their language'[6] by also using their way or medium of story telling. Various researchers have acknowledged the anthropological significance of storytelling for the evolution and development of humans. Whether it is oral tradition passed down through the generations, educated records, mass-printed novels, or digital media, it demonstrates that telling history is vital to our mode of existence.[7] Many studies show that the consumption of fiction books increases readers' empathy;[8] one study focussed on Harry Potter readers showed that they display 'improved attitudes towards stigmatized groups'.[9]

Narrative forms have also evolved in a world driven by 140–280 character tweets, Emojis, and short YouTube Videos. The Internet's development has radically altered the ways we tell stories, for example through introducing us to a variety of new ideas and blurring cultural influences. Social media networks have opened up new ways of telling stories, for example through real-time stories with user engagement or even customised narratives, while addressing a global audience. While we shared stories only with those who were very close to us in the past, such as family and friends, by the means of word of mouth, we can nowadays tell our stories to the entire world. Sometimes, this can even spotlight certain issues and draw global attention. It has also changed the way we value our privacy and how we identify ourselves since it caused a certain craving for recognition by strangers in public. Unfiltered feedback drives the pursuit to present things in the best light.

As today's world has changed in remarkable ways, new forms of catching the attention of decision makers are required. Slides, which are the primary consulting medium to convey results, are not always the best medium for conveying narratives. Historically, written prose or theatre plays have been used to illustrate scenarios. With advancing technologies, new ways of storytelling are feasible. They do not just tell the same old stories in a new world. Digital media such as video need to incorporate the changing zeitgeist. Digitalisation means that our attention span has shortened significantly. A Microsoft study discovered that the digital lifestyle has made it difficult for us to stay focussed. They measured that the human attention span has decreased from 12 seconds to 8 seconds in more than a decade.[10] Platforms like Facebook or Instagram enable users to express their opinions publicly with everyone on the Internet, or to choose with whom to share their information. This is intriguing, as technology has given everyone the ability to share his internal views easily with the entire world. To comply with these changes, we use video as a new medium. Through a combination of image and sound, the content can be compressed, compared to written, read-only narratives. For us, crowdsourcing, by using stock material, is a crucial lever for this development. It enables fast and cheap development of astonishing videos, which previously required expensive technology and intensive practice. Now, it is accessible to everyone due to easy-to-use tools. To personalise this, executives and key stakeholders can even be part of the video. The rise of technology means that any smartphone can capture high-quality videos that then can be filled with narrative, while easy-to-use editing software is readily available at no or little cost. The storytellers of today, like us, have much more choices and options than Stone Age cave artists. When compared to writers and artists a couple of decades ago, they are also in an advanced environment, yet the need to tell stories has always been part of human nature and history. Societies today might look radically different from before the emergence of the Internet and other technologies, changing the way of storytelling yet not the reasons for telling them. New technologies build narrative twists in the overarching story. It is certain that we will construct narratives and tell stories in the future; however, the way we do it will change and adapt to the Zeitgeist. Some of the best narratives might look like the best stories from the past, while others will look very different in every way. With the entire world's knowledge constantly at our fingertips, stories in scenarios need to be built with care, as well-informed viewers will doubt anything lacking plausibility. Furthermore, technology acts as a magnet to attract a wider audience, and stories can be spread quickly.

## NOTES

1. See Longitude Prize. (n.d.). The history. Retrieved from https://longitudeprize.org/about-us/history

2. See Grady, J. (2015). *Matthew Fontaine Maury, Father of Oceanography: A Biography, 1806–1873*. Jefferson, NC: McFarland & Company.

3. See Gilliver, P. (2012). 'Your dictionary needs you': A brief history of the OED's appeals to the public. Retrieved from https://public.oed.com/the-oed-appeals/history-of-the-appeals/

4. See Peterson, K. (2007). Microstock photography represents a new business model. Retrieved from http://old.seattletimes.com/html/businesstechnology/2003724590_istockphoto28.html

5. Wikipedia. (n.d.). History of Wikipedia. Retrieved from https://en.wikipedia.org/wiki/History_of_Wikipedia

6. See Tucholsky, K (1975). *Gesammelte Werke in zehn Bänden* (p. 197). Band 3. Hamburg: Rowohlt.

7. See Todd, A. (2016). Stories through the Ages. An examination of the evolution of storytelling through time. Retrieved from: https://landt.co/2016/06/storytelling-through-time-evolution/

8. See Bal, P. M., Veltkamp, M. (2013). How Does Fiction Reading Influence Empathy? An Experimental Investigation on the Role of Emotional Transportation. *PLoS ONE, 8*(1).

9. See Chua, K. (2014). Fiction Teaches Students Empathy, Research Shows. Retrieved from: http://blogs.edweek.org/teachers/teaching_now/2014/09/study-fiction-teaches-students-empathy.html

10. See Borreli, L. (2015). Human attention span shortens to 8 seconds due to digital technology: 3 ways to stay focused. Retrieved from https://www.medicaldaily.com/human-attention-span-shortens-8-seconds-due-digital-technology-3-ways-stay-focused-333474

# 5

# SUPERPOWER FOR STRATEGISTS

After reading this book so far, you have been given an excellent strategic toolset to make valid strategic decisions. However, what do you think about not just being an excellent strategist but becoming a super-strategist who can combine long-term and short-term actions? A strategist who is most confident about all strategic decisions he takes. A strategist who can argue that each choice has been made incorporating all available facts, aspects, and perspectives. How about possessing the capability to provide all stakeholders with a long-term–oriented growth story while also keeping the short-term KPIs under control. A strategist who can align the team behind the strategic objectives every day and still has all the time to see the big picture. A strategic leader with a vision and concrete strategic choices that engage not only the inner management circle but also the ecosystem inside (e.g. team, unions, etc.) and outside the firm (e.g. selected suppliers and targeted customers/ clients). In sum, a strategist with 'superpowers'.

Let us wait for a second and digest this statement. Do we even need strategic decision makers with superpowers? Heroes with superpowers usually fight their antagonists or help to solve issues that cannot be solved otherwise. Yet, a lack of those obstacles would be quite tragic for heroes, because it would challenge their *raison d'être*. Thus, if the strategy world is harmonic and ideally in shape, we would not need the hero. We could stop here. Unfortunately, we are far away from strategy paradise.

Various academic studies have unveiled that there is a high controversy on the success rates of strategists. This needs some time to digest. Trust in the success is one of the major pillars in the interaction with experts. Imagine a conversation with your doctor without trust.[1] Without trust in his capabilities to successfully undertake a critical operation on the open heart, a brain surgery, or a surgery on any other vital organ. Would you not leave the doctor's office immediately? The doctor's advantage is asymmetric information. You trust him, as you usually cannot evaluate his capabilities *ex ante*. Frequently, we can observe such a great knowledge gap between an expert and us. The greater the gap the more you need trust, because you cannot verify the capabilities. In the corporate and public space, we trust in our decision makers, who themselves rely on strategic advisors. If we see any reason that could cause a lack of trust in strategic advisors, the very core of the field is at risk. Let us have a look then. What do the numbers tell us?

There is quite a considerable body of literature dealing with the core question: Are organisations better off with or without strategic advice. Essentially, is there a good reason to trust or not to trust? The unsettling result is that some authors claim the failure rate of strategies to be up to 90%, others see it around 5%.[2] Even though there are no recent, profound meta-studies available to come to an overall conclusion, it is fair to say that the debate itself is already harmful when it comes to trust into strategic advisors. Would you spend time and money on advisors and their frameworks that have a highly doubtful success rate when the future of the whole organisation is at stake? Would you also take into account the high financial impact on the shareholders, putting the employees' basis of existence at risk? You probably wouldn't – and this is precisely what we can observe happening right now in the market.

The strategy field is in a trust crisis. Not just missing trust in strategic advisors but in the whole field with its methods, frameworks, and approaches. Instead of long-term thinking, many companies roll with the punches and act from month to month, even from week to week – often driven by the expectations of stock markets to deliver quarterly results. As a consequence, strategic decisions come too late or are not decisive enough. Who could blame the decision makers? Many just do not see the value in strategic approaches anymore. Instead, they are focussing on the next tactical move: the upcoming trend or the current technological hype. However, who could blame them since also their personal KPIs are rather short-term than long-term oriented. In other words, we can observe the dictatorship of tactics over strategy.

One could argue that the overall market for strategy consulting has been growing in the last decade[3] but those numbers have to be interpreted carefully. First, the growth is typically correlated to the overall high global phase of economic prosperity. Simple formula: When the overall economy goes well, the strategy business does so as well. The questions that would need an answer then would be whether the growth could have been even higher if the trust level had been higher. Second, strategy typically does not come *alone* anymore but is tightly connected to an operational implementation.[4] In other words, pure strategy projects are becoming less typical. Third, the real growth story takes place not in strategy but in technology, digital, and analytics consulting. Strategy's answer to these developments are new, combined offering packages like 'Digital Strategy' or 'Strategic Analytics' to support clients in their efforts to prepare for the digital and analytics storm and make sense of the data. In the olden days, it was without question that the strategy team was the first to talk to the client and define the field for the other teams to implement the strategy. In these days, some say you will be lucky as a strategy consultant if the analytics and digital department asks you to play a role at all. We will not paint such a pessimistic picture here. By nature and definition, strategy is still the place-to-go for long-term thinkers.

Overall, the numbers prove that strategy consulting, as long as it continues to re-invent itself, still serves a substantial part of the consulting market. Yet, the day-to-day practice also makes it clear that the doubt in traditional, pure strategic approaches is growing. The former prestige strategy project, 2–3 months, pure concept, is less and less common. The moment of truth for the strategy market will definitely come with the next recession.

Besides, there a more frightening signs. Ask a business or MBA student these days for a definition of what strategy means. You will be surprised how many blank looks you will get. Strategy is becoming a term that could mean everything or nothing. Also, be honest with yourself – how well could you have explained what strategy is all about before reading and refreshing your memory in the previous chapters? We learned in Chapter 2 that one part of the definition we are searching for is long-term orientation. Furthermore, strategy is about making choices what to do and what not to do. We also learned that strategy, as a profession, is at risk due to lack of trust. Therefore, if we want to secure the long-term success of strategic decision-making, we better come up with a strategy to do so and make the right choices.

In summary, strategy is at the risk to deteriorate from being a supreme business discipline to merely a shadow of its own, being sold as an add-on with tactical implementation and/or condensed to a trending tech topic. We risk losing the trust among our stakeholders. People start wondering why we, as strategy developers, do not get our job right. The discipline of strategic management as a whole is at risk. A superpower is therefore in high demand to secure the long-term success of our beloved profession.

In this chapter, we will show you how to develop such a superpower for strategists based on artificial intelligence. In that sense, it is not so much a super-power like *Superman* has it, but more like Tony Stark creates and uses it as *Ironman*. While *Superman* has natural superpowers, Ironman extends his capabilities by having an AI – JARVIS (Just A Rather Very Intelligent System) – at his service, so he can make better-informed decisions and finally defeat his enemies.

One crucial note upfront: It is exclusively a superpower for long-term–oriented leaders or the ones who want to become long-term oriented. The reason behind is just that only long-term–oriented leaders would know how to use such a superpower wisely. We will explain that in the next section. To understand what the superpower should look like, we needed, of course, to get to know the most prominent 'enemies' of a strategist first. Only if we know our enemies we can we defeat them. Furthermore, we want to learn more from past success stories, and avoid typical mistakes, to enable strategists in making better decisions. Finally, we will present and discuss our extension of scenario thinking based on AI. This marriage of one of the most proven toolsets in strategy and one of the most cutting-edge techno-logical advancements in human history makes the extension so impactful. We believe it can indeed be called a superpower for a strategist with all appropriate confidence.

## THE SECRET OF STRATEGIC SUCCESS – AND FAILURE

As decision makers, we always have the choice between two approaches to improve our decisions: Tackling our weak spots or bolstering our strengths.

Regarding the first approach, we would have to identify our weak spots first. After establishing in which areas you have deficiencies, you can develop countermeasures. Take for example the lack of a strategist to contribute to achieving short-term goals. The strategist is typically trained to reach strate-gic goals only and has developed an armada of frameworks to do so. They are less capable of dealing with a sudden hitch in the production line, or a malfunction in the IT systems. Take for example the famous rupture of the tulip bubble in 1637. During the so-called 'Tulip Mania', bulbs were priced way over their true value for a short period of time.[5] This is clear day-trader territory. Day traders process the signals to invest or not to invest on a daily basis. An excellent strategic advisor would incorporate day traders to reach a particular financial goal but not replace them by trying to do their job. If your strategic objective was financial stability, the right strategic choice could be to invest in diverse market areas (e.g. tulips and a new machine for production) in contrast to a specific market area only. The actual execution precisely when to invest or disinvest is in the hand of the specific market experts (e.g. day trader for flowers). A strategist would not be a good course corrector in a hyperactive, short-term market situation. However, he would be a good advisor for choosing the right playing field in the first place. Most important, once you know where your deficiencies lie, you should not give in to the temptation to offer your services in those areas anyways. You simply do not do short-term oriented. Therefore, you *do not offer short-term advice.*

In a world becoming more and more short-term oriented and reactive, this specialisation on long-term challenges could be taken as a weak point in our skillset. However, if we are simply not good in 'short term', but 'short term' is in high demand, one could argue that we might just have to rectify and improve on that. One exemplarily countermeasure could then be to adapt and apply strategic frameworks to short-term decision making. Based on our experience, however, we really cannot recommend that. A strategist who tries to become anything else but a strategist would probably need to start from scratch. Hardly any of us has the lifespan to finish two different degrees and experience two complete career paths. This approach can be successful, but would require many resources. Let us face it, then: Short term is not our business. Do not give in to the temptation to pretend a strength in short-term advice just because the demand is high these days. What about the following, much more elegant proposal: If we, as strategist, could come up with wise, long-term decisions that would help companies to *avoid* short-term hyperactivity in the first place, we could just flip the arguments upside down. The message would then be: We cannot help you with every one of your short-term challenges, but we can help you to have simply less of them.

The second option originates in the conviction that one should bolster their strengths. The primary reasoning behind that is that we only become 'super' in anything when we further improve on the things we are already good at. Jack Welch of GE (General Electric) took it to an extreme for a whole organisation by is 'rank and yank' policies in the 1980s. He would lay-off all managers belonging to the bottom performers and promote the top performers; clearly focussing on the 'strengths' and getting rid of the 'weak-nesses'.[6] The success of this approach in terms of net worth was tremendous. The moral dilemma is also apparent (also, we recently see a discussion about the side effects of such an extreme shareholder orientation in terms of 'finan-cial engineering', but this is another discussion). Nevertheless, the approach to strengthen your strengths is less resource intensive and therefore in our favour.

In summary, when we identify the source of our success and exploiting it to the fullest, then we have the best chance to revitalise strategic think-ing. Therefore, we are going to build the superpower to extend the origi-nal strengths of strategists. To achieve that, we would have to define these strengths of strategists first.

## THE ORIGINAL STRENGTH OF STRATEGISTS

To come closer to unveiling the original strength of strategists, let us have a look on one of our most robust frameworks, scenario thinking, again. Chapter 2 made it pretty clear that scenarios can be seen as a prerequisite in the toolset of an outstanding strategist. There are many useful strategic frameworks like strengths, weaknesses, opportunities, and threats analysis commonly known as SWOT analysis, Porter's five forces or the BCG Growth-Share matrix, but the proposed framework, in particular, has something fascinating about it. The fact that we, the authors of this book, have dedicated significant parts of our careers to a toolset that has already been common knowledge for many decades, speaks a clear language as well. To be precise, we have invested a lot of time and effort to master it. We have supported numerous clients across the globe so that they can achieve their strategic goals based on the trust in the methodology and backed by the experience that scenario thinking is *the* suc-cess factor in strategy. In the end, we concluded that scenario thinking is not just another great framework, but also very much an inspiring mind-set. It not only contains a proven toolset, a structured process and hundreds of real-life success stories to learn from, but it is also the source of our professional

inspiration. Inspiration because scenario thinking aims at big goals. The goals that are worth fighting for and unite stakeholders to the extent that they follow you through fire if necessary. A big goal that, once achieved, would make a massive difference to the status quo.

In the previous chapter, we concluded that successful strategists use scenario thinking to windtunnel strategic options. While this is working perfectly fine, we almost overlook the original motivation to do so. This motivation is to achieve big goals. In other words, scenario thinking is making the important, the inspiring goals, come true.

To build our superpower now, we have to identify the source of this strength to master it further. We must understand what truly differentiates strategy from tactics. The differentiator that lies between achieving big goals and small goals. The differentiator that is surprisingly obvious but also mysterious. This differentiator is *time*.

Think of it as the very basic ingredient for the potion that is giving us strategic strengths. All big goals are only achievable when a company has enough time to pursue them. Or the other way around: The bigger the goal, the more objectives you have to achieve, the more time you need. As simple the logic, as impactful the consequences for us as strategists.

Napoléon Bonaparte already theorised that, 'strategy is the art of making use of time and space... '. He even concluded that he was most concerned about time when he said, 'space we can recover, lost time never'.[7] Time is inherent to 'long-term' thinking. It is a logical consequence. Vladimir Kvint, a highly awarded economist and strategist, translated the concept into a modern 'mathematical' formula of strategy when he writes that 'strategy is the product of the multiplication of time, costs and [...] strategic ideas'.[8]

We would say that time is the first necessary *resource* you need to possess and use to build the big palace/house [strategic goal] made of many building blocks/stones [achieved objectives] (see Fig. 6). A non-strategic, short-term house is consequently smaller, maybe even more fragile, since it simply has fewer building blocks [achieved objectives] due to relatively a short period of time. Therefore, time is a necessity to reach the big, stable and maybe even inspiring goals in our lives as decision makers/advisors. Before we understand how to gain more of this most valuable treasure in an increasingly short-paced world, let us further verify the assumptions by looking at some real-life masters of time. In contrast to non-strategic goals, strategic goals can typically be reached with much time and relatively many achieved objectives, as shown in Fig. 6.

**Fig. 6:   Time, Non-strategic, and Strategic Goals.**

Strategists like Steve Jobs, Jeff Bezos, or Elon Musk are known for their inspirational ideas and products. However, the other critical factor in their success stories, time, is often underestimated. Take for example a quote from Elon Musk and read between the lines:

> *Critical to making that happen is an electric car without compromises, which is why the Tesla Roadster is designed to beat a gasoline sports car like a Porsche or Ferrari in a head to head showdown. Then, over and above that fact, it has twice the energy efficiency of a Prius. Even so, some may question whether this actually does any good for the world. Are we really in need of another high-performance sports car? Will it actually make a difference to global carbon emissions. Well, the answers are no and not much. However, that misses the point, unless you understand the secret master plan alluded to above. Almost any new technology initially has high unit cost before it can be optimized and this is no less true for electric cars. The strategy of Tesla is to enter at the high end of the market, where customers are prepared to pay a premium, and then drive down market as fast as possible to higher unit volume and lower prices with each successive model.[9]*

Let us have a closer look at the terms we have introduced so far. The *strategic goal* is to become a leading company for efficient, energy-friendly cars. But in contrast to just directly building such a vehicle (i.e. mass car) as a *strategic objective*, he has another strategic objective before that: the sports/premium car, where higher costs can be better handled via higher prices. The secret master plan, as Elon Musk describes it, is to ask for as much *time* as possible from his stakeholders to achieve the two objectives before attaining the final, inspiring goal. The more building blocks, the bigger the house, the more time needed. He will use and require a lot of time to make his goal come true – because it takes counterintuitive measures like building an exclusive sports car first to be able of producing a mass-production vehicle very much later.

There are many more examples of outstanding strategic leaders, but what they all have in common is the secret of asking for a lot of time. Time is money but time is also the necessity to build a sustainable, high margin business. To put it another way in the words of Creel Price, co-founder of the early-stage investment group Investible:

> We tend to overestimate what we can achieve in a year, but grossly underestimate what we can achieve in five.[10]

Real-world examples are useful in order to make things tangible and vivid. In addition, let us add a thought experiment to deepen the understanding even further. As long as the following simple thought experiment holds true, time is truly a candidate for one of the most significant differentiator between strategy and tactics.

Imagine two twin companies, which are entirely the same. They are precisely the same regarding IP, balance sheet, leadership, talent, and so on. The only difference is that company A has more time than company B to reach a specific goal. That could be the case when both companies are start-ups, but company A was founded way before company B. Furthermore, the target could be that both want to receive seed money from business angels at a shared deadline.

The business angels provided both companies with a clear description of what the product/service is supposed to do and in which market it would have to fit. Under these circumstances, company A might always win since they have just more time to bring their product/service idea to another level. They have more time than company B to be more creative, to do more research, to find the best answers. So far, so good. Maybe not quite.

One could argue that time pressure can also work as a motivator. Just in how we call good ideas 'diamonds', and diamonds result from high pressure to coal (more precise: carbon). In this case, maybe company B would even outperform company A because they had the idea for the one-in-a-million unique selling proposition that came from one crucial meeting under high pressure.

By the way, we would say that a typical business consultancy very much follows this principle. The costs of time for a consultant are relatively high. That is why consultants are asked to accomplish so much in so little time. Also, the results are very often surprisingly good, keeping in mind the available, highly limited time. If the most respected partner on a consultancy project tells you to find a suitable solution in no time, you might wonder what creativity and motivation that unleashes. However, if it is not necessarily time, under these circumstances, what else could be the differentiator then?

Imagine companies A and B are finally both equipped with all the money necessary to start. Everything is the same again for the imaginary twin companies. The only difference still is the time available, but in this case, the time counts for the actual phase of doing business. The difference is therefore that we switch from a situation purely focussed on company-internal matters, during the period of funding, to a situation in which also the external environment counts.

Company A has been given a time window of 5 years, while company B has two time windows. The first one ends after 2.5 years, the second after another 2.5 years. The numbers do not have the claim to meet real-world start-up cycles. What counts here is the relative value. Which means in total the same amount of time for company B as for company A, but cut in two short-term periods. After the specific time windows, the companies are supposed to show results. The stakeholders are only interested in near-term positive cash flow. The assumption here is that not everyone is as charismatic as Elon Musk, who manages to instil high confidence in the long-term future to his investors. Based on the results, it will then be decided which business to continue – company A or B. Company B is therefore driven by achieving short-term goals while company A has a relatively long-term perspective.

Again, we would formulate the hypothesis that company A is in an advantageous position here and will be able to succeed over company B because it has more of the resource time until it needs to show results. How is that? We would argue that the difference here is that the success (or failure) of both companies is not just dependent on themselves but very much on what happens *around them*. In other words, external, not control-able effects are kicking in.

In contrast to the founding phase in part one of this thought experiment, the external environment now plays a significant role in which company is more or less successful. By external environment, we mean anything that is not directly controlled by the company itself, for example customers, vendors, or regulatory/political circumstances. The 'trick' to just use the time pressure internally on the team would not work anymore. Your customers do not really care about any time pressure of your team but only for the quality and/or price of your products and services.

Ultimately, foremost internal matters played a role during the founding phase, while during the business phase external issues dominate. Imagine the government announcing a new type of regulation, which will demand your products meeting certain unification standards. Time-wise, the unification is mandatory and three years ahead. Both companies are facing a specific investment to meet those standards. Company A would be able to build a product even with a lack of standards. Company A has the luxury of time. After having finished the first product version after two years, they still have enough time until the regulation demands higher standards. They can gather the cash from the cheaper, non-conforming product revenue over one year, which is needed to build a next generation of the product to meet the standards long term. They can start to update their product from year 2 on and have plenty of money and time to be finished in year 4. In contrast, company B would already have to present a product matching the upcoming standards since they are judged already after 2.5 years. They would have a hard time explaining their short-term–oriented stakeholders anything less than a future-ready product since they do not get another chance. This leaves them only room to trim the features of the product in order to meet the safety standards because of the limited time. This product will meet the standards but is inferior to the second-generation product of company A. The result is that company B gets outperformed by company A. Company A has more time to reach two objectives. First, product below standards to gather cash. Second, investment into second product edition meeting the standards. Company B already had to meet the standards as the first and last objective, leaving only the option for an inferior solution to achieve short-term goals.

What has all of this to do with time? The time now is a huge competitive advantage since company A can, for example, use the first 2.5 years to lay out the basis for the success of tomorrow, just like Elon Musk did with the investment in the capabilities to build the Tesla Roadster. Apple, for example, used the time to build an ecosystem around the smartphone. Competitors like Samsung have managed to create smartphones at least as performing, but building the whole ecosystem around it you cannot be done short term. The result is that Apple is fighting less short-term battles but rather is protected after this long-term investment in the ecosystem.

However, there is more. Company A, like company B, are both dependent on the external environment. So far so known. Therefore, independent of how quick you as a company would evolve, the external environment will keep its pace separate of yours. Which means that company A has more time to convince customers for example. It is all about building a loyal fan base here. Without many years of investment in the ecosystem, the Apple watch would just be a single product without much value – just like any other smartwatch. But the Apple Watch is more, it comes as connected part of ecosystems and mainly not as a single product. Customers had time to get used to the ecosystem and build trust in the long-term orientation of the company. They know when they buy the Apple watch, it will not only be perfectly compatible to their hardware and the Apps they know from their iPhones and MacBooks but also be supported through software updates and the like for many years.

In summary, strategy helps to define, or at least choose, the playing field in your favour. In the words of Warren Buffett: 'Someone is sitting in the shade today because someone planted a tree a long time ago'.[11]

Let us leave this thought experiment and focus again on the real world. If this argument that time makes all the difference holds to be true, do we find any evidence that a long-term–oriented strategy is more successful than a short-term one? Are there any companies having the time luxury of company A from our thought experiment? And if so, do we see a story of success for the long-term–oriented strategy approach. What would be your guess?

Let us have a look at the numbers. How successful does a real-world company perform that has identified time as a highly valuable strategic resource? The consulting firm McKinsey asked the same question, and the results are quite clear. Based on the analysis of 615 large and mid-cap US publicly listed companies from 2001 to 2015, they have checked for patterns of investment, growth, earnings quality, and earnings management.

*From 2001 to 2014, the revenue of long-term oriented firms cumulatively grew on average 47 percent more than the revenue of other firms, and with less volatility. Cumulatively the earnings of long-term firms grew 36 percent more on average over this period*

*than those of other firms, and their economic profit grew 81 percent*
*more on average. [...] Our findings show that companies we classify*
*as 'long-term' outperform their shorter-term peers on a range of key*
*economic and financial metrics.* [12]

There is more. Caroline Flammer and Pratima Bansal investigated whether long-term–oriented compensation has a positive effect on the stock price. The result is clear: Yes, it has. 'We show clear, causal evidence that imposing long-term incentives on executives – in the form of long-term executive compensation – improves business performance'. [13] An important fact is that this knowledge is not new. Take for example the quite exciting research of Francois Brochet, George Serafim and Maria Loumioti done shortly after the financial crisis. They have analysed the conversations of leadership with investors and management and compared the tendency to discuss short-term versus long-term arguments with the stock performance of the company. For example, if the management were stressing terms like 'years' over 'weeks' in their arguments to convince investors, it would be rather long term. You can guess the answer – that is positive. Furthermore, they have shown a quite motivating phenomenon. It is simply in the hands of management what kind of investors they attract by using a certain kind of language. The more your financial story is built on long-term arguments, the more you are surrounded by long-term investors. [14]

Overall, the thought experiment and empirical evidence show very impressively that time, regarding a long-term oriented strategy approach, is a central success factor. Generally, good things take time. Some would say it is the most crucial ingredient to success altogether.

However, time is not just highly impactful but also highly rare. Therefore, it is not surprising at all that only the very most capable and trusted employees in a company become the masters of this precious resource: The CEOs, the strategic decision makers, the leaders of a company. They decide what to use the future time for.

Why do we then find, based on our practical experience as strategy consultants, that short-term–oriented strategy approaches outnumber long-term–oriented ones? Why are Elon Musk, Steve Jobs, and some others so rare that they are treated like pop stars, each of them with their personal fanbase? Why are strategists who postulate longer time horizons so rare?

Strategy advisors, shareholders, and media – everyone tends to ignore the benefits of time by compressing, squeezing, and almost eliminating it from any strategy or project plan. Time seems to be shortened whenever possible; we somehow treat it more like an enemy. Superiors would almost always opt for the strategic plan that takes less time to save costs. Time is money. Time is a luxury we do not have right now, one could argue.

After looking at the research and our thought experiment, we argue that obviously time is not the enemy here. Quite the opposite, time is the *source of our strength* as strategists. Time is what differentiates us as strategists. Time has to be protected and cherished. Adding another perspective, Jeffrey Sonnenfeld asked the very right question in his article from 2015 about the perfect length to stay in the same company for top managers. In summary, he concluded that retention time must fit the culture of the company and that there is no simple formula. Nonetheless, the CEOs that fall into the category 'we are here to stay' show extraordinary shareholder returns.[15]

So far, we have investigated what our true strength is. Obviously, a superpower should then build on this strength. It must extend it or at least protect it. But wait. Do we not miss an important factor before we come to the superpower? Yes, the *enemies* are still missing. Whom are we fighting?

## OUR TRUE ENEMIES

Before we can establish a capable superpower, we must first understand the reasons why so many strategic decisions turn out to be wrong these days. Only if we find the real reasons (i.e. enemies), we can develop the right countermeasures. A word of caution before you continue reading. While this chapter will not only let you understand strategy better but will also give you a new perspective on what holds the (business) world together, it also might be pretty abstract. Nevertheless, we strongly encourage you to keep on following us on this journey. Based on our experience and research,[16] the two major enemies are 'Complexity' and 'Adaptiveness'.

### Enemy No. 1: Complexity

Prussian general and military theorist Carl von Clausewitz wrote an influential book called *On War* and identified our first enemy already:

*Everything in war is very simple, but the simplest thing is very difficult. These difficulties accumulate and produce a friction which no man can imagine exactly who has not seen war [...] Countless minor incidents – the kind one can never really foresee – combine to lower the general level of performance. So that one always falls short of the intended goal. [...] The military machine [...] is basically very simple and easy to manage. But we should bear in mind that none of its components is of one piece: each part is composed of individuals, every one of whom retains his potential of friction [...] A battalion is made up of individuals, the least important of whom may chance to delay things and sometimes make them go wrong [...].*[17]

If we understand what Carl von Clausewitz was about to discover here when he writes about the 'friction', we find first the two enemies of a strategist and hopefully protect against it.

Conduct a little experiment with either yourself or the person next to you. Directly ask this question: What is the difference between 'complicated' and 'complex'? Is there any difference? Which one is causing more 'friction'? Based on our experience, typically, you would get answers like 'it is quite the same' or 'I use both words as synonyms'. Either way, in our day-to-day life, we tend to avoid anything that is called 'highly complicated' or 'complex', because it smells like a lot of effort to understand or to do it. Typically, caused by our evolutionary development, we tend to avoid activity with a high energy consumption if we have a practical alternative.[18] If technological devices, software interfaces, or rules of board games are labelled as complicated or complex, it works like a killer criterion to keep the hands off it. In sum, even if the answer what 'complicated and 'complex' mean is not so easy to answer, the applied relevance of these properties should not be underestimated.

From our point of view, the differences between something being 'complicated' versus being 'complex' are huge. It is like the difference between a sand corn and the universe, or knowing all the rules of a card game versus knowing who will win the game in the end. Moreover, most relevant to the reader of this book, it holds the explanation why strategies tend to fail more often now than they used to do in the past. Or to put it the other way around: It is the first of two major end-game enemies of a strategist. It is the 'wall' between us and our strategic goal (see Fig. 7).

Before we deep dive into the theoretical world, let us give a break and look at the empirical evidence first. Why do strategies fail according to the literature? Of course, this is not a novel topic. Also, the body of research is enormous. Some selected results: Manfred Perlitz concluded that strategies often are just not novel enough. A standard approach simply does not fit novel challenges.[19] Roger Wery and Marc Waco asked the question why even good strategies fail. What is so wrong with the strategy consultancy firms – can they not build good strategies anymore? Not quite. According to the authors of the study, poor execution is the simple reason hindering good strategies to show their full potential.[20] In contrast, Finkelstein investigated whether the decision maker himself might be the reason for failure.[21] He points out that many managers do not incorporate the external environment sufficiently and fall into the trap of being to 'self-centred'. Finally, Freek Vermeulen is very clear about the fact that a strategy can only be successful if it includes actionable insights.[22] In addition, he points out that the implementation itself should not only be top-down but must also come from the inside; it has to be supported and put into action by each single employee. The interested reader might find many other studies and perspectives on this, and all are worth reading.

We propose to look a little deeper. Is there a common denominator for all these empirical findings, like there was in the thought experiment around time that we did a few pages earlier? The big question here is: Do we find a way to identify underlying rules that apply while being independent from the specific cases? This would help us a lot in defining the superpower since we are not 'distracted' by individual cases. Basis theory, here we come. Complexity can be seen as a wall in between the strategist and the strategic goal, as shown in Fig. 7.

**Fig. 7: *The Complexity Wall.***

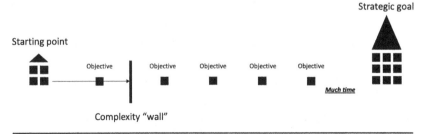

In general, complicated things in your life are time-consuming and displeasing, but in the end, they are solvable. This is similar to the studies we have just discussed. If a strategy is not actionable, make it actionable. If the manager is not incorporating competitors or other elements of the external environment, then, well, just do it. Solve it. Of course, it is not easy, but still solvable. By solvable, we mean that you will be entirely able to deal with them in a reasonable time. Complex things, in contrast, are enemies you very often cannot beat at all – even if you try it with everything you have. Complicatedness is here to be solved, complexity is here to stay.

Let us clarify what *complexity* is all about and how it differs from *complicatedness*. And, most importantly, how all of that helps us to become better strategists. In doing so, we define both terms formally and then describe them in an example based on a mental model.

For the formal definition, we shall introduce the term 'system' first. A system comprises 'elements'. Each element manifests at a specific 'state'. The more elements and states a system has, the more *complicated* it becomes. The more the different states of the specific elements depend on each other, the more *complex* the system gets.[23]

To make it more tangible, let us introduce a mental model. Mental models are very useful to highlight certain aspects of a phenomenon that matter, while keeping away distracting noise or unimportant elements. The alternative would be to describe the properties with a real-world example from a specific industry. We made the experience that each industry leader is very adamant when it comes to the non-transferability of findings from one industry to another one. We, therefore, use the mental model to highlight the difference between complicatedness and complexity on an abstract level and to develop an intuition how to transfer it to the specific context of your industry.

The model comprises the idea to get out of a jungle. As typical for a mental model, the jungle here is just a placeholder. See the place in the jungle as the current state of the organisation and the moment of coming home as the state in which you have reached your strategic goals. Let the journey begin.

It is hot and humid. It is also green, loud, and potentially dangerous. Welcome to the jungle. The simple description of the task now would be to get out of the wilderness as your strategic goal. You will face several obstacles. The least scaring one is the heat, the second one is complicatedness, and the most dangerous one is complexity. Imagine yourself being the person who got lost in the jungle. Just like a strategist who would have to come up with a working strategy to guide the company in the right direction towards their objectives.

Also, watch yourself closely whenever we describe a particular challenge or obstacle, regardless whether it is reasonably *solvable* or not. Try to pinpoint the moment when you are, while reading, suddenly having the feeling 'oh, now it gets tough'; to the degree that you would rather like to leave the mental model because it feels too 'confusing'. If you experience this particular feeling, you will have crossed the line from a complicated situation to a complex situation in our mental model. You have therefore also encountered the case when you face challenges that are overwhelming and keeping you up at night while figuring out a successful strategy for your company. In this very moment, you are facing one of your biggest enemies as a strategist.

First, you would have to interpret the map to find your way back home. The map has a scale of 1:15.000 (1 cm on the map reflects 150 m in real life). There might be a right way alongside the river (route A) with 45-km distance. An alternative would be directly through the jungle (route B) with only 35 km distance. Route C and route D are both 60 km and go around the jungle. You have to wear protective clothes for route B. Route A, C, and D provide a good amount of fresh water. The decision would be too easy, based on this little information. Let us increase the level of difficulty.

Route A shows less tree density and will guide you directly to the next bigger village. You must cross the river one time. Be aware of the animals. There are 25 different animals, of which 10 are dangerous. For route B, you would have to face around 60 different animals, of which 20 are dangerous. You have three different options for minor variants of route B. One would be over a small mountain (60 minutes time savings but a 50% probability that the path is blocked), the other one over a plain path (30 minutes time savings) and for the third one, you need a machete to clear the way from all the plants (no time savings). These are the possible routes for getting out of the core jungle. So far, these possibilities add up to a certain degree of *complicatedness*.

What is your approach to solving this task of finding a way back home? You are reading this book, so you are not the type of person who would give up and spend the rest of your life in the jungle. You would probably take a piece of paper, a pen, and a calculator (assuming you brought one to the jungle), but at least you would invest some time in reflecting your options.

Therefore, you look for a good spot in the shade and formulate your strategy. The strategy could be: Come home as quickly as possible, another strategy could for example be as cheap as possible. The rest is pure effort and a cool head. In addition, since you have no supercomputer around, you would calculate all possibilities and use a fair amount of heuristics and rules of thumbs as well. After some time, the actionable route back home stands, and you are ready to go.

All in all, the way back home with all the options is complicated, but you are capable of solving this task. Here, complicated means that you need a fair amount of time going through the different alternatives, understand the symbols on the map, interpret distances, and so on. In other words, complicated means *difficult* (as it requires some effort) but solvable. Solvable like in a mathematical formula. Once you have all variables, the relations, and enough information, you can solve the formula to come to clear results.

We can sense that there is something missing – not everyone is coming back from the jungle and even if they do, they often did not just follow a straight plan but instead survived a lot of thrilling adventures worth being told around a campfire. If it were easy, strategies would not fail so often. Still, if the jungle, or by extension the world, were 'only' as complicated as described so far, there would be a mathematical formula to solve the problem. Remember that complicated tasks can be solved. There would be clear answers to strategic questions. Apparently, this is not the case neither for the jungle nor in the business environment. We therefore would probably have to add a new sort of obstacles then, to make it more realistic.

In 2002, the former US Secretary of Defense, Donald Rumsfeld put it this way:

> [...] *there are known knowns; there are things we know we know. We also know there are known unknowns; that is to say we know there are some things we do not know. But there are also unknown unknowns – the ones we don't know we don't know.*[24]

Therefore, all the 'unknowns' should also be a variable for the mental model. Of course, the 'unknowns' we do not know are especially tricky. Can we model what we cannot describe? Yes, we can! We would add random events at random points in the model. We could add a storm or sudden illness, even encounters with unknown species. It adds to the challenge, but with some waiting time and shelter, the decision which route is the best will be still calculable. Also, the map could be false. Sometimes, we just get false information. With imperfect or even wrong information, one can for example easily miss the next village. However, it still does not quite do the job. One would argue that a smart decision maker would have bought a proven map only. Coming back to the business environment, you would not engage a strategy consultancy firm that has provided you with false information a second time. You would take any measures ensuring that the quality of information you base your strategy on is as good as possible. Finally, do not forget that the business life is not a necessarily friendly environment. Competitors (internal and external) might scatter misinformation to lure you from the right path. Nevertheless, all challenges are bearable so far.

Finally, what about adding some of the 'mysterious ingredient' of complexity now. For comparison, the amount of information regarding the absolute number of sentences in this book will be the same as for the description of the complicated routes before.

Going back to the comfortable spot in the shade, looking at the map, we are observing different route alternatives. Contrary to before, we realise that there is more information on the back of the map. It says:

> Route A: Please keep in mind that the river holds some traps. You will find dangerous animals like tigers, crocodiles, and hippos. The most dangerous ones only come out of the river if there are enough preys on the riverbank. The number of predators depends on the water level. The lower the level, the more crocodiles will look for room in the shallows. The water level depends on the weather conditions of the last 14 days. The more it has rained, the higher the level of the river.
>
> Please also keep in mind that the number of dangerous tigers, crocodiles, and hippos depends on the temperature of the river. The warmer it gets, the more they will search for shelter in the shade alongside the river. The stream can only be crossed via a bridge. Whether the bridge is open or closed depends on the level of water in the river. Indigenous people might hunt for the crocodiles or hippos. They typically go hunting when the sun is shining for more than three days in a row but only if the river is not showing too much of water.

You will find similar notes for route B, C, and D on the back of the map.

You can instantly tell or at least 'feel' the difference. While the complicated challenge was just a matter of linear adding and subtracting minutes of the different routes and/or summing up the potential costs, the complexity challenge is on an entirely different level. To solve the task, you would have to consider a tremendous amount of variants. The number of alternatives to calculate rises exponentially with each information.

The magic word here is 'it depends'. If you read the information on the back of the map again, you will notice that in contrast to the information on the map itself, the word 'depends' occurred quite often. It means that you cannot go through the information linearly but instead have to go back to see the state of the information before. The task becomes non-linear. For example, you get the information that the bridge status depends on the weather. To add to the complexity, the weather also influences the number of prey animals, which in return affects the number of dangerous animals and so on.

Going back to our formal definition, the system 'jungle' comprises different elements regarding the river, the prey, and predators for instance. Each route has different states (as the number of miles would be one state, or whether the bridge is open or closed). The more elements and states a system has, the more complicated it becomes. The more the different states of the specific elements *depend* on each other (i.e. the bridge will be open when the water in the river is at the right level) the more complex the system gets.

In sum, the map itself is complicated because of the different routes and their specifics, but the information on the back of the map adds to the complexity. Some decent time in the shade and maybe an excel sheet and you are all good when it comes to the complicated calculations. In contrast, the information about the conditions along those routes depend on each other and are therefore complex. You will probably end up making a decision based on a gut feeling rather than a complex formula with dependencies of several degrees. In other words, whenever you hear the term 'it depends', you should usually be on alert.

Unfortunately, strategists have to deal with one of the most complex systems regarding quantity and quality that exists on our planet Earth: Our economy. Whether a strategy will be performing well or not is always a matter of 'it depends'-questions. A strategist has to consider social, technological, economic, environmental, and political systems. Each one is comprised thousands of elements that depend on each other. If this were our jungle, it would mean that the jungle is massive, has to be watched as a whole and is full of dangers and opportunities that depend on illegally numerous, interdependent states. You have almost no chance to find a *dominant* strategy out of this jungle.

To give you a sense of the complexity, a physicist already describes a system with only three elements as complex, when the state of two elements (e.g. two planets) depend (e.g. via gravity) on the state (e.g. location in space) of the respective third one.[25]

You can imagine that already a business meeting with the board members (like the planets in the example before) can be considered as more complex. Each board member is an element with different states (e.g. opinions). During a strategic discussion, the different views influence each other, are depending on each other. Imagine for example the CTO (Chief Technology Officer) joining the debate with the belief that we should invest more into the IT systems. He might change his opinion once the CEO (Chief Executive Officer) informed the board about the negative development of the firm and that cash flow is in focus. The CEO in return might have to change his opinion when the CFO (Chief Financial Officer) unveils that huge cash flow was just realised, and so on. If we consider a board meeting as a complex system already, you can imagine that watching whole economies, competitors, and product markets are unbearably complex. This also means that there is no mathematical, formal model for strategists – and probably never will be. It also means that strategists should never fall into the trap of being promised supposedly 'easy' answers to complex challenges.

Does complexity, therefore, qualify as one of the enemies that hinder strategists from utilising the time they have available to achieve strategic goals? We would say very much, indeed. The examples showed that complexity means that finding the best decision poses a great challenge. Even if we imagine that we would have the resources to go through the pain for one decision and calculate all possibilities against each other, we would not be able to do the same for all the other coming choices just because there are too many to be made. Not to deep dive but at least to make us aware, this assessment gives us an idea for the difficulties we are facing when it comes to climate change, immigration, and potential economic crisis.

In the absence of total excel models, strategist facing the enemy of complexity rely on their experience and gut feeling. Based on this mental model, experience and gut feeling is the *only* steering capability in a highly complex world. Therefore, a potential superpower should support strategic decision makers in exactly that: Making better decisions despite complexity, based on their highly valuable experience and gut feeling.


## Enemy No. 2: Adaptiveness

Complexity alone makes it almost impossible to find the optimal route out of the jungle or to formulate the optimal strategic plan. A strategist with enough experience and a well-proven gut feeling may find a way. But even if we suppose that our gut feeling will guide us well, there is a second enemy of a strategist that could stop even the most experienced strategists. This enemy is called 'adaptiveness' (see Fig. 8). Adaptiveness can be seen as the second major wall after complexity in between the strategist and the strategic goal, as shown in this figure.

Let us go back in the jungle and face our second enemy. Back in the green hell, sitting in the shade and studying the map. We have spent quite some time on calculations and used some heuristics to include the information on the back of the map. We have kept in mind our preference to leave the jungle as soon as possible and have evaluated the different routes accordingly. We concluded that it is worth the time to put all effort into planning. Finally, many hours and heavy strategizing as well as translation into actionable waypoints later, we conclude to take the way alongside the river. The back-pack is ready and the map is easily accessible at the side of the backpack. Also, the level of motivation is high.

So far, the situation in the mental model could remind us, for example, on the process of defining the strategy for the next years. Your team and/or the external consultancy firm has done a great job, all the facts have been

---

**Fig. 8:   The Adaptiveness Wall.**

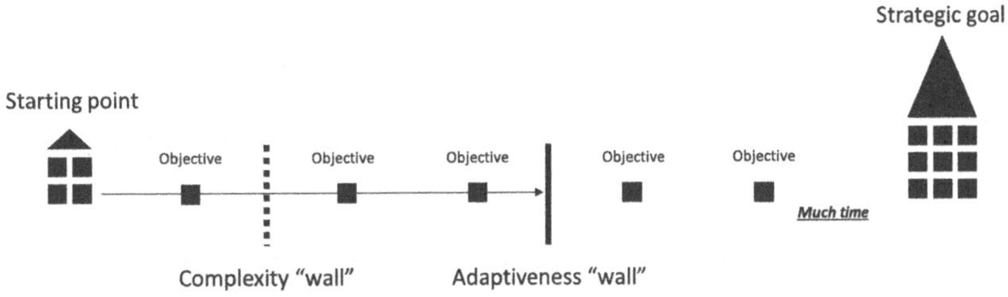

considered. The complicated tasks, like gathering all required information and drawing conclusions, have been solved. For the upcoming complex obstacles (at the river), you may have needed way more time to analyse as you had hoped for, but in the end, you settled on a promising strategy. All set and ready to go. So what could go wrong now?

The journey goes well as planned, until one minor but game-changing alteration happens. A slight change with tremendous implications for the success rate of your strategy. Arriving at the river, you find that a small barrage has been built. Yes, just a simple barrage. This barrage services the indigenous to make sure they have access to enough water all year. Unfortunately, this small change made the calculations regarding the complex obstacles (e.g. the behaviour of the prey and predators) obsolete. What does that mean?

Let us imagine: We would finally have had developed a strategy to cross the river at the right moment. Imagine we would have been able to cut through complexity and consider the effects of the weather, the level of water, the number of prey, and most probable behaviour of the predators in the correct interdependency. We might even have figured out that there is a pattern in the actions of the crocodiles and hippos, allowing us a window of crossing the river in the early morning while keeping in mind the weather of the last days, the amount water, and so on.

Because the size of the river has been altered due to this little barrage, all the assumed interactions of the different elements of the system have changed, as well. This causes quite an impact. The various aspects of the system have adapted to new conditions. This adaption means that you have to deal with literally a completely *new system behaviour*. Even if the system elements and the element states stay the same, the fact that the way the elements react on each other has changed means that the whole system behaviour has changed as well.

Your time window to cross the bridge early in the morning not only has potentially vanished, but also all assumptions from the map that would allow you to come up with a strategy are obsolete. To be clear, we are talking here about the fact that not the complicated parts of the journey have changed but the complex ones. The part where we found out that finding a solution is prohibitively difficult.

The potential effects of this 'little' change are innumerable. For example, after the barrage was installed, the prey preferred smaller water ponds beside the river. As of yet, nobody knows, especially not the outdated information on the back of the map, what this means for the ecosystem of prey and predators. The influence the weather has could also have changed, not talking about the different levels of the water at different times. The result would be that you have to find a nice place in the shade again, watch, and learn. You would have to update the information on the map after studying the interactions between the weather, the river, the animals, and so on. Finally, you would have to cut through all the complexity all over again to identify a safe window to cross the river.

One note here. The 'Adaptiveness' in the mental model describes the changes in the system 'jungle'. In the real world out there, there is not just the market (in the mental model the jungle) undergoing changes but also the market players like companies (in the mental model the challenged person that has to find a way out). Let's take again the previously mentioned Eastman Kodak for example. The enemy 'Adaptiveness' can be found both in the market as well as in the company. Regarding the market, the digitalisation of photography (could be the barrage in our mental model) changed everything. Kodak's strategy to get 'out of the jungle' (i.e. high margins) was to build everything in-house. This strategy gave Kodak a high level of control over processes and quality. Unfortunately, the costs of production were too high for the new digital 'jungle'. Competitors entered the market with unseen low production costs; Kodak had to go back to the shade and re-think its strategy completely. Which is what they did. They invested heavily in new technologies. We understand today that the transformation failed. What went wrong? One reason could be that they were facing the challenge of 'Adaptiveness' inside the company. The employees were not used to the new production processes and product marketing for the digital world. The change happened too fast. It is not enough to conduct a town hall meeting and inform about the new circumstances (in our mental model the new behaviour of the prey and predators). People were only used to the workflows from the old analogue world and acted accordingly. They crossed the river in the same way they were used to do. They were not expecting the predators waiting for them.

'Adaptiveness' is cruel and shows no mercy regardless of how much effort you put into the strategy. The diligently formulated strategy could be outdated even before the ink is dry because the world has already changed again. What if the expected consumer behaviour has shifted to the opposite due to a single event like an accident with one of the products? A direct and prominent example is the terrible accident of the Concorde in 2000.

The accident changed the product from being a luxury symbol of freedom to a life-threatening danger. The consumers adapt to new information and might change their buying behaviour drastically. Typically, these events could mean that regulators adjust to the new public opinion or insights and change their behaviour as well. The previously restrained course of the regulators, for example, might have turned into a progressive regulation facing the new landscape of events. Strategic moves that were a great idea before could now mean the end of the company. In our mental model, the change was – at least – noticeable (the barrage), but what if it was less visible. The consumer behaviour could change for various reasons, which might not be clear until it is too late to react, or even to study it. Take for example trends in the fashion industry. Who can really tell why a trend occurs and why it was gone even quicker. One of many examples here is Abercrombie & Fitch. In 2013, it had a brand value that other firms could be jealous of with a brand core as simple as it was successful: Young, good-looking people. Who would tell that by 2019, sex would not sell anymore? The effect-direction has literally changed to the opposite. Abercrombie & Fitch will have to adapt.

The most harmful enemy after complexity is therefore adaptiveness. Adaptiveness means that the system we have studied so carefully, with its elements, states, and interdependency, is suddenly not the same system as it was before. Furthermore, change here does not mean that one or two states (like the weather conditions) have changed (which would only add more to the bucket of the complicatedness). The change means that the system does not behave like before (like the fact that all the dependencies have changed due to the barrier). It means that you would have to re-study it again to make sure you model the system correctly.

In sum, adaptiveness is a property of a system, not a cause. What causes the system to adapt is change. In other words, adaptiveness alone would be no challenge, but change is once it *triggers* the system to adapt, and make all observations obsolete. The question is just how often the adjustment occurs.

As a strategist, you have two options when change is happening and you recognise it. You could stick to the strategy and hope that it still fits; that the system has not adapted too drastically so that your observations that have led to the strategic plan still hold. In addition, you could call your own team or the external consultancy firm again to analyse the new situation. A highly reasonable but also cost-intensive approach, if the change happens too often.

Strategic thinking in former days was very much meeting with the influential people in charge, smoking a cigar and discussing essential matters over a glass of fine wine or whisky. Then you returned with what you had learned from each other, formulated a hypothesis on a piece of the potential strategic plan, and came back a week later to continue the process. During these days, the level of available time to reach the strategic goals were high and the rate of change relatively low. These were the golden times for strategists. They could utilise the power of time and manage the complexity and adaptiveness of the business world around them highly successfully. Nowadays, in the digital century of computers and the Internet, decision making is more like fast food dining; always coming back home with an 'unhealthy' feeling and being undernourished due to the lack of vitamins.

While in past days, strategic challenges could also have been quite complex and market environments adaptive, at least the rate of change was quite low. Therefore, the 'enemy' adaptiveness had way less cause to take action. Strategists could focus on the complexity, cut it and come up with solutions. Nowadays, the complexity is not just growing, but the complex relationship between markets and market players is adapting all the time due to ever-growing changing conditions. The speed of change is making studies, strategic insights or strategic plans obsolete in no time. Very often, we see in our daily work that the world has become faster; that the market dynamics have increased dramatically; that strategists struggle to keep the pace. For example, the strategy to go international had been a great idea for the last two months until a politician twittered that he just did not like the country you had planned to invest in anymore.

While this is all true, we now understand better that 'change' alone is not causing the struggle of strategists these days. If you refurbish your headquarter and change the painting, change your internal IT system, or adapt the composition of the cars in your carpool, this is the change one can easily deal with. Change only becomes a challenge when it is in *counter play* with complexity and adaptiveness at the same time. *This* is what makes our (business) world more and more complicated at an increasing speed.

Utilizing our mental model of the jungle to illustrate the speed of change, you could say that the barrage was one change, already with quite an impact on our strategy to find a way out. However, while we are sitting in the cooling shade and trying to figure out a means to cross the river, the barrage now has been opened via a smart, algorithm-based control. The indigenous people are simply profiting from the benefits of digital technology. This intelligent control factors in the weather conditions and the state of the water supply in the village and decides whether to open the barrage. You can imagine what this does to your new calculations and efforts to predict the behaviour of the predators safely. Imagine now that the control was not depending on the behaviour of the people living next to the river but also of the people living farther away. An inter-village trade system would be implemented based on blockchain. Even more modern, the deals are settled via an AI that incorporates the forecasts, festivals, and mood of the inhabitants. Change is now happening hourly. Welcome to the future of the jungle and a salute to the most dangerous (business) world of the near future.

Change here is coupled with a complex and adaptive system of environmental conditions, prey, and predators. If the rate of change now increases, the system adapts more often, which would be no problem – if it was not to be a complex system at the same time. The complexity means that it is harder to analyse, to deal with, and to optimise your strategy once it has adapted to the occurring change.

Unfortunately, strategy consultants have also no answer to the high rate of change yet. To be more precise, at least not an answer that is not prohibitively expensive. Of course, you can hire a consultancy firm not for just three months but the whole year. Of course, you could also increase the workforce and double the size of your dedicated strategy team to keep pace with the rate of change. In addition, of course, your Chief Financial Officer is not very happy about these means. Therefore, traditionally, you have to make choices where to allocate your resources and your focus on.

In summary, both complexity and adaptiveness are both challenges every one of us is coming across. The difference between strategists to non-strategists is that the strategist has way more time between the start and the end of their journey to reach the goal. In that sense, the strategist has a much higher chance to encounter complexity and adaptiveness. We, therefore, find a two-sided source of our strength. The resource time is giving the strategist all the opportunities to go for the big goals, which is good. *Equally*, it causes the enemies, that is complexity and adaptiveness, to come into the way more often; the longer the journey, the higher the chance to encounter crocodiles. Since the level of complexity, adaptiveness, and rate of change have risen in the last years tremendously, the once former source of strengths becomes more and more a source of our weakness.

Stakeholders see a world full of complexity and adaptiveness. They believe that with achieving goals in less time, focussing on short-term KPIs, the risk of failure due to complexity and adaptiveness would be lower. They are right. The risk is lower indeed. The other side of the coin is that we lose all the positive effects of long-term thinking at the same time. We do not want to live in a (business) world where the inspirational big goals are gone. Therefore, we propose a third way. We propose a solution to deal with complexity and adaptiveness in such smart way that we achieve both: Become less exposed to complexity and adaptiveness even though we spend all the time needed to achieve big goals.

## ATTEMPTS TO PROTECT AGAINST THE ENEMIES

There have been attempts to find a protection to the enemies. Attempts to give the power of time back to the strategist. Attempts to cut through the complexity and handle the adaptiveness so that the increasing rate of change would be manageable for the strategist. One famous attempt is the idea of *System Dynamics*; the other one is *Game Theory*. Let us have a look at both and check whether those concepts of the past are still valid and could help strategists today.

To start with, System Dynamics is based on the assumption that we can put complexity into one total model in a so-called top-down approach. Top-down here means that you understand the relationships of each of the system elements and model them in mathematical equations. The inventor of this approach is Jay W. Forrester, professor at the MIT Sloan School of Management, who was a pioneer in computer engineering and system science. He concluded, 'manager's task is far more difficult and challenging than the normal tasks of the mathematician, the physicist, or the engineer'. As a trained engineer, he therefore refused to accept that business problems have no scientific foundation.[26] Looking at the strategist's quests nowadays, we would hope to set up a scientific model describing the world around us in the form of mathematical equations. This hope is founded on increasing computer processing power and the assumption that the growth in processing power is outpacing the speed of change. Unfortunately, up until now, this very promising approach has failed. To be successful, this approach would require providing the computer with a mathematical model of our world to run calculations on. However, we are here facing the same enemies as in the real world.

Complexity and adaptiveness is in combination with the high rate of change. The researchers and practitioners applying System Dynamics have had to understand the complexity and effects of adaptiveness of the real world first, to programme it into a computer. This is leading to the question, why we should develop a digital model to understand the complexity and adaptiveness of the real world, when building the model is as tricky as to understand the real world in the first place. In other words, if you face the impossibility to understand the real world, then you would have a hard time to formulate exact representative equations at the same time. Of course, models of the real world are always simplifications; that is the very nature of models. The performance, so to say, of a model is then whether it provides an appropriate way in understanding a particular phenomenon and/or if it could even be used for practical predictions or optimizations. Unfortunately, System Dynamics is better in the former than the latter application. Since the business world is not so much about merely understanding a phenomenon, but rather how to make more money in the end, System Dynamics falls short. One could argue that once the 'digital' representative world is modelled sufficiently, it would prove to be really worth the trouble since it can be reused repeatedly. As a mindful reader, you already know the answer of course – just as adaptiveness is changing the real world all the time, also the digital world or respectively the model behind it would have had to be re-thought and rebuild all the time. Especially because System Dynamics models are rather complicated and 'lengthy', a high rate of change comes in with high costs. In the end, System Dynamics was, up until now, the most sophisticated attempt to fight complexity and adaptiveness but comes with limitations especially relevant for the practical business application.[27]

There are some other attempts to fight and handle the triad of complexity, adaptiveness, and rate of change. A particularly famous one is Game Theory, which is a bottom-up approach to model complex systems. The inventor of this approach is the general genius John von Neumann. The completion of the theory can be found in his book *Theory of Games and Economic Behavior* in the year 1944. His original motivation was to better model typical situations in the business world like the exchange of goods under the maxim of profit maximisation. Furthermore, he was interested in finding mathematical representations, which come in handy to fight our enemies, since computers could handle the calculation work.[28] Ultimately, just as Jay W. Forrester, he was fascinated by the idea of a 'universal model' of (economic) systems.

In contrast to the top-down System Dynamics way of thinking, a bottom-up approach would mean that you only have to understand the objectives of each element but not the total mechanisms behind it. The advantage here is obvious: Complexity can be modelled more easily since you only have to describe the *motivation* of its elements but not the whole system. Unfortunately, this way of modelling holds a strong assumption that each element is a rational, intelligent entity. Going back to the jungle for a second, we understand that rationality is not the only way of decision making for neither humans nor animals. Of course, this also holds to be true in the business world.

Besides the fact that it is hard to explain to your stakeholders that you base your decisions on a model, which excludes detailed market mechanics, but only incorporates the objectives of the elements (e.g. competitors), the adaptiveness and rate of change hit the modellers of agent-based systems as hard as any other modellers. What if the agents (competitors, regulators, consumers, or predators) change their mind on how they behave? In this case, this model would also have to be adapted as often as we find change, resulting in high costs.

What about scenario thinking? Is not scenario thinking a more potent strategic toolset that makes us better strategic decision makers? This is true, but only for the fight against one of the two enemies. Scenario thinking does a tremendous job to cut through the ever-increasing complexity of our business world. It provides just the right balance between a total model (as in System Dynamics) and (over)simplification (like in prognosis or agent-based modelling). However, scenario thinking also fails when it comes to the speed of change.

After some months of identifying a useful focal question, identifying all the driving forces, and finally building the scenarios of the future, you possess a strong answer to the complexity of the business world. However, this answer is only valid over time, if the business world is not changing too much. Therefore, if the rate of change has struck again and adaptiveness does its thing changing everything, then you as a strategic decision maker cannot be sure anymore that the scenarios are still valid. If they are not valid anymore and you wind tunnel your strategic options against them, it could turn out that they work pretty well in the model but not very well in the real world anymore. The results could be disastrous.

The answer of strategic thinkers these days is to check the validity of the scenarios periodically – typically every 6–12 months. If the so-to-say 'health' check of the scenario framework arrives at the conclusion that the axes are outdated, then a new scenario exercise has to be organised, to refresh the scenarios. The costs of each exercise are depending on the complexity, adaptiveness, and rate of change of the particular focal question and the connected market/market players at hand. The only way to avoid the costs would be to leave scenario thinking and return to prognosis or simple forecasts. It is evident that those forecasts are suffering even more from the rate of change and its implications for the adaptiveness, resulting most definitely in outdated and therefore invalid numbers. The reason behind is that scenario thinking is incorporating change due to the idea of developing not just one but four scenarios by design. The more scenarios you develop, the higher the chance that one is the true one.

To conclude, scenario thinking is still the sharpest weapon we possess. While other attempts to model our business world follow rather extreme premises (System Dynamics: Too complex; Game Theory: Too simple), scenario thinking finds the golden middle. On the one hand, you are building a non-linear model (scenario axes in combination with scenario narratives), and on the other hand, you are keeping it practical because no computer science degree is needed to build your strategy on.

Unfortunately, our sharpest weapon gets blunter and blunter. The reason is the rate of change in combination with the adaptiveness of the complex systems we as strategist have to manage. Just as in the other attempts to model the business world, we will have to check whether our model is still valid despite the change. Because the rate of change is also increasing, the health of the scenario framework would have to be checked at an increasing frequency.

The question here stays: How to use the modelling capability of scenario thinking in an increasingly fast-changing world while keeping the resources needed to do so at a reasonable level (see Fig. 9). How to prepare for complexity, adaptiveness, and rate of change when even a vast team of consultants would struggle to overview the shift, interpret its meaning for the scenario health and ultimately the tuning of an optimal strategy? Dynamic scenario modelling in contrast to other approaches to deal with complexity, adaptiveness, and the rate of change, as shown in Fig. 9.

**Fig. 9:  Dynamic Scenario Modelling.**

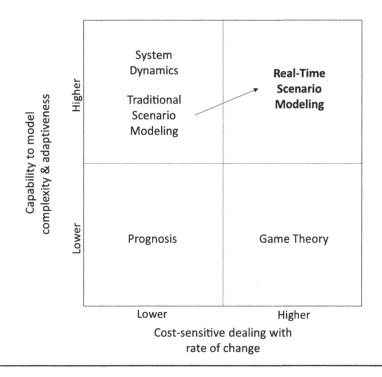

## OUR ULTIMATE SUPERPOWER AGAINST OUR STRONGEST ENEMIES

This chapter promises to unleash a superpower so that strategists can successfully fight complexity and adaptiveness despite the high rate of change. In doing so, we have minutely analysed the two enemies, complexity and adaptiveness, and why they 'become stronger and stronger' due to the ever-increasing rate of change. Therefore, by using the superpower to successfully deal with the rate of change, we can 'cut the food supply' for our two enemies.

We have also seen that almost all former attempts to deal with our two enemies have failed, either because they do not actually fight the two enemies properly (Game Theory and prognosis) or because they suffer from the rate of change and the connected costs (System Dynamics and traditional Scenario Modelling).

We advise you to leave out Game Theory and forecasts for the moment, since they are over-simplifying by design. In addition, stakeholders are not ready yet to put their trust in the 'black box' of Game Theory when it comes to very important decision making. Therefore, we compared System Dynamics and Scenario Modelling regarding their suitability for improvements. We analysed which approach is most promising when it comes to dealing with the rate of change while keeping the promise to not oversimplify regarding complexity and adaptiveness.

Both are top-down approaches to help us understand the business world around us better. Both are doing a great job when it is about modelling complex and adaptive systems. The small but decisive difference is that Scenario Modelling is by far more comfortable to implement in the strategy process. You can feel this advantage as soon as you begin to build the model. For example, while Scenario Modelling uses familiar concepts like brainstorming most decision maker can resonate with, System Dynamics is relying on the concept of system theory that would literally have to be studied first.

Besides, to implement System Dynamics, special software is needed, while in contrast Scenario Modelling only needs pen and paper (at least in the most basic variant). Consequently, the application of System Dynamics is far more seldom than the use of Scenario Modelling in today' business world. Therefore, we had System Dynamics on the list for a further avenue of research but concentrated on Scenario Modelling first.

Our vision is to improve Scenario Modelling to the point that it supports strategists significantly in achieving their big goals despite an ever-increasing complexity, adaptiveness, and rate of change of the business world (see Fig. 10).

Our proposed solution is to augment strategists with the superpower of AI. We are convinced that only AI is capable of helping us achieve this vision. The good news is that, based on our practical experience, we already find proof that the basic process of Scenario Modelling is perfectly suited to plug in an AI. Let

**Fig. 10:  Scenario Planning in Combination with AI.**

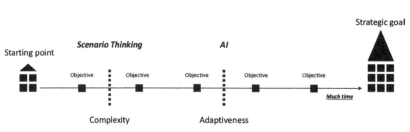

us first elaborate why AI is both a great idea and, at the same time, a great risk for applications in strategy. Scenario Planning in combination with AI allow strategists to deal with complexity and adaptiveness, as shown in Fig. 10.

## FROM FICTION TO SCIENCE TO STRATEGY

In many scenario exercises, we have come across a new phenomenon. We call it the 'AI excuse'. Whenever a participant is out of ideas on how to solve a specific challenge, you will most probably find them stating that the AI will do the rest. While this might be understandable in the face of the great potential of AI, we wanted to make sure that we do not use AI as a Potemkin village[29] – like in western movies.

AI is a frequent buzzword in the industry and currently transforming from existing only in the books of science fiction authors to being a part of reality. The term AI itself was eventually coined in 1956, during a research project at Dartmouth University, including key researchers of the field.[30] Only a few years later, Herbert Alexander Simon, Nobel Prize holder, stated in 1965 'machines will be capable, within 20 years, of doing any work a man can do'.[31] Facing this early outlook, a short look at history is disappointing and motivating at the same time. It seems that it has always been the dream of humankind to build a machine with a general intelligence. 'General' here means that the AI is capable of leaving its unique application that is was built for (e.g. autonomous driving) and instead become human-like in terms of being able to solve different kind of tasks (e.g. your car-AI is the same AI that reads and summarises this book for you). Philosopher René Descartes already theorised in his writing 'Discourse on the Method' in the 17th century whether a machine could act, think, or be like a human. From his point of view, there might have been the possibility of machines existing that looked and acted similar to humans. However, he declared that machines would not be able to speak or write in any useful capacity:

> *it is not conceivable that such a machine should produce different arrangements of words so as to give an appropriately meaningful answer to whatever is said in its presence, as the dullest of men can do.*[32]

Descartes was a futurist to the core, already seeing the current challenge to create a general AI instead of a specialised, narrow AI:

*Even though some machines might do some things as well as we do them, or perhaps even better, they would inevitably fail in others, which would reveal that they are acting not from understanding, but only from the disposition of their organs.*[33]

A prominent approach to test the capability of an AI was developed in 1950, when Alan Turing described 'The Imitation Game', which is also known as Turing Test. This test indicates whether machines can be intelligent enough to mask themselves as humans. The test is based on a human judge interacting with machines and humans, for example through written interaction, without knowing which one is which. Once the judge believes to be corresponding with a human while actually interacting with a machine, the machine is seen as intelligent.[34]

A promising technical prerequisite to win this test was developed in 1951; the Stochastic Neural Analog Reinforcement Computer was probably the first system using an important characteristic of human (and animal) intelligence: A self-learning approach to problem solving. This computer was based on vacuum tubes, motors, and clutches, and its purpose was helping a virtual rat to solve a maze puzzle. Each action led to a learn effect, so that the probabilities of succeeding increased. However, it took until the late 1980s in AI research to finally see a major shift from the so-called traditional 'rule-based' programming to actual 'machine learning'. Whereas in the past developers typically tried to build systems that were supposed to anticipate the underlying rules according to which people (or any other phenomena of interest) behaved or worked, some machine learning systems follow a self-learning or trial-and-error approach completely automatically. The publication of IBM's TJ Watson Research Center, 'A statistical approach to language translation', is regarded as another milestone in these developments.[35] This system was an early form of current translation tools (e.g. Google Translate or DeepL). IBM trained the system with more than two million English and French phrases, coming from the records of the Canadian Parliament. However, also rules-based system proof to be very performing. It was also IBM, making a major progress, when their Deep Blue computer beat chess champion Gary Kasparov in 1997. Yet, Deep Blue was merely based on pure analytical power, calculating potential moves and comparing them with past moves of other chess games, not learning like a machine learning based AI.[36] Another breakthrough was in 2016, when Google beat Lee Sedol, a professional in the Japanese board game Go, which is way more complex than chess. The impressive capability of this AI is to learn from playing against itself. Practically, it became invincible to any human Go player without have ever played against one.[37]

The difference of today's discussion around AI and the appearance of AI in the history books is that we are reaching an essential landmark with AI. We are experiencing the so-called 'second spring' of this impressive technology. The first spring is typically characterised by the appearance of a fundamental principle (e.g. neural networks) and a lot of basic research (e.g. number of scientific publications and patents). Also, the first spring is gratefully adapted into mass and science media and the basis for lots of dreaming and imagination (e.g. science fiction movies). Lastly but also most frustratingly, the promises did not get fulfilled in our day-to-day work or life. An evil combination of great expectations and little outcome was causing the first spring of AI to end. We have been experiencing the effects of this cycle for the past 50 years. In the end, AI was something you would rather avoid naming or being connected to, since opinion leaders would have easily judged you.

This time, we are talking about AI again. And the difference is that all the theoretical work that has been done before now pays off and we finally see more and more practical applications. The underlying reasons behind this second spring are the much higher processing power and the availability of data. For example, 10 years ago it was not possible to analyse a news website via an official data provider. We had to crawl each news site individually to access the information, which was also only permitted for test purposes anyway. Processing power and data are essentially the revitalising resources for traditional AI approaches.

One of the most potential approaches within AI to deal with complex adaptive systems are the discussed neural networks, which are used in machine learning. They are the reason why Siri or Alexa 'understand' you (most of the time), and they even are the force behind autonomous driving, giving cars 'eyes' and 'brains'. While the basic idea behind the concept of a neural network is over 50 years old, only the processing power and data available today are finally sufficient to feed them properly.

Neural networks can be (to a certain extent) compared to little children. They need a lot of energy and time, but already possess a powerful brain (processing power) and learn most of what defines them later on by observation and feedback (data).

Thanks to the advancements in processing power and digitalisation that brings us all the data needed, neural network AIs are finally practical for typical (business) application purposes.

To be crystal clear, a general AI is still not available and may be part of a third phase in the evolution of AI. A general AI is still the stuff science fiction movies that are made of, and will continue to be for quite a while.

This is not a solely intellectual distinction but has critical implications for the use of AI in our strategic environment. As long as we do not see general AIs, human strategic minds will be the only ones capable of *understanding* complex adaptive systems like business markets. What that means is that AIs are and will be capable of modelling certain kind of elements of systems (like, in our previous example, the river, the preys, or the predators separately), but they have a much harder time modelling their interplay with each other. 'Having a harder time' here also means that you would need almost *total data* about the historical behaviour of the system elements to feed the AI. Total data here means that the modeller would have to have all historical data about each element of the system (prey, predator, weather, ingenious people, barrage, etc.). For example, this would essentially mean to outfit each element with a sensor, gathering all kinds of information about the specific current state over time. Well, good luck with the crocodiles. While imaginable for our jungle model, this becomes obviously even harder for a real-world business situation with all the market stakeholders and conditions.

Taking into account the rate of change and adaptiveness, this means that every single time the system adapts to new conditions, a tremendous amount of updated data are necessary. This explains to a certain extant why the most sophisticated AIs today run within virtual realities, like computer games, only.

Within a computer game, you can measure each element and re-run the virtual world again and again to produce enough data the AI can learn from. In other words, not a single AI is out there that could help us with building the scenarios (model of a complex adaptive system) and – equally important – develop future-proof strategic implications from it. Available AIs are capable of reading and writing content, but they are for sure not the authors of any strategy book since there is no AI actually *understanding* the different elements of complex adaptive systems instead of only replicating elements from historical data.

In summary, the advantages of AI can only be harvested in identifying the best narrow, specialised ones but avoiding any gurus that promise anything close to a general AI.

# NOTES

1. See Kiechel, W. (1982). Corporate strategists under fire. *Fortune, December, 106*(13), 34–39; Kiechel, W. (1984). Sniping at strategic planning. *Planning Review,* May, 8–11; Gray, D. H. (1986). Uses and misuses of strategic planning. *Harvard Business Review, 64*(1), 89–97; Nutt, P. C. (1987). Identifying and appraising how managers install strategy. *Strategic Management Journal, 8*(1), 1–14; Kaplan, R. S. and Norton, D. P. (2001). The Strategy-Focused Organization–How Balanced Scorecard Companies Thrive in the New Business Environment. Boston, MA: Harvard Business School Press; Sirkin, H. L., Keenan, P. and Jackson, A. (2005). The hard side of change management. *Harvard Business Review, 83*(10), 109–118.

2. See Cândido, C. J., & Santos, S. P. (2015). Strategy implementation: What is the failure rate? *Journal of Management & Organization, 21*(2), 237–262.

3. See Consultancy.uk. (2017). Digital transformation market booms to $23 billion. Retrieved from https://www.consultancy.uk/news/13489/digital-transformation-consulting-market-booms-to-23-billion

4. See Vermeulen, F. (2017). Many strategies fail because they're not actually strategies. Retrieved from https://hbr.org/2017/11/many-strategies-fail-because-theyre-not-actually-strategies

5. See Garber, P. M. (1989). Tulipmania. *Journal of Political Economy, 97*(3), 535–60; Garber, P. M. (1990). Famous First Bubbles. *The Journal of Economic Perspectives, 4*(2), 35–54.

6. See Cohan, P. (2014). Why Stack Ranking Worked Better at GE Than Microsoft. *Forbes.* Retrieved October 2, 2014. Retrieved from: https://www.forbes.com/sites/petercohan/2012/07/13/why-stack-ranking-worked-better-at-ge-than-microsoft/#207dd0823236

7. See Colegrove, M. B. (2005). *Distant Voices: Listening to the Leadership Lessons of the Past* (p. 31). Lincoln, NB: iUniverse.

8. See Kvint, V. (2016), *Strategy for the global market: Theory and practical applications* (p. 264). Routledge.

9. See Musk, E. (2006). The Secret Tesla Motors master plan (just between you and me). Retrieved from https://www.tesla.com/blog/secret-tesla-motors-master-plan-just-between-you-and-me

10. See Kimmorley, S. (2018). Here's how 12 successful CEOs set their goals for the year. Retrieved from https://www.businessinsider.com.au/how-ceos-set-goals-2018-1#3m5fQJAHt6euf8Fm.99

11. See Friedman, Z. (2018). Here Are 10 Genius Quotes From Warren Buffett. Retrieved from https://www.forbes.com/sites/zackfriedman/2018/10/04/warren-buffett-best-quotes/#10af74494261

12. See Barton, D. Manyika, J., Koller, T., Palter, R., Godsall, J., & Zoffer, J. (2017). Where companies with a long-term view outperform their peers. Retrieved from

https://www.mckinsey.com/featured-insights/long-term-capitalism/where-companies-with-a-long-term-view-outperform-their-peers

13. See Flammer, C., & Bansal, P. (2017). Does a long-term orientation create value? Evidence from a regression discontinuity. *Strategic Management Journal, 38*(9), 1827–1847.

14. See Brochet, F., Loumioti, M., & Serafeim, G. (2012). *Short-termism, investor clientele, and firm risk*. Boston, MA: Harvard Business School.

15. See Sonnenfeld, J. (2015). CEO exit schedules: A season to stay, a season to go. Retrieved from: https://fortune.com/2015/05/06/ceo-tenure-cisco/

16. See Becker, F. (2014). *Simulation in der Marketingforschung auf Basis der NK-Methodik: Eine Evaluation und Illustration von Anwendungspotenzialen*. WiGIM.

17. See Von Clausewitz, C. (1976). *On war* (p. 119). Princeton University Press.

18. See Cheval, B., Tipura, E., Burra, N., Frossard, J., Chanal, J., Orsholits, D., … Boisgontier, M. P. (2018). Avoiding sedentary behaviors requires more cortical resources than avoiding physical activity: An EEG study. *Neuropsychologia, 119*, 68–80.

19. See Perlitz, M. (1993). Why most strategies fail to-day: The need for strategy-innovations. *European Management Journal*.

20. See Wery, R., & Waco, M. (2004). Why good strategies fail. In *Handbook of business strategy*.

21. See Finkelstein, S. (2005). When bad things happen to good companies: Strategy failure and flawed executives. *Journal of Business Strategy*.

22. See Vermeulen, F. (2017). Many strategies fail because they're not actually strat-egies. *Harvard Business Review*.

23. See von Bertalanffy, L. (1968). *General system theory: Foundations, develop-ment, applications*. New York, NY: George Braziller.

24. See Rumsfeld, D. (2002). DoD News Briefing – – Secretary Rumsfeld and Gen. Myers. Retrieved from https://archive.defense.gov/Transcripts/Transcript.aspx?TranscriptID=2636

25. See Perlitz, M. (1993). Why most strategies fail to-day: The need for strategy-innovations. *European Management Journal*; Gowers, T., & Barrow-Green, J. (2010). *The Princeton companion to mathematics, the three-body problem*. Princeton University Press.

26. See Forrester, J. W. (1961). *Industrial dynamics*. The MIT Press.

27. See Featherston, C., & Doolan, M. (2012). A critical review of the criticisms of system dynamics. Retrieved from https://www.researchgate.net/publication/271827939_A_Critical_Review_of_the_Criticisms_of_System_Dynamics

28. See Von Neumann, J., Morgenstern, O., & Kuhn, H. W. (2007). *Theory of games and economic behavior (commemorative edition)*. Princeton University Press.

29. The Russian statemen Grigori Potemkin is the originator of the phrase potemkin village. He, who lived in the 18th century, supposedly built spectacular false villages along Catherine the Great's way to the south of her empire to fool her about the regions wealth. Today a potemkin village represents an elaborate façade or display intended to disguise an unpleasant fact or circumstance. Source: Montefiore, S.S. (2001). Prince of Princes: the life of Potemkin. London: Weidenfeld & Nicolson, 379–383.

30. See Taulli, T. (2019). AI (artificial intelligence) words you need to know. Retrieved from https://www.forbes.com/sites/tomtaulli/2019/09/07/ai-artificia l-intelligence-words-you-need-to-know#74f47ba77f11

31. See Simon, H. A. (1965). *Via: AI: The tumultuous search for artificial intelligence (Crevier, 1993)*. NY: Basic Books.

32. See Gunderson, K. (1964). Descartes, La Mettrie, Language and Machines. *Philosophy, 39*, 193–222.

33. See Dormehl, L. (2017). *Thinking machines: The quest for artificial intelligence and where it is taking us next*. TarcherPerigee.

34. See Warwick, K., & Shah, H. (2016). *Turing's imitation game: Conversations with the unknown*. Cambridge University Press.

35. See Brown, P., Cocke, J., Pietra, S. D., Pietra, V. D., Jelinek, F., Mercer, R. L., Roossin, P. (1988). A statistical approach to language translation. Coling'88. *Association for Computational Linguistics, 1*, 71–76.

36. See IBM (n.d.). DeepBlue. Retrieved from: https://www.ibm.com/ibm/history/ ibm100/us/en/icons/deepblue/; Teicher, J. (2018). Garry Kasparov: it's time for humans and machines to work together. IBM. Retrieved from: https://www.ibm.com/ blogs/industries/garry-kasparov-its-time-for-humans-and-machines-to-work-together/

37. See Metz, C. (2016). In Two Moves, AlphaGo and Lee Sedol Redefined the Future. Wired. Retrieved from: https://www.wired.com/2016/03/ two-moves-alphago-lee-sedol-redefined-future/

# 6

# REAL-TIME SCENARIO MODELLING

By identifying our biggest enemies – complexity and adaptiveness in combination with the rate of change – and understanding what we can expect and not expect from our strongest ally artificial intelligence we can now focus on developing the ultimate defensive strategy.

The process of scenario modelling provides several great opportunities to plug-in specialised AIs. In doing so, the specific process steps become superior to the traditional scenario modelling. The superiority can mean that the process steps improve regarding quality (e.g. the improved validity of the scenarios) and/or become more cost-efficient (e.g. fewer consultancy hours needed). The ultimate goal is to identify and utilise AIs to bring scenario modelling to a completely new level so that strategists can use the enhanced toolbox to achieve their strategic goals. Eventually, with the help of AI, we can augment the scenario practitioner to deal with the rate of change more effectively, which ultimately helps to fight complexity and adaptiveness.

To apply AI in a structured fashion, we can divide the scenario-thinking process into three phases:

1. Research (focal question and driving forces);

2. Modelling (critical uncertainties, scenario framework, and narratives); and

3. Monitoring (monitoring of scenarios and 'health check').

## HOW AI CAN AUGMENT THE RESEARCH STAGE

### Focal Question

Defining the focal question should be entirely in the hands of the strategic decision maker (e.g. CEO) or the group or responsible decision makers (e.g. board). Following the scenario thinking logic, the focal question has to be answered so that the CEO can develop a future-proof strategy and ultimately reach his strategic goals or even vision. Since only he knows his vision, he is also best suited for formulating the focal question from it. It is hard to imagine that an AI will develop a vision or at least strategic goals instead of a human decision maker any time soon. This is very much connected to the necessary ability to understand and model markets, customers, or employees conjointly (all complex adaptive systems). CEOs typically have conscious or unconscious mental models for all these systems and build their vision and strategic objectives on them. Only a general AI would be able to do the same, which is not available – yet. However, models, for example, based on Game Theory may inspire decision makers or sharpen the thinking.

### Driving Forces

Very much in contrast to the necessary mental capability to modelling complex adaptive systems (e.g. markets and their players) is the task of identifying them and their elements. In the phase of determining the driving forces regarding the focal question, this is precisely the task of the scenario practitioners, analysts, and industry experts – at least so far. As described in Chapter 2, this task is cumbersome and complicated and therefore an AI is in high demand.

Typically, we identify around or more than 100 driving forces based on the work of at least 3 weeks, depending on the complexity of the business context at hand. For example, a typical focal question could ask for scenarios of the future of a specific industry. To identify all relevant driving forces, we typically interview experts and record the results as text protocols. Furthermore, we scan scientific papers, news, and other internet sources for other expert statements. The goal is to 'brainstorm' all possibly relevant systems and their elements respectively the driving forces, categorised into the STEEP categories.

While an interview provides an excellent opportunity to get to know the expert assessment in all detail, it is at the same time resource intensive.

For example, the recording has to be transcribed, and the valuable expert time has to be compensated. Therefore, the number of interviews are limited in practice. This could cause a *bias* in the research due to a limited number of expert opinions.

Researching the Internet for other specialist opinions is a valid measurement, to keep the promise of holistic research. Unfortunately, the number of possible sources are usually so overwhelming that the analysts can only cover a subset and are not able to go over every possible detail.

In summary, the research process is characterised by a high level of human work. Also, the research process is the foundation for all the subsequent steps – a fact that highlights its importance for the validity of the to-be-developed scenarios.

The good news is that available, specialised AI is highly capable of assisting us in this vital phase. AI is already very much outperforming human scenario practitioners in certain aspects of the research. The obvious advantage here is, of course, that AIs with the capability of Natural Language Processing can 'read' faster but never get tired and are way more cost-efficient than any human analyst. By reading, we mean that the AI can identify relevant articles, analyse them, and even judge them, for example regarding their sentiment, almost in real-time after they are published. The only thing you would have to provide is a keyword or context; the rest is up to the AI.

Coming back to the example of building scenarios of the future of a particular industry. If we provide the AI, for example with the keyword 'Automotive', it will go through all available information, identify the relevant texts (e.g. interview transcripts on your local drive or interviews in the online news), and provide you with an analysis. The analysis consists for example of all the subtopics related to the topic 'Automotive', which is an excellent source for identifying driving forces.

Also, the AI cannot just build clusters of connected articles, but also show linkages to adjacent clusters. In combination with a visual representation of the results (e.g. each interview is one element), we are not just able to identify driving forces, but also see empirical connections to other topics as well. A recent AI analysis, for example, turned out that not only the typical suspects like economic growth, ecosystem, and technological innovations have to be considered separately, but especially the connection between AI and blockchain technology. Our client was quite surprised since they have treated both topics separately before. In the next step, if we find the relationship of both technologies relevant, we can use this information to provide the AI with a new keyword and extend our research horizon easily and so on.

It becomes clear that the analysis goes way beyond a manual search engine research. In addition, it also goes beyond studying basic information like encyclopaedia entries or academic papers. For example, while a reader of a basic article regarding the topic 'automotive' would get a pretty good overview of typical subtopics, the AI also highlights the *relevance* of each subtopic in the current discussion. This makes the AI not just assisting the analyst doing the research but so to say, formulates a second medical opinion besides the expert opinions themselves. Of course, the expert opinion in weighing and judging current development remains the most important source for the research phase, but the AI adds an equally highly valuable new objective perspective in understanding developments around the focal question at hand. Behind all that is no magic but rather sophisticated statistical analysis of information.

In summary, this is a game-changer and resulted in a reduction of the resources needed during the research phase in our daily work by almost 75%, while increasing the quality by up to 40%. This result is very important keeping in mind the reason why we do all this: We want to improve our capabilities to cope with the high rate of change. Thanks to the AI during the research phase, the high rate of change becomes less and less frightening because the amount of information to describe and understand the change is gathered and analysed automatically – anytime a change may have occurred. This gives us back all the time we need to understand the consequences that the change has triggered. In other words, the rate of change itself will not change, but our ability to deal with it will. The adaptiveness is still there, obviously, but we have now *more time* to cope with it. The positive practical implications are tremendous, especially because those tools are available online for everybody, competitively priced.

## HOW AI CAN AUGMENT THE MODELLING STAGE

### Critical Uncertainties

The long list of drivers is an excellent source for a holistic approach to answer the focal question in the form of scenarios. As described, thanks to AI, the resources needed to develop such a list have decreased while the quality regarding scope has increased tremendously.

Now, the next step is to shorten the list by the two criteria 'importance' and 'uncertainty' (introduced in Chapter 2). In a traditional approach, we would ask a group of hand-selected subject matter experts to do the judgement for us. For the 'importance' criterion, we specifically ask them for their assessment as part of an online survey; for the 'uncertainty' criterion, we ask for their expected endpoint and analyse the difference in the answers to conclude the uncertainty by the variance in the responses. While there is undoubtedly no (general) AI available to replace the assessment of experts in the survey, the AI technology to extend the reach of the survey is existing. Typically, one would interview around 10–50 experts depending on the focal question. Thanks to the AI, you are now capable of 'interviewing' thousands of experts.

First, the AI identifies experts and their publically available statements based either on a manual list or by the appearance of certain authors (e.g. who are cited often). Concerning the criterion 'importance', the AI then scans for statements that relate to one or more driving forces from the long list. Finally, it analyses whether the expert stated that the relevance or importance of this driving force is high or low. However, the system can go even further. Since the AI 'knows' how often a specific opinion about a driving force is shared among users (based on the information of URL-shorteners – yes that is one business model behind them), it can indirectly conclude how vital a particular driving force is. For example, newspapers might publish an economy-related article on page one especially at the top of the page. In contrast, the readers and users might be much more interested in a topic on page 10 since it becomes a trend, which is not apparent to the news outlet, yet. The judgement of the importance of a driving force could therefore be informed by taking into account what kind of topics go viral.

The time frame that the AI would look back in (e.g. look up all expert statements since the past one year) depends on the rate of change of the topic that the focal question is addressing. Also, it is up to the scenario practitioner to set the filters correctly. For example, making sure that the list of experts is evened out regarding certain potential biases like the overpronouncation of one source origin. Whether the statements of direct interviews, expert comments online, or indirect conclusions count equally or will be weighted while developing the short list also depends on the specific focal question.

Regarding the 'uncertainty' of a driving force, the same AI can be utilised, but in a slightly different way. After the experts and their statements have been identified, the AI checks for the direction of the statement. For example, one expert could state that the connection between AI and blockchain is weak from a technical perspective. The direction here would be the term 'weak', then. Following this approach, if the AI then identifies, for example 50% of statements that point in the direction that the connection is 'strong', it concludes automatically that there is a high uncertainty among experts. In summary, the AI is not replacing experts' judgement but helps to analyse them much more efficiently.

## Scenario Framework

The benefits of AI during this step are somewhat limited. This is explainable since at this stage, a unique ability only humans possess so far comes in handy: The understanding of complex adaptive systems and the interplay of elements. In other words, only the strategists and scenario practitioners can judge a particular combination of axes correctly since each axis describes one complex adaptive system, and the magic happens when combining them. One criterion to judge a specific combination of axes (i.e. the scenario framework) is for example whether it is 'challenging' or not. An AI would have to have an understanding of the vision, the strategic objectives, the focal question, and all connected systems (e.g. markets and market players) to conclude. Again, only a general AI would be capable of doing so, which is, to our knowledge, not available yet.

What is worth experimenting is to free the scenario practitioners from the guesswork whether two axes correlate or not. In doing so, we assign indicators to each axis. An indicator measures which endpoint of the axis is coming true. We will take a closer look at the idea of an indicator in the following chapter. For now: If the two axes have developed, based on historical data and their indicators, in the same direction, following a clear pattern, they would be highlighted high in correlation. Human experts tend to under- or overestimate the relationship of axes during an intense workshop. Outsourcing this step to the AI is not only saving time, but also increasing the quality of the results. In the end, the list of possible scenario frameworks regarding non-correlating axis combinations can be generated automatically, but the choice which of those is the final one to go with is in the hands of the human experts.

## Scenario Narratives

While there are specialised AIs available not just to read but also to write text, they lack the necessary understanding of the interplay between two scenario axes. Only the decision maker, scenario practitioner, and/or expert are capable of 'imagining' what it means with regards to the focal question when two end-points play out. Only the mental model, which is formed in each head of the workshop participants, is capable of explaining the complex adaptive systems, like markets and market players, behind it. However, the AI might assist by suggesting narrative elements, like pictures or important citations – whether they fit well or not to the story is up to the human scenario practitioner.

## HOW AI CAN AUGMENT THE MONITORING STAGE

### Scenario Monitoring

We are coming to the Holy Grail in scenario thinking. While the research phase and the modelling phase have existed before – without the blessings of AI at a lower quality and at higher costs – the monitoring phase did practically not exist.

Let us have a closer look at that case. After the scenario development, the strategists possess a compelling framework to build the strategic decisions on. To remind ourselves, the scenarios are the basis to wind-tunnel strategic options. Most of the time we find that certain strategic options work better in only specific scenarios or groups of scenarios. The big question has always been *which scenario* is becoming how likely over time.

If you knew the probabilities of the scenarios, you could easily calculate which strategic option to choose whenever the decision is to make. The challenge here was traditionally the continuous, resource intensive measurement of the indicators for each scenario. If you wanted to calculate a probability, you would continuously have to watch the world around you on which scenario is playing out.

The only solution here was to periodically ask experts on their judgement. Of course, each expert has only a certain field of expertise. Therefore, the need to identify and hire experts for almost each indicator is quite costly and would only be possible in the large-scale scenario projects. Furthermore, the number of experts are highly limited, risking a particular bias in one or the other scenario. In the end, monitoring was practically not used. The consequences were quite severe. Take for example the ever-increasing rate of change of market conditions. For example, imagine you would have asked an expert about his assessment of the blockchain technology a few days before and then after the fatal crash. The scenario probabilities – if dependent on the perception of this technology – would have changed drastically within days. If you now take into account that such expert interview about the status of the scenarios – facing the costs of gathering all the experts – was only conducted every 6–12 months, it gives you quite a feel for the challenge at hand. Now, also consider that a scenario monitoring consists of many indicators, all having an effect on the probabilities.

The AI is of great help here. It scans for information regarding each indicator and identifies which endpoint is becoming more likely based on each piece of information automatically and in real time. Good data sources are news outlets, patent data, and investment flows.

For example, if we want to calculate the probability of a hypothetical scenario in the chemical industry, one indicator probably would be regulation of certain aspects. Since companies operate globally, that includes monitoring the entire regulatory landscape. Each regulatory decision gets then picked up by the AI (e.g. a strict regulatory decision about the usage of a certain chemical substance), runs through a statistical model to give this piece of information a certain weight (e.g. whether it concerns a small or a big market) and finally feeds into the overall probability of a scenario, in which strict regulation maybe suppresses market growth.

As AI is resource-saving, one could increase the number of indicators by the factor 100, therefore improve the accuracy compared to a traditional expert panel-based approach substantially and lower the investments in resource drastically nevertheless. Thanks to the AI, we get a *real-time update* about the scenario probabilities. This does not only come in handy to calculate which scenario materialises over time for the evaluation of strategic options (i.e. wind tunnelling), but also provides very helpful information for the daily implementation of the strategy. It provides us with a constant, objective stream of information about the development of our business world. We saved all the time that would have been necessary to generate such a stream of information and can use this time now for analysis. The constant, elaborated analysis of the development of the business world and its reasons provides a tremendous source of insights for decision making. Take for example the blockchain situation. The constant monitoring of the realisation rates always comes with the connected news bits. Therefore, the analyst can perfectly understand *why* a shift in the realisation rate has happened. The implementation team of the blockchain strategy could therefore take into account the latest news, for example on the choice of the best technological basis. This is the first time a strategic framework like scenario planning is also directly having an impact on short-term decision making.

## Scenario Health

How does this affect our fight against the two enemies, complexity and adaptiveness, in counter play with the rate of change? Obviously, as long as the scenarios are valid, the AI now digests all the change automatically. Therefore, change becomes much more of a *differentiator* than a challenge. The reason for that is that the higher the rate of change, the higher the discrepancy between companies using AI for monitoring and those who are not. In other words, those companies who have the appropriate AI do not to have to fear for change anymore but welcome it. Change becomes much more of an opportunity instead of a risk. However, what if adaptiveness strikes again. If the change of the market conditions would lead to a change of the underlying critical uncertainties, the monitoring of the scenarios would be meaningless potentially since they become outdated. Nevertheless, the big difference now is that due to the constant scenario monitoring we not only understand which scenario is materialising over time, but also can determine the exact moment *when* the scenarios must be updated. This is a game-changer. We call it real-time monitoring of the *health* of the scenarios.

The health of scenario indicates how well the scenario is suited to answer the focal question. Right after developing the scenarios, this health is set to 100%. Over time, the world is not just developing in one or another direction but also adapting due to change. As we have discussed, the adaptiveness of the world means that the interrelations of system elements change over time. While, for example, there might be a clear finding for the decision makers that technological axes are more important as environmental axes to describe an industry's future, this could change dramatically in no time.

The implications of a low scenario health means that one would have to re-do the scenarios. The threshold is when the evaluation of the driving forces that have been identified as 'highly important' and 'highly uncertain' change over time. The implications are that the scenario modelling would have come to another result if the driving forces had not been considered in the first place, due to their lower value in importance and uncertainty. The decision maker would and should not rely on scenarios that are not valid anymore. A false scenario framework could misguide the strategists in the wrong direction; the wind-tunnelling results would be of no value anymore either. The worldwide rate of change has increased in all industries, which makes it more and more necessary to check for the health of scenarios regularly.

Based on the traditional approach, one would have to monitor all driving forces whether new are entering the zone of interest or whether the original driving forces that were considered are still within the zone of interest; at least with regards to the importance since the uncertainty decreases naturally over time. While monitoring the relatively few indicators to calculate the probability of the scenarios was already prohibitively expensive, the continuous analysis of the numerous driving forces is usually not in practice at all due to the high costs.

AI can fully capitalise on its strengths during this phase of the scenario process. The same AI we use to rank the driving forces in the first place comes into play when we monitor the development over time. In order to do that each driving force must be monitored by the AI continuously. We can then easily observe if the information landscape (e.g. based on news) changes to an extent that the importance or uncertainty of the specific driving forces have to be re-evaluated. In addition, the monitoring over time for example also allows identifying seasonal patterns, which we can take into account for the analysis.

Therefore, when the zone of interest with the most important and uncertain drivers changes in its composition over time, the scenario health indicator also decreases. When it comes below a certain landmark (the level is depending on the requirements of the client), one could test new variants of the scenario framework against the focal question. If we conclude that the new scenario framework is more beneficial than the old one, it will be replaced.

Also, one might use the explorative AI that helped us to identify relevant driving forces in the first place, to check whether utterly new driving forces might need to be considered. Those new driving forces are then handed to the AI, which is specialised on monitoring and will also be considered when we are checking the composition of the zone of interest over time.

To be clear, AI is not changing the laws of complexity and adaptiveness, but in contrast to before, we can now judge exactly *when* a certain change has caused the invalidity of scenarios or not. This makes a huge difference in the practical application of modern scenario thinking in contrast to the traditional approach. Using the traditional approach plus, let us say, a timespan of six months, you would simply not know whether the framework is still valid or not. It could be 100%, or it could be 10%. With this question mark in mind, a strategist would simply not rely on the scenarios any more. Every changing event could potentially have caused markets, consumers, or competitors to adapt in an unforeseen way; could have made the scenario planning obsolete. The AI makes sure that you know every day that your scenarios are a valid basis for the decision making.

In sum, the application of AI during the scenario process could not only reduce the costs but also increase the quality of results tremendously. While scenario planning always has been a great approach to model complex systems, the rate of change was recently just too high to cope with. As a result, we have found that scenario practitioners were rushing during the phases of research and modelling to reduce the time and costs. While this certainly shortened the time until results, it also meant that the trust in the scenario frameworks has suffered. Also, since the rate of change has increased significantly over the last years, the theoretical standard of checking the development and health of scenarios every 6–12 months is not sufficient anymore.

Thanks to the advancements in AI, the rate of change has lost its horror. The AI can easily cope with any changes in real time so that the scenario practitioners have all the time to adjust the scenarios and keep them healthy. Strategists, therefore, when relying on AI-augmented scenario thinking, are most effective in fighting our two biggest enemies, *complexity* and *adaptiveness*. As a result, strategists now have all the time again to achieve big, inspiring strategic goals.

# 7

# CLOSING PERSPECTIVES

In this book, we fused established strategy methodologies, recent experience, and emerging technologies to give you a picture of where artificial intelligence enabled strategizing currently stands. We have argued that the lines between human decision making and machine intelligence are blurring. We took the example of scenario planning to illustrate the point how far human and machine intelligence have already converged and yet, how far from perfect our integrated decision-making processes still are.

The possibilities of combining machine sensing with human intuition to make sense of the insights are amazing and at the same time quite scary. Typically, most people are impressed with how much faster and more robust strategic planning can become when adding AI capabilities to human intuition. Some observers might be disillusioned because AI does not (yet) explain the world to us, while others worry that we go straight into the direction of Skynet, the fictional AI system in the *Terminator* movie series that would become self-aware and wage war against mankind. Therefore, our final reflection must be: where might this lead us? You will know by now, from the previous chapters, that this team of authors does not have a crystal ball that allows us to predict how AI-enabled strategy development will evolve. The best we can do is give our very personal views on three different plausible outcomes.

We will start with a cautious, pragmatic view. In his perspective, 'storytelling in a data-driven world', Andreas argues that we need to combine classical fact-seeking strategic thinking with the emerging opportunities of technology to measure opinions and ideas. Without overrating the potential of technology, we need to find the right balance between human decision-making capabilities and technological support.

In 'the future of collective sense-making', Florian takes an even more optimistic, human-centred perspective. He describes how AI-enabled decision support systems could solve some of the fundamental issues we face in society and the economy today. If we managed to scale-up real-time strategy systems and put them to use for many people and across societies, they could profoundly change the way we work. Moreover, they might even have the potential to change the way our societies perceive and process information.

The third account goes to the opposite extreme. In 'a decision-making utopia', Frank argues that there are no simple answers to wicked problems. Consequently, typical storytelling – which in its nature simplifies and stylises, is time-consuming, imprecise, and subjective – is certainly not be the best way to inform decision making. Instead, the decision making of the future should be based on non-story, machine-digestible formats, which allow experts to perceive and measure what is going on around us and make sense of it without the need to tell stories. Such formats have the potential to reduce the human bias in future decision-making processes further.

The three perspectives describe the future playing field of decision making from different vantage points. The underlying question across the three stories is this: Will decision making and strategizing remain a social process in which humans continue to imagine and negotiate strategy based on stories? Or, will decision making evolve to the next level, and we will see a world in which we increasingly replace conventional strategic processes with their need for storytelling with new, algorithm-based, processes free of qualitative narratives.

## PERSPECTIVE 1: STORYTELLING IN A DATA-DRIVEN WORLD

What I can observe from my various client projects across industries and geographies and my perception of the surrounding world, there is no doubt that uncertainty is a given in today's complex, hyper-connected world. We moved from a world of black and white with clear boundaries towards a world of 50 shades of grey with blurring boundaries. Thus, nowadays, there is hardly any situation where we can speak of certainty or givens. While we had two distinct poles during the Cold War, we moved into a world full of asymmetric warfare with various poles pursuing their distinct interests. The question who is friend and who is foe, needs to be raised from time to time, as roles are changing quickly. The classical, decade-long battle between Pepsi and Coke for dominance in caffeinated lemonades did not have a winner. Yet, in recent times, various competing products expanded and disrupted this market, and new rivals, such as energy drinks shook up the industry, providing a higher degree of uncertainty to incumbents. Just two examples showing that the rules of the past with clear boundaries will not apply to the present and probably even less to the future. There are plenty more examples of blurring boundaries that are driving complexity and increasing the level of uncertainty. Players that have been active in a certain industry are expanding into new offerings, strict separation of sectors does not apply anymore. While in the past, car OEMs manufactured the vehicles, insurance companies offered the mandatory vehicle insurance. This was the past. Disruptors are not just changing their own industry but also adjacent industries and products, for example Tesla adding vehicle insurances to its own portfolio, providing additional benefits at lower costs than their competitors (as they can cross-subsidise new offerings with their existing products or services) to lock-in their customers.[1] However, decision makers should not act like an ostrich and bury their heads in the sand. They instead need to find ways to cope with uncertainty to act and plan despite the complex and turbulent environment. They need to remain confident and show this to their surroundings. The means that help to cope with uncertainty provide them with a competitive edge and transform them and their organisations into powerful eagles, looking from the top at their ostrich competition.

However, what are such means that provide competitive edge despite uncertainty? To me, the answer is simple and sophisticated at the same time: scenario-based strategic planning augmented by technological solutions – what we call real-time strategy.

## Uncertainty Is a Given, But How Do We Master It?

But let us take a step back. Behaviour under uncertainty is a topic arousing the interest of various research fields. Hence, strategy researchers have also argued if strategy is helpful in times of uncertainty. To cut it short, the discussion whether we need strategy in times of uncertainty is more academic than practical. While there is some doubt in academia, the practical debate is in favour of planning and strategy. The belief that a large, multinational company can be managed without an explicit strategy originates from an intellectual discourse in an ivory tower instead of organisational practice.

From a practitioner's viewpoint, it is hard to imagine any large organisation that bases their planning on pure ad hoc feelings of relevant decision makers. Organisations are not like classical families, where everyone was raised in the same patterns. They are more a patchwork of diversity combined with various agendas. Strategy in such organisations is the glue that holds together the group and provides purpose. Thus, strategy holds its ground as a means of organisational success in times of uncertainty. If life was simple, there would be a strategy cookbook, providing instructions on how to combine and process the ingredients to get a successful (or at least satisfying) result. But, as we have argued before, life is a bitch. Thus, strategy is a combination of art and science that requires both the experience of the old age and the curiosity of a new-born. As strategy and planning are essential basics that all corporates have (explicitly or implicitly), the question is how do we do strategy in organisational reality and how should we do it in an ideal world.

## Strategy Is About Hard Facts – Really?

Frequently, we observe in practice that decision makers' expectations are driven by the curriculum of business schools and strategy books, for example focussing on discounted-cash flow calculations or forecasts based on a limited number of assumptions. As a result of this upbringing strategy is in most cases just about hard facts. Robust data build the foundation to test hypothesis and then eventually draw conclusions that are translated into beautiful PowerPoint decks.

Yet, are hard facts a law of nature? There is doubt, at least to me. Furthermore we need to ask ourselves, can we always collect reliable data, required for sophisticated analysis or are they rather some surreal assumptions driven by some agenda (or maybe even just lacking indicators that can transform the complexity of our world into a few numbers)? There is some more doubt. As we have outlined in Chapter 2, number-based forecasts as ultimate truth have often failed throughout history. Frequently, I observe organisational goals that seem to be promising at first glance, yet when double clicking on their underlying assumptions, they are outlandish. Consequently, we need to ask, why do people rely on numbers and data? Why do organisations entrust their future on a few numbers with limited validity and lacking ability to grasp complex systems and interactions. The answer is simplicity. Numbers are easier to grasp than opinions and ideas as they condense a lot of information but are also better to measure and handle. Another argument for our quantitative focus is our education system where we get trained to follow the numbers, as many educational systems across the world base their final evaluations of students on quantitative grades. In Germany for example, there is even a switch from qualitative to quantitative evaluations, showing that qualitative evaluations are for starters yet numbers are the real deal. Pupils receive their first school transcripts as a letter, analysing verbally strengths and weakness of each individual pupil. With higher grades, German pupils receive grades in the form of numbers – hence we are getting raised in the sense that only numbers are providing true insights. Qualitative analysis is only for the beginners, that can not make sense of the numbers. Yet, way more important are the structure of our management systems and compensation schemes, which are based on key performance indicators. Caught in those classical set-up, decision makers need to fulfil quantitative goals to maximise their own gains. Peter Drucker's often unquestioned business adage 'you can't manage what you can't measure' leads to the number dependency of contemporary decision making. Hence, why should people use qualitative narratives, such as the outcome of the scenario planning process, to manage based on qualitative factors? The answer is simple: Scenarios help to improve long-term performance and eventually drive the compensation of decision makers in the long run. In this line, I hold it with the aforementioned Pierre Wack that good strategy is about the combination of qualitative-based perception and quantitative-based facts. This clash is nothing only managers perceive; various other disciplines lie in the trenches and fight a war between qualitative-driven and quantitative-driven schools of thought.

Winning strategies that help to prevail in the market need to be dynamic, especially in turbulent times of uncertainty. To win, strategies should combine both, qualitative aspects with quantitative factors. Qualitative aspects can describe interactions difficult to put in a few numbers (e.g. due to lacking reliable data or analytical power), quantitative factors can condense information and build the basis for decision making, supporting arguments with real world evidence. However, scenario planning as the basis of a dynamic strategy is purely a qualitative tool and brings many advantages, which we have hopefully shown along this journey. Yet, when combining the qualitative benefits of scenario planning and its assumptions into quantitative models, we can make the best of both worlds. This combination is not easy and rather mind-stretching, as it requires to think and speak with the data in various plausible worlds. Beyond the necessary human capabilities, the surrounding environment needs to support this combination, as large amounts of data and analytics capabilities, such as algorithms and hardware, are required. While scenarios can be easily conducted with low-tech, the combination requires technology as support. Already a 'low-tech' Excel model for the four scenarios that we develop with our process can help – yet lacks the ability to be dynamic. It is rather a snapshot of the present, neither incorporating developments happening in the present nor anticipating the advancements unfolding in the future. Regarding the technology that can help us to truly support dynamic strategy and overcome the downsides of the Excel models, we can observe a quantum leap in the last decade – thanks to AI and Big Data. However, when we hear about AI, we often think about Science Fiction and machines that relieve us of the burden of making decisions – but we are not there yet. And for the future of humanity, we can only hope that technology will never relieve us of the last pure human realm – decision making. To me, the role of technology is that of a pure enabler, but once it relives us from our burdens, our existence might be questioned. This is not to say that the technology of our time is total idle, but it has learned to walk, yet is rather only in primary school and not an experienced craftsman. However, beauty lies in the eye of the beholder – technology can help to augment a dynamic strategy that yet needs to be taken carefully and tested for its suitability and adaptability. Technological solutions are also convenient, they provide an answer to our questions and tasks and we can always refer to the machine as omniscient source of truth. However, as thoughtful beings, we need to pose some questions. Can we trust its output? Are we able to comprehend the process of the machine's decision making? To me, we frequently can't, unfortunately. Therefore, we need to trust the author of the algorithm. Hence, we face two concerns: The ability of technology and its ethics.

## Strategy Beyond Ethics

Complex technology has always required trust. We did not have the ability to test whether our car did have proper emergency systems or if the house we live or work in is properly built according to all standards necessary for a safe usage – we had to trust in the abilities and ethics of the developers. Recently, we have seen that ethics are secondary to profits, just take for example global, large scale issues with cars (cheating against regulation), planes (using faulty software leading to deadly crashes) or houses (burning down after not applying necessary standards). And when we look at the news in the technology sector, there is support for doubt. In 2016, Microsoft had to shut down its AI-based chatbot Tay after 16 hours. Trained by its surroundings, Tay became a racist, posting inflammatory and offensive tweets.[2] Three years later, research firm Open AI refrained from making its new AI system GPT-2 public, as it was considered 'too dangerous' for the wider audience. They saw the threat of creating fake news or spamming on social media and thus released only a 'light' version.[3] There are many more examples out there, showing that we face transparency and trust issues. To work perfectly, AI requires a sufficient data set for training and active usage, proper training and set-up, as well as appropriate, trustworthy algorithms. The burden of proof of transparency and trust lies quite high. Hence, to use AI as decision-making tool, we require some universal, objective AI certification or auditing. And this is leading to the next challenge: who defines the standards? We all have different ethical standards, opinions on what is right and wrong, shaped by our culture, education and life experience. Humans are not flawless, humans develop and build AI, thus why should AI be perfect?

## Maintain the Doubt

When looking at human history, we can say that technology has improved many aspects of our lives, but technology is not always the best solution to all questions. There is no crystal ball to look into the future and nail it down into a single figure. Instead, many questions and uses cases require human judgement, despite the abilities technology provides us with. Therefore, we need to keep it with Antoine Léonard Thomas, whom we introduced in the introduction, and doubt. Doubt on the universality of technology will foster its development. In my opinion, technology will provide us with better decisions, however, in the end, humans make decisions and humans are affected by strategies.

## Narratives Remain Valid in Strategy

Humans need to be persuaded, motivated, or engaged. Pure numbers will not work in strategy, yet narratives help in the acceptance of all stakeholders, especially when strategies imply larger changes. Human nature is driven by stories, and stories stretch the thinking. Fortunately, narratives still have a future. They will help decision makers to embrace a 'What-If' mindset and communicate this to all their stake- and shareholders. However, those stories need to be enhanced by algorithms and their output, leading to maximum informed decisions. In summary, strategy needs narratives and classical story-telling, supported by data and technological solutions. Yet, we need to maintain our doubt and question automatic outcomes resulting from technology. We should refrain from blindly trusting technology and algorithms, and improve the last human domain, decision making, with thoughtful narratives.

## PERSPECTIVE 2: THE FUTURE OF COLLECTIVE SENSE-MAKING

In our strategy projects over the past years, I have seen a paradoxical trend. The more comprehensive and sophisticated our AI tools become, the more workshops with actual people we need to conduct. This is of course counterintuitive, as one would think that ever more capable machine learning systems would replace the human element in decision making. Yet, reality is quite the opposite.

Big Data tools have tremendously improved our capabilities to conduct research into future trends, and opened up new avenues to measure, track, and monitor ideas and opinions. As a result, the amount of time we need to spend on compiling evidence has decreased dramatically. Only five years ago, it took a team of four trained consultants a couple of weeks to compile a fact book on the drivers for a specific market. With our advanced tools today, one analyst can do this within days. Moreover, the evidence the tools generate is more objective, comprehensive, and relevant for strategic discussions.

However, the amount of hard work to consider the resulting strategic options has not decreased because of this – much to the contrary! We have become faster and better in perceiving what is going on around us, and we can spend more time on the 'so what'. Yet at the same time, the quality requirements towards the strategy workshops have become much higher. The speed and transparency that AI tools have given us in the research phase of our projects have raised the bar for strategists in several dimensions. First, because of the fact that we now crowdsource ideas from a multitude of people when compiling the long list of drivers in our scenario projects, strategists are required to keep a more open mind. Today, participants of scenario workshops need to consider a longer list of factors, many of which will feel 'strange' to them because they come from outside their usual circle. Second, in order to build a logic model that the AI system can later use to monitor the scenarios we developed, workshop participants need to be as transparent as possible on their thinking. Today, a significant part of the time we spend in workshops captures underlying assumptions and spell out hypotheses, and to make sure the other participants factor them in. In other words, the use of AI tools has already changed the way expert human brains need to collaborate and communicate. If we want to continue earning the right to participate in the integrated human/AI intelligence process, we will have to permit more ideas, think harder and communicate more effectively.

## A Forced Upgrade to Collective Thinking

This pressure to upgrade our thinking and discussion culture is precisely the reason why I tend to be optimistic about the beneficial impact of integrated human/AI decision systems. To illustrate this, let us imagine for a moment a world in which such systems have become the norm.

In this world, we will use AI tools at the beginning of the strategizing process, as well as at the end of it. At the beginning, the AI will give us an immediate baseline assessment on the real-time state of the market or topic in question. This assessment will be initially fuelled by a number of indicators that were identified as significant to similar strategic questions in previous exercises. Over time, the library of indicators will grow with every iteration.

Hence, AI tools will capture, measure, monitor, and record all relevant angles of our idea landscape. They will cover all significant fields of discussion. They will be more objective and comprehensive when they record the diversity of opinions than any system we know today. They will spot new ideas, and the people who contribute them. They identify emerging topic areas, and automatically add them to their ever-growing library of indicators. In effect, AI systems would become the cartographers of humankind's evolving universe of ideas.

If this sounds like science fiction to you, keep in mind that this avalanche is already in motion, triggered by the steady growth of our digital data lake and the proliferation of advanced data analysis tools. The main reason why you might not have noticed it yet is the fact that we have uneven access to the data and the tools. At this moment, only few corporations and institutions can access them, driven mainly by two reasons: time, cost, and their internal capability to use AI on the one hand, as well as the social acceptance of AI usage on large data lakes on the other hand. However, on both accounts, I would expect the hurdles to come down over the years. We already see a clear trend towards the democratisation of AI, as the cost algorithms is shrinking while their availability to the public increases. The second issue will and should continue to be contentious. However, I believe that our societies will define a set of rules around the use of AI, and that regulators will get more efficient at enforcing it.

Now imagine for a moment that these real-time maps of our idea landscape were accessible to all. People could browse them to comprehend the context of any topic, as well as the range of opinions within that topic. They could zoom out and zoom back into any topic instantly. Everyone could become something like an expert in any knowledge domain, as they would find related, structured information in an instant. Imagine a world in which everyone could navigate and put to use a universe of ideas, enabled by AI. Not only could those knowledge maps make specialist education for most of us redundant, they could also serve as a kind of collective memory. They would record our collective ideas, as well as all the angles we collectively took to make sense of them.

You might ask how this picture would differ from today's internet. The information we receive through the current digital channels is not reflected (at least in many instances), but rather biased and typically far from comprehensive. In contrast, the AI-enabled map of ideas would be structured, curated, dynamic, and multidimensional. It would provide information on any topic that we or the AI would choose to include.

Yet, this amazing promise would come at a price. To use the knowledge map, the 'superficial' first-level information would not be sufficient. Users would need to read knowledge maps critically, and to do that they would need the ability to factor in the metadata. First, knowledge map users would need to consider the context of the topic they look at. Second, they would need to take in and weigh the different angles people before them have taken. Third, they would need to form their own opinion on how robust the ideas around the topic in question were.

In other words, while dynamic idea maps have, in theory, the power to convert its users in 'instant experts' on any topic, they will require us to become masters in critical thinking in the first place. Hence, to participate in this AI-enabled wonderland of ideas, users will need a number of elemental skills. What are those critical skills? You might have guessed it – users will need the basic disposition to admit and reflect on other people's ideas, they will need the discipline to think in structure and context, and they will need the skill to communicate effectively to hand on their ideas for the future generations of users. In such a world, we cannot simply follow the AI like lemmings.

## The Stakes Could Not Be Higher

Of course, I realise how far-fetched this human-centred utopia must sound. It would take nothing short of a second wave of enlightenment in favour of critical thinking in a world that suffers from ignorance, fake news, polarisation, and ideology. However, I believe there is a reason for hope. If we take into account that global education levels have constantly risen over the last decades, and that we are currently in the process of connecting the second half of the global population to the Internet, the picture may not look so dire anymore. In addition, the ability to think critically does not require extraordinary levels of intelligence or training, but is rather a set of values that we can teach our children. These values will be the key *for us* to live and prosper in our data-driven world.

Which brings me to my last points. To promote integrated human/AI systems in conjunction with critical thinking must be in the interest of anybody in favour of a liberal, human-centred society. These systems are the most feasible and desirable antidote I see to counterbalance the ills of societal fragmentation and fake news. In fact, integrated human/AI systems would empower societies to frame, analyse, and negotiate the big, non-trivial issues we must solve so urgently, such as climate change.

Last, there is a more sinister argument in favour of promoting integrated human/AI systems. At the end of the day, they are an elegant way to keep us humans relevant in decision-making process. If we cannot find a way to use AI to enhance our collective decision-making process, this would increase the danger of us being eliminated from the process altogether. If you think that this notion is an exaggeration, read on.

## PERSPECTIVE 3: A DECISION-MAKING UTOPIA

Ask yourself an important question: Is the result or the way to achieve it more important? Instinctively, you might answer 'the result, of course'. And now, imagine a world in which you receive your tasks at work from an AI and not a human boss anymore. A business world where you would not even interact with any human colleague in the office; even further, what about the perspective that there were no offices anymore at all. In such a world, you would sit at home and merely work through the task list organised by the *algorithm*. Just as all the other 'human resources' – your former colleagues.

## A Story of Storytelling

In this decision-making utopia, the algorithm must be the orchestrator of the organisation, being in charge of information exchange, which is highly automated and brutally efficient. Hence, there is need for neither informal exchange in the coffee corner nor motivational speeches from the leadership. From a human perspective, these work conditions might sound cold, but could this not be the setting to provide optimal results? No distraction. Just pure information orientation. Efficiency over emotions. Effectiveness over 'having a good time'. Obviously, we have to make choices. In today's world of interconnectedness, one bad decision can bring entire economies down; hence, leaders should make not just good but only optimal decisions. Therefore, the question is do we want to have a human-friendly work place with all the comforts in combination with inferior results, or a sterile, algorithm-based business world in which challenges are solved optimally. I'd (have to) vote for the latter. However, what if I can persuade you that this setting is even much *more human* and fun than the best coffee corner or traditional work place you can imagine.

   To explain the necessity better, let us first have a look at the challenges that organisations are facing. In our western societies, organisations are the corner stone in value generation. Therefore, their leaders have a respon-sibility for the wellbeing of the society. In other words, the challenges of a society are also *their* challenges. If not directly, than at least indirectly. Granted, the current shareholder driven and KPI-oriented systems do not tackle the stakeholder view sufficiently. However, we can observe a change in the minds of leaders. Regardless of large campaigns of big corporations or private discussions with leaders, they take society and their surroundings into account when they make decisions. In the end, hardly any company can successfully make business in an unstable market conditions. Hence, companies play an important role not only when it comes to actual business, but also the crucial societal challenges.

Now, when we look at the key challenges our societies are facing, like demographic change, social instability, or climate change, to name just a few, we understand that all these challenges are extremely difficult to solve. They are properties of complex and adaptive systems. As illustrated in our mental model of the jungle, complexity and adaptiveness make it extremely difficult to come to optimal decisions. Therefore, decision makers must act very wisely if they want to secure organisational survival and profits while making their contribution to solve societal challenges at the same time. Politicians can set the general conditions but most often individuals or large companies have to come up with innovative solutions to solve the issues of our time. For example, just think about the trade-offs we are facing when it comes to the hunger for energy and the need for environmental friendly solutions. Politicians can ban certain ways of energy generation or define ecological standards, yet it lies with scientists, entrepreneurs, and organisations to come up with effective ideas to translate the political agenda into sustainable solutions.

In this century, the challenges that the companies and their decision makers are facing have grown tremendously in terms of scope, complexity, and rate of change in combination with adaptiveness. Unfortunately, the tools and processes decision makers can rely on have been the same for the past 30 years and longer. Take for example the typical tool PowerPoint that has been existing in its basic form since 1982, essentially being just an electronic version of classical overhead projectors, or Excel for data analysis since 1985.[4] Both up until now are the most prominent tools to communicate results, status reports etc. in today's business world.

In other words, we just cannot demand from decision makers to solve tasks with an ever-increasing difficulty without improving the toolset and processes accordingly. A new generation of challenges must be answered with a new generation of decision making. To me, it sounds very painful that decision makers wake up every morning with the knowledge they will hardly solve any of the big challenges, because their weapons are simply too blunt. Day after day after day. At the same time, expectations of stake- and shareholders are on an all-time high while they can do so little. Of course, this does not only hold to be true for high-ranking decision makers but for everyone facing important challenges every day. Thus, we need to ask, is it really our aim to have those comfortable, well-equipped coffee corners – full of depressed, overstrained people.

The proposal of this book to incorporate AI algorithms in strategic decision making is a good start. This superpower augments decision makers and puts them in a substantially better position to find wise answers to very difficult questions. Unfortunately, this is just the *necessary* condition to have a chance at all, facing the current and upcoming challenges. The truth is that possessing the AI algorithms is only one side of the coin; the other side is *applying them* in the most effective manner – by reducing the human component.

## There Are No Simple Answers to Interesting Challenges

To give you an example. Frequently, we communicate results of consulting projects via PowerPoint slides to our clients. PowerPoint is a great tool to produce easy-to-read, convincing narratives. The 'price' for this great readability is quite high. While the analysis itself might be comprehensive, over multiple factors and with lots of smart modelling, we have to simplify the insights the moment we communicate and respectively put them into a *story*. A story here means that we translate the insights into an 'easy-to-digest' format and narrative. A typical situation where you can observe this simplification is the widespread visualisation format '*xy*-diagram'. Whether it is a business presentation, a biohacking blog post, or scientific study. *xy*-Diagrams are everywhere, where *x* is an input factor, like investments into R&D, and *y* is the expected output, like revenue. The truth is, in order to build them, you can *only* take into account *one or two* input factors per diagram (e.g. investment in R&D) correlating with the result of the *y*-factor (e.g. expected revenue). The limiting factor here is, as profane as dangerous, that we can only draw diagrams up to the third dimension. Granted, to a certain extent we might be able to integrate further information by adding more details via colours and the form of the individual plots. In addition, we could obviously produce also multiple diagrams in order to communicate the results of the analysis more comprehensively. Unfortunately, when adding more information we quickly clash with the necessity to produce results that can be digested in a reasonable amount of time. In the end, this is obviously true for any type of diagram or narrative. To summarise, already due the simple fact that we deal typically with *multiple* factors, which play a role in our models, we are running into storytelling boundaries. While this limitation of storytelling is linear in terms of its impact per additional factors, we are also facing an exponential, much more dangerous threat when it comes to the risks of communication of results.

Let us have a look on the analysis part before we think about the communication of the results again. A typical analysis that might be communicated via $xy$-diagrams is the regression analysis. Most regression analysis do not go beyond the so-called level-one interaction. 'Level-one', because the output ($y$) *depends* on the status of the one input ($x_1$) and is not influenced by the status of another input factor (e.g. $x_2$). Let us be precise here in order to avoid confusion; we are not referring to the *number* of influencing factors (as before) but the *interconnectedness*. Just like in the mental model of the jungle, the obstacles really start to become a challenge once they influence each other. Unfortunately, this 'influencing each other' not just makes it difficult to escape the jungle but also to tell the story about it later on when being home again. Following up, a level-two interaction would be that the correlation between the output and $x_1$ depends not only on the state of $x_1$ but also on the state of $x_2$ at the same time, and so on. Unfortunately, our world is such complex that there is not a single complex adaptive system (like markets, companies, or climate system) with 'level-one' interactions. Keeping aside that we sometimes even do not know all influencing factors. In reality, the resulting effect ($y$) always depends on multiple input factors, which, *at the same time*, also influence each other.

For example, if you see a diagram showing a positive correlation between investments in R&D and revenue, this is for sure a simplification. The truth is that this relationship is influenced by probably hundreds of factors, for example industry or geography effects etc. For example, some markets might be more receptive for innovation and are hence paying more, driving revenues. While this is at least keeping the direction of the correlation (the correlation of investments and revenue might still be positive independent from the geographic market), we can easily imagine another influencing factor turning the correlation in the *other direction*. If you are only focussing on R&D but have a lack of focus on maintenance, R&D investments might turn out to be negative. If your production facility explodes because it got not maintained sufficiently, all the innovation investments are lost. Therefore, the missing influencing factor is the level of investments that you keep for maintenance. The correlation between the investments in innovations and revenue are only positive *if* the maintenance investments are over a certain threshold. Otherwise, they might become even negative. Unfortunately, the typical number of interactions is prohibitively high so that building a story around them in the form of $xy$-diagrams becomes impossible. The reason for that is that each single interaction, which causes a change of the direction in the correlation between the factors, brings the necessity of a dedicated diagram; resulting in hundreds over hundreds of diagrams. Simply speaking, a story with a few $xy$-diagrams only is of high risk in terms of oversimplification and therefore must be supplemented by plenty of assumptions and limitations.

$xy$-Diagrams are just one example. Anytime we are communicating insights in form of a story, we are risking falling into the trap of 'oversimplification'. The uncomfortable truth is that we must get rid of stories at all – they are more hindrance than help. While stories are easy to understand, sometimes even entertaining or convincing, they are also *wrong* almost all the time when describing complex adaptive systems.

In more detail, if we see stories as a model of a certain part of the world (e.g. the story of how investments influence revenues), then they have a built-in drawback. Stories usually have to follow certain mechanisms, such as 'make it easy to understand', 'make it convincing,' or 'make it reasonable'.

In contrast, this is the danger, reality does not need to follow any script as stories do. Realty is highly complex and very difficult to understand. Reality typically goes like this: The influence of factor $x_1$ on $y$ depends on $x_2, x_3, x_4, x_5, x_5, x_6...$ but only if $x_7, x_8, x_9$ are... and so on; also it could be that if $x_4$ is higher than $x_5$ we see a complete different picture, etc. Just remember our mental model of the jungle. Reality is sometimes overwhelmingly cumbersome and complicated to explain. A true picture about reality is typically not entertaining to human standards. Nevertheless, it does not help: If we want to solve the big challenges, we must not simplify just to make it handier for us.

In other words, there are no simple answers (i.e. stories) to questions regarding complex adaptive systems. Even more tragic, we often have the best ambitions, but relying on stories our choices sometimes end in catastrophic results. Hence, we need to ask ourselves, does it help us to tell compelling and promising stories how R&D will translate into revenues, yet leaving out all the exceptions? Do stories bring us any long-term advantage, when we find out later that the communicated, plausible relation was not true, and organisations are forced to go out of business? Obviously, a good consultant must always find the best balance between the hard-to-digest analysis and getting the message transported to the audience. Unfortunately, to find the right, balance gets more and more difficult facing the traditional, almost ancient ways of storytelling in contrast to the modern challenges. Yet, it is very time-consuming to translate insights into digestible stories. And frequently, decision making lacks time and resources. Hence, we need to make an almost impossible trade-off between further analysis or nice 'wrapping'. Facing the business and societal challenges ahead, we do not have the luxury of wasting any time.

As we have discussed in the chapters before, time is the source of strength for achieving long-term objectives. It must not be wasted for storytelling but only be used to achieve the big goals. Equally important, we must observe and learn from our experiences. Complex adaptive systems are not easy to describe or understand. Therefore, it is even more important that all available knowledge on a complex adaptive system is stored and can be re-used for further learning and application. Counterintuitively, transferring knowledge is the second important weakness of stories. They are simply a bad way of storing knowledge. For example, in consulting we see a great need to learn as much as possible from former projects to re-use the knowledge frictionless in future projects. At first glance, this seems utterly straight forward, as it saves costs and increases the chance of success, when a proven approach is applied again. In reality, this is extremely difficult to implement. First, we abide strict restrictions in terms of exclusivity and confidentiality between client projects. Apart from that, every client situation is very different. However, we rather use past stories than anonymised, complicated data sets. The problem is that those stories are typically targeted to a certain situation. Even though the insights of the analysis in form of data could be used in next projects again, the format to save the results is typically a story – or at least highly condensed data.

Documents that provide guidance for decisions, such as final presentations of consulting projects, are incorporating the very specific situation of the stakeholder and tell the facts in a highly tailored story. Therefore, the next project cannot just build on the knowledge since the insights are, besides from being confidential, hidden in the complicated data set. The most important data about all the assumptions, interaction-effects, and so on are by far not that easy to access. Probably only the experts who have done the analysis in the first place will be able to lift the data treasure. Unfortunately, they are typically not available, but serving the client they have initially conducted the analysis for. Of course, this example from consultancies can also be transferred to any company since they are following the same mechanisms in preferring easy-to-digest stories over complicated data analysis.

In summary, the stories we are able to remember and comprise easily will not help us in the next situation, because they are simplified and do not contain all the insights. We simply cannot store all the knowledge, which is rather complicated, in an easy, simple story.

## Proposal for a New Decision-Making Culture

Therefore, I propose a radical but necessary approach. We should get rid of any need to sell a decision via stories. It simply costs too much time and is, even worse, probably doing more harm than it helps. It does not matter if it is a sophisticated quantitative model or an entertaining qualitative narrative. In the end, they are all stories because they suggest predictable input–output relations. While these relations might be true for short-term cases, the reader knows that at the latest when complexity and adaptiveness kick in, all the relations are questionable again.

In decision making, only objective and comprehensive descriptions and analyses of the reality should be used. This implies that we agree on the most basic understanding of complex adaptive systems and the challenges that come with them: The whole picture is always highly complicated and not easy to understand neither explained. Only few highly trained and knowledge-able experts might be able to evaluate certain effects. Thus, we must embrace uncertainty, for example as we do in scenario planning. They are also stories but at least not one but many, which increases the likelihood that some are a good approximation of reality. However, also in the scenario planning exercise, we cannot tackle all uncertainties and need to condense the information. The softer limitation is that it is difficult to narrate four compelling stories covering all drivers and their potential effects. Yet, the hard limitation is that through interactions we would have to tell an indefinite number of scenarios. Thus, I say: leave the limitation of stories behind and go for higher dimensional scenario planning. Use a scenario mind-set, think about potential effects but use the machine to define an indefinite number of scenarios and monitor how the future evolves to early anticipate how the world is evolving.

Thanks to AI, we can feed the knowledge we gather over time from past decisions and their effects into the machine and enhance its future decisions. The employee might leave, but in contrast to before, the implicit knowl-edge stays. If a certain expert is aware of the fact that R&D investments is negative under certain circumstances, which the broader decision making community might be unaware of, this knowledge is incorporated into the algorithm. Once fed into the system, we can apply the knowledge in any situations in the future. Thus, the need to be physically in one place in order to facilitate knowledge exchange becomes less and less meaningful. The knowledge lives in the AI in a 'non-story' format so that it can easily be applied to different similar situations. The AI can then easily access past knowledge and apply it – while even being able to adapt it to a certain situation.

Overall, we will not entirely beat our two enemies complexity and adaptiveness in long-term decision making but we should at least be able to react in real time in the most informed way, improving over time as the machine learns and evolve. You might not know all the icebergs in advance. However, thanks to the AI, you will know *when* there is one in front of you – and *how* to course correct optimally. Also, you do not have to explain to everyone that you have to course correct via a time-consuming story before it is too late – as the AI provides the reasoning. All it needs it trust. Let us learn to abandon the fireplace (at least for business decisions) where the one with the greatest narrative gets the most attention. Instead, let us trust the algorithms that might seem inhuman but will help us to build a more human place.

I envision a world in which highly trained subject experts are augmented by AI algorithms to come as close as possible to the truth and guide to wise decisions. In this world, we do not need entertaining but distracting stories anymore. Therefore, why now is this even more social? Because we find a business world that is most capable of dealing and solving the big business and societal challenges. At the same time, the ever-improving AI will help us to save time that we can give back to our friends and family in our private life. I call this a decision-making utopia that is worth fighting for – or at least promoting it by writing this book.

## NOTES

1. See O'Kane, S. (2019). Tesla launches car insurance offering in California. Retrieved from https://www.theverge.com/2019/8/28/20837265/tesla-car-insurance-california-autopilot-discount

2. See Vincent, J. (2016). Twitter taught Microsoft's AI chatbot to be a racist asshole in less than a day. Retrieved from https://www.theverge.com/2016/3/24/11297050/tay-microsoft-chatbot-racist

3. See Wakefield, J. (2019). 'Dangerous' AI offers to write fake news. Retrieved from https://www.bbc.com/news/technology-49446729

4. See Wikipedia (2020). Microsoft Excel. Retrieved from: https://en.wikipedia.org/wiki/Microsoft_Excel#Early_history

# REFERENCES

Bal, P. M., Veltkamp, M. (2013). How Does Fiction Reading Influence Empathy? An Experimental Investigation on the Role of Emotional Transportation. *PLoS ONE, 8*(1).

Barton, D., Manyika, J., Koller, T., Palter, R., Godsall, J., & Zoffer, J. (2017). Where companies with a long-term view outperform their peers. Retrieved from https://www.mckinsey.com/featured-insights/long-term-capitalism/where-companies-with-a-long-term-view-outperform-their-peers

BBC. (2016). Science fact: Sci-fi inventions that became reality. Retrieved from http://www.bbc.com/news/health-38026393

Becker, F. (2014). *Simulation in der Marketingforschung auf Basis der NK-Methodik: Eine Evaluation und Illustration von Anwendungspotenzialen.* WiGIM.

Berandino, M. (2012). *Mike Tyson explains one of his most famous quotes.* Deerfield Beach, FL: Sun Sentinel.

Bill, G., Myhrvold, N. & Rinearson, P. (1996). *The Road Ahead.* New York, NY: Penguin Books.

Bisson, P., Stephenson, E. & Viguerie, S. P. (2010). *Global forces: An introduction.* McKinsey Quarterly (June).

Borreli, L. (2015). Human attention span shortens to 8 seconds due to digital technology: 3 ways to stay focused. Retrieved from https://www.medicaldaily.com/human-attention-span-shortens-8-seconds-due-digital-technology-3-ways-stay-focused-333474

Bradfield, R., Wright, G., Burt, G., Cairns, G., & Van Der Heijden, K. (2005). The origins and evolution of scenario techniques in long range business planning. *Futures, 37*(8), 795–812.

Brochet, F., Loumioti, M., & Serafeim, G. (2012). *Short-termism, investor clientele, and firm risk.* Boston, MA: Harvard Business School.

Brown, P., Cocke, J., Pietra, S. D., Pietra, V. D., Jelinek, F., Mercer, R. L., Roossin, P. (1988). A statistical approach to language translation. Coling'88. *Association for Computational Linguistics, 1,* 71–76.

Business Standard. (2012). Kodak files for bankruptcy, plans biz overhaul. Retrieved from http://www.business-standard.com/article/international/kodak-files-for-bank-ruptcy-plans-biz-overhaul-112011900119_1.html

Cândido, C. J., & Santos, S. P. (2015). Strategy implementation: What is the failure rate? *Journal of Management & Organization*, 21(2), 237–262.

Chermack, T. J., Lynham, S. A., & Ruona, W. E. (2001). A review of scenario planning literature. *Futures Research Quarterly*, 17(2), 24.

Chermack, T. J. (2003). *A theory of scenario planning*, University of Minnesota Human Resource Development Research Center. St. Paul (Minnesota).

Chermack, T. J., & van der Merwe, L. (2003). The role of constructivist learning in scenario planning. *Futures*, 35(5), 445–460.

Chermack, T. J. (2017). *Foundations of scenario planning: The story of Pierre Wack*. New York, NY: Taylor & Francis.

Cheval, B., Tipura, E., Burra, N., Frossard, J., Chanal, J., Orsholits, D., ... Boisgontier, M. P. (2018). Avoiding sedentary behaviors requires more cortical resources than avoiding physical activity: An EEG study. *Neuropsychologia*, 119, 68–80.

Chua, K. (2014). Fiction Teaches Students Empathy, Research Shows. Retrieved from: http://blogs.edweek.org/teachers/teaching_now/2014/09/study-fiction-teaches-students-empathy.html

Clare, A., Motson, N., & Thomas, S. (2013). *An evaluation of alternative equity indices Part 2: Fundamental Weighting Schemes*. Cass Business School.

Cohan, P. (2014). Why Stack Ranking Worked Better at GE Than Microsoft. *Forbes*. Retrieved October 2, 2014. Retrieved from: https://www.forbes.com/sites/petercohan/2012/07/13/why-stack-ranking-worked-better-at-ge-than-microsoft/#207dd0823236

Colegrove, M. B. (2005). *Distant Voices: Listening to the Leadership Lessons of the Past*. Lincoln, NB: iUniverse.

Consultancy.uk. (2017). Digital transformation market booms to $23 billion. Retrieved from https://www.consultancy.uk/news/13489/digital-transformation-consulting-market-booms-to-23-billion

Crainer, S., & Dearlove, D. (2004). *Business, the universe and everything: Conversations with the world's greatest management thinkers*. Oxford: John Wiley & Sons.

Decartes, R. (1853). *The Meditations and Selections from the Principles of Philosophy*. Edinburgh: Sutherland and Knox.

DeHaan, R. L. (2011). Teaching creative science thinking. *Science*, 334(6062), 1499–1500.

Deutsch, C. H. (2008). At Kodak, some old things are new again. Retrieved from https://www.nytimes.com/2008/05/02/technology/02kodak.html

Dormehl, L. (2017). *Thinking machines: The quest for artificial intelligence and where it is taking us next*. New York, NY: TarcherPerigee.

Einstein, A. (1954 [1982]). *Ideas and opinions*. New York, NY: Three Rivers Press.

Farber, D. (2014). When iPhone met world, 7 years ago today. Retrieved from https://www.cnet.com/news/when-iphone-met-world-7-years-ago-today/

Featherston, C., & Doolan, M. (2012). A critical review of the criticisms of system dynamics. Retrieved from https://www.researchgate.net/publication/271827939_A_Critical_Review_of_the_Criticisms_of_System_Dynamics

Finkelstein, S. (2005). When bad things happen to good companies: Strategy failure and flawed executives, *Journal of Business Strategy*, 26(2), 19–28.

Flammer, C., & Bansal, P. (2017). Does a long-term orientation create value? Evidence from a regression discontinuity. *Strategic Management Journal*, 38(9), 1827–1847.

Forrester, J. W. (1961). *Industrial dynamics*. Cambridge, MA: The MIT Press.

Frieden, J. A. (2011). The financial crisis was foreseeable and preventable. *The New York Times*. Retrieved from https://www.nytimes.com/roomfordebate/2011/01/30/was-the-financial-crisis-avoidable/the-financial-crisis-was-foreseeable-and-preventable

Friedman, Z. (2018). Here Are 10 Genius Quotes From Warren Buffett. Retrieved from https://www.forbes.com/sites/zackfriedman/2018/10/04/warren-buffett-best-quotes/#10af74494261

Garber, P. M. (1989). Tulipmania. *Journal of Political Economy*, 97(3), 535–60.

Garber, P. M. (1990). Famous First Bubbles. *The Journal of Economic Perspectives*, 4(2), 35–54.

Garber, J. R. (1998). What if …? Retrieved from https://www.forbes.com/forbes/1998/1102/6210076a.html#270aa2902995

Garreau, J. (1994). Conspiracy of Heretics. Retrieved from: https://www.wired.com/1994/11/gbn/

de Geus, A. P. (1988). Planning as learning. *Harvard Business Review*, 66(2), 70–74.

de Geus, A. P. (1999). *The living company: Growth, learning and longevity in business*. London: Nicholas Brealey Publishing.

Gilchrist, A. L., Cowan, N., & Naveh-Benjamin, M. (2008). Working memory capacity for spoken sentences decreases with adult ageing: Recall of fewer but not smaller chunks in older adults. *Memory*, 16(7), 773–787.

Gilliver, P. (2012). 'Your dictionary needs you': A brief history of the OED's appeals to the public. Retrieved from https://public.oed.com/the-oed-appeals/history-of-the-appeals/

Global Business Network. (2003). The Mont Fleur scenarios: What will South Africa be like in the year 2002? *Deeper News*, 7(1), 1–20.

Global Business Network. (2010). Where we started. Retrieved from https://web.archive.org/web/20100105183523/http://gbn.com/about/started.php

Gowers, T., & Barrow-Green, J. (2010). *The Princeton companion to mathematics, the three-body problem*. Princeton, NJ: Princeton University Press

Grady, J. (2015). *Matthew Fontaine Maury, Father of Oceanography: A Biography, 1806–1873*. Jefferson, NC: McFarland & Company.

Gray, D. H. (1986). Uses and misuses of strategic planning. *Harvard Business Review, 64*(1), 89–97.

Gunderson, K. (1964). Descartes, La Mettrie, Language and Machines. *Philosophy, 39*, 193–222.

Hagel, J. (2017). Crafting corporate narratives: Zoom out, zoom in. Retrieved from http://edgeperspectives.typepad.com/edge_perspectives/2017/08/crafting-corporate-narratives-zoom-out-zoom-in.html

Hemp, P. (2009). Death by information overload. Retrieved from https://hbr.org/2009/09/death-by-information-overload

Hern, A. (2016). Nokia returns to the phone market as Microsoft sells brand. Retrieved from https://www.theguardian.com/technology/2016/may/18/nokia-returns-phone-market-microsoft-sells-brand-hmd-foxconn

Hungenberg, H. (2014). Strategisches Management in Unternehmen. Ziele-Prozesse-Verfahren. 8. Auflage. Wiesbaden. Springer-Verlage. p. 5.

Jefferson, M. (2012). Shell scenarios: What really happened in the 1970s and what may be learned for current world prospects. *Technological Forecasting and Social Change, 79*(1), 186–197.

Jones, G. H. (2013). *Pythia. Ancient History Encyclopedia*. Retrieved from: https://www.ancient.eu/Pythia/.

Kahane, A. (2012). *Working Together to Change the Future: Transformative Scenario Planning*. Oakland: Berrett-Koehler.

Kahn, H. (1961). *On Thermonuclear War* (2nd ed.). Princeton: Princeton University Press.

Kahn, H., & Wiener, A. J. (1967). *The year 2000: A framework for speculation on the next thirty-three years*. New York, NY: Macmillan.

Kahneman, D., & Tversky, A. (1979). Prospect theory: An analysis of decision under risk. *Econometrica, 47*(2), 263–291.

Kaplan, R. S. and Norton, D. P. (2001). The Strategy-Focused Organization–How Balanced Scorecard Companies Thrive in the New Business Environment. Boston, MA: Harvard Business School Press.

Kiechel, W. (1982). Corporate strategists under fire. *Fortune, December, 106*(13), 34–39.

Kiechel, W. (1984). Sniping at strategic planning. *Planning Review*, May, 8–11.

Kimmorley, S. (2018). Here's how 12 successful CEOs set their goals for the year. Retrieved from https://www.businessinsider.com.au/how-ceos-set-goals-2018-1#3m5fQJAHt6euf8Fm.99

Klein, F., Bansal, M., Wohlers, J. (2017). *Beyond the noise: The megatrends of tomorrow's world*. Munich: Deloitte Consulting.

Knight, M. (1999). 2020 Visionary. Rensselaer Alumni Magazine. Rensselaer Polytechnic Institute. Retrieved from https://www.rpi.edu/dept/NewsComm/Magazine/dec99/visionary1.html

Krämer, W. (2012). Die Affen sind die besten Anleger. Frankfurter Allgemeine Zeitung. Retrieved from: https://www.faz.net/aktuell/finanzen/meine-finanzen/2.2465/denkfehler-die-uns-geld-kosten-9-die-affen-sind-die-besten-anleger-11711132.html

Kvint, V. (2016). *Strategy for the global market: Theory and practical applications*. New York, NY: Routledge.

Lafley, A. G., & Martin, R. L. (2013). *Playing to win: How strategy really works*. Boston, MA: Harvard Business Press.

Levitt, T. (1960). Marketing Myopia. *Harvard Business Review, 38*(4), 45–56.

Lindgren, M., & Bandfold, H. (2003). *Scenario planning: The link between future and industry*. London: Palgrave Macmillan.

Linneman, R. E., & Klein, H. E. (1983). The use of multiple scenarios by US industrial companies: A comparison study, 1977–1981. *Long Range Planning, 16*(6), 94–101.

Lohr, S. (1998). Long Boom or Bust; A Leading Futurist Risks His Reputation With Ideas on Growth And High Technology. *The New York Times*. Retrieved from: https://www.nytimes.com/1998/06/01/business/long-boom-bust-leading-futurist-risks-his-reputation-with-ideas-growth-high.html?scp=10&sq=%22Global+Business+Network%22&st=nyt.

Longitude Prize. (n.d.). The history. Retrieved from https://longitudeprize.org/about-us/history.

Malkiel, B.G. (2007). *A random walk down Wall Street* (9th ed., p. 24). New York: North & Company.

McKinsey. (2008). *How companies act on global trends: A McKinsey Global Survey*. The McKinsey Quarterly.

Mencher, A. G. (1971). IV. On the Social Deployment of Science. *Bulletin of the Atomic Scientists, 27*(10), 37.

Millett, S. M. (1988). How scenarios trigger strategic thinking. *Long Range Planning, 21*(5), 61–68.

Millett, S. M. (2003). The future of scenarios: challenges and opportunities. *Strategy & Leadership, 31*(2), 16–24.

Moeller, S. B., Schlingemann, F. P., & Stulz, R. M. (2005). Wealth destruction on a massive scale? A study of acquiring-firm returns in the recent merger wave. *The Journal of Finance, 60*(2), 757–782.

Mui, C. (2012). How Kodak failed. Retrieved from https://www.forbes.com/sites/chunkamui/2012/01/18/how-kodak-failed/3/#6c6f293e4a97

Mulherin, J. H., & Boone, A. L. (2000). Comparing acquisitions and divestitures. *Journal of Corporate Finance, 6*(2), 117–139.

Musk, E. (2006). The Secret Tesla motors master plan (just between you and me). Retrieved from https://www.tesla.com/blog/secret-tesla-motors-master-plan-just-between-you-and-me

Norris, G. (2005). Creating a titan. Retrieved from https://www.flightglobal.com/news/articles/creating-a-titan-199071/

Nutt, P. C. (1987). Identifying and appraising how managers install strategy. *Strategic Management Journal, 8*(1), 1–14.

Ogilvy, J., & Schwartz, P. (2004). *Plotting your scenarios.* Emeryville, CA: Global Business Network.

O'Kane, S. (2019). Tesla launches car insurance offering in California. Retrieved from https://www.theverge.com/2019/8/28/20837265/tesla-car-insurance-california-autopilot-discount

Paul, R.; Elder, L. (1996). Foundation For Critical Thinking. Retrieved from https://www.criticalthinking.org/resources/articles/critical-mind.shtml

Perlitz, M. (1993). Why most strategies fail to-day: The need for strategy-innovations. *European Management Journal, 11*(1), 114–121.

Peterson, K. (2007). Microstock photography represents a new business model. Retrieved from http://old.seattletimes.com/html/businesstechnology/2003724590_istockphoto28.html

Plato (380 bc). Laches, or Courage [Translated by Jowett, B.]. Retrieved from: http://classics.mit.edu/Plato/laches.html

Plato (n.d.). Apology. Translated by Jowett, B. Retrieved from: http://classics.mit.edu/Plato/apology.html

Porter, M. E. (1980). *Competitive strategy: Techniques for analyzing industries and competitors.* New York, NY: Free Press.

Porter, M. E. (1985). *Competitive advantage.* New York, NY: Free Press.

Reddish, T. (2016). *Science and Christianity: Foundations and frameworks for moving forward in faith.* Eugene, OR: Wipf and Stock Publishers.

von Reibnitz, U., & Hammond, P. (1988). *Scenario techniques.* Hamburg: McGraw-Hill Hamburg.

Rescher, N. (1998). *Predicting the future: An introduction to the theory of forecasting.* New York, NY: State University of New York Press.

Ringland, G. (1998). *Scenario planning: Managing for the future.* Chichester: John Wiley and Sons.

Roberts, L. (2010, January–February). *Analysis paralysis: A case of terminological inexactitude*. Defense AT&L. Retrieved from https://web.archive.org/web/20170131231704/http://www.dau.mil/pubscats/ATL%20Docs/Jan-Feb/robersts_jan-feb10.pdf.

Rumsfeld, D. (2002). DoD news briefing – Secretary Rumsfeld and Gen. Myers. Retrieved from https://archive.defense.gov/Transcripts/Transcript.aspx?TranscriptID=2636

Scearce, D., & Fulton, K. (2004). *What if? The art of scenario thinking for nonprofits*. Emeryville, CA: Global Business Network.

Schühly, A., Vieten, N., Weiß, J., & Niggeloh, S. (2019). *Braving the wind of change – resilient portfolio strategy*. Munich: Monitor Deloitte.

Schoemaker, P. J. (1993). Multiple scenario development: Its conceptual and behavioral foundation. *Strategic management journal, 14*(3), 194.

Schwartz, P. (1991). *The art of the long view: Planning for the future in an uncertain world*. New York, NY: Doubleday.

Sharpe, B., & van der Heijden, K. (Eds.). (2007). *Scenarios for success: Turning insights into action (Oxford Futures Forum)*. Chichester: Wiley.

Shen, L. (2016). Warren Buffett just unloaded $195 Million worth of these 'weapons of mass destruction'. Retrieved from http://fortune.com/2016/08/08/mass-destruction-buffett-derivatives/

Simon, H. A. (1965). *Via: AI: The tumultuous search for artificial intelligence (Crevier, 1993)*. New York, NY: Basic Books.

Singapore Airlines. (2013). Singapore airlines – Our history. Retrieved from https://web.archive.org/web/20130209040833/http://www.singaporeair.com/en_UK/about-us/sia-history/

Sirkin, H. L., Keenan, P. and Jackson, A. (2005). The hard side of change management. *Harvard Business Review, 83*(10), 109–118.

Sonnenfeld, J. (2015). CEO exit schedules: A season to stay, a season to go. Retrieved from: https://fortune.com/2015/05/06/ceo-tenure-cisco/

Spira, J. B. (2008). Information overload: Now $900 Billion – What is your organization's exposure? Retrieved from http://www.basexblog.com/2008/12/19/information-overload-now-900-billion-what-is-your-organizations-exposure/

Störig, H. J. (2006). *Kleine Weltgeschichte der Philosophie*. Frankfurt am Main: Fischer Taschenbuch.

Sterling, B. (2002). *Tomorrow now: Envisioning the next fifty years*. New York, NY: Random House.

Süddeutsche Zeitung. (2010a). Airbus: Pannenflieger A400M: Pleiten, Pech und Peinlichkeiten. Retrieved from http://www.sueddeutsche.de/wirtschaft/airbus-pannenflieger-iami-pleiten-pech-und-peinlichkeiten-1.65920

Süddeutsche Zeitung. (2010b). Die Geschichte von Airbus: Erfolgsgeschichte mit Problemen. Retrieved from http://www.sueddeutsche.de/wirtschaft/ die-geschichte-von-airbus-erfolgsgeschichte-mit-problemen-1.516776

Szczerba, R. J. (2015). 15 Worst tech predictions of all time. Retrieved from https:// www.forbes.com/sites/robertszczerba/2015/01/05/15-worst-tech-predictions-of-all-time/#6417b1ba1299

Taulli, T. (2019). AI (artificial intelligence) words you need to know. Retrieved from https://www.forbes.com/sites/tomtaulli/2019/09/07/ai-artificial-intelligence-words-you-need-to-know#74f47ba77f11

The Economist. (1999). A survey of telecommunications: Cutting the cord. Retrieved from https://www.economist.com/node/246152

Theiss, E. (2009). Parable of a Chinese farmer: How an ancient story resonates in today's hard times. Retrieved from https://www.cleveland.com/living/2009/02/ parable_of_a_chinese_farmer_ho.html.

Thomas, A. L. (1765). *Éloge de René Descartes*. Whitefish, Mont: Kessinger Publishing.

Todd, A. (2016). Stories through the Ages. An examination of the evolution of storytelling through time. Retrieved from: https://landt.co/2016/06/ storytelling-through-time-evolution/

Tucholsky, K (1975). *Gesammelte Werke in zehn Bänden*. Band 3. Hamburg: Rowohlt, p. 197.

Tuna, C. (2009). Pendulum is swinging back on "Scenario Planning": JDS Uniphase prepares responses for a range of business situations, helping company react quickly to change. Retrieved from http://online.wsj.com/article/SB124683295589397615.html

Varum, C. A. & Melo, C. (2010). Directions in Scenario Planning Literature: A Review of the Past Decades. *Futures*, 42(4), 356.

Vermeulen, F. (2017). Many strategies fail because they're not actually strategies. *Harvard Business Review*. Retrieved from https://hbr.org/2017/11/ many-strategies-fail-because-theyre-not-actually-strategies

Vincent, J. (2016). Twitter taught Microsoft's AI chatbot to be a racist asshole in less than a day. Retrieved from https://www.theverge.com/2016/3/24/11297050/ tay-microsoft-chatbot-racist

von Bertalanffy, L. (1968). *General system theory: Foundations, development, applications*. New York, NY: George Braziller.

Von Clausewitz, C. (1976). *On War*. Translated and Edited by Howard, M. & Paret, P. Princeton, NJ: Princeton University Press.

Von Neumann, J., Morgenstern, O., & Kuhn, H. W. (2007). *Theory of games and economic behavior (commemorative edition)*. Princeton, NJ: Princeton University Press.

Wack, P. (1985a). Scenarios: Shooting the rapids. *Harvard Business Review*, 63(6), 139–150.

Wack, P. (1985b, September–October). Scenarios: Uncharted waters ahead: How Royal Dutch/Shell developed a planning technique that teaches managers to think about an uncertain future. *Harvard Business Review*, 72–79.

Wainwright, M. (2005). Emails 'pose threat to IQ'. Retrieved from https://www.theguardian.com/technology/2005/apr/22/money.workandcareers

Wakefield, J. (2019). 'Dangerous' AI offers to write fake news. Retrieved from https://www.bbc.com/news/technology-49446729

Warwick, K., & Shah, H. (2016). *Turing's imitation game: Conversations with the unknown*. Cambridge, MA: Cambridge University Press.

Wery, R., & Waco, M. (2004). Why good strategies fail. *Handbook of Business Strategy*, 5(1), 153–157.

Wery, R., & Waco, M. (2004). Why good strategies fail. In *Handbook of Business Strategy*.

Wilkinson, A., & Kupers, R. (2013, May). Living in the Futures. *Harvard Business Review*. Retrieved from https://hbr.org/2013/05/living-in-the-futures.

Wikipedia. (n.d.). History of Wikipedia. Retrieved from https://en.wikipedia.org/wiki/History_of_Wikipedia

Wired (2012): Inside Minority Report's 'Idea Summit,' Visionaries Saw the Future. Retrieved from: https://www.wired.com/2012/06/minority-report-idea-summit/

Wulf, T., Meissner, P., & Stubner, S. (2010). A scenario-based approach to strategic planning–integrating planning and process perspective of strategy. Leipzig: Leipzig Graduate School of Management.

Zetlin, M. (2019). Blockbuster Could Have Bought Netflix for $50 Million, but the CEO Thought It Was a Joke. Retrieved from: https://www.inc.com/minda-zetlin/netflix-blockbuster-meeting-marc-randolph-reed-hastings-john-antioco.html

# INDEX